Supercook

Marshall Cavendish London & New York

Contents

Volume 13

This edition published 1982

© Marshall Cavendish Ltd 1978, 1977, 1976, 1975, 1974, 1973, 1972
58 Old Compton Street, London W1V 5PA

Printed and bound in Singapore by Times Printers Sdn. Bhd.

ISBN (for set) 0 85685 534 0
ISBN (this volume) 0 85685 547 2
Library of Congress catalog card number 78 – 52319

Supercook

USEFUL TERMS FROM THE EUROPEAN COOK'S KITCHEN

Foreign Terms — American equivalents

Foreign Terms	American equivalents
bacon rashers	bacon slices
demerara sugar	pale brown granulated sugar
fillet steak	filet mignon
heatproof baking dish	flameproof casserole
icing	frosting
kitchen paper	paper towels
minced meat	ground meat
pastry case	pie crust
salad cream	salad dressing
to grill	to broil
to whisk	to beat
veal escalopes	veal scallops
single cream	light cream
double cream	heavy, whipping cream
cake tin	cake pan
frying pan	skillet
greaseproof paper	waxed paper
sieve	strainer
tea towel	dish towel
starter	appetizer
entree	main course
pudding	dessert

Foreign ingredients — American equivalents

Foreign ingredients	American equivalents
aubergine	eggplant
bicarbonate of soda	baking soda
biscuit	cookie
castor sugar	super fine sugar
cornflour	cornstarch
chutney	relish
cos lettuce	romaine lettuce
courgettes	zucchini
digestive biscuits	graham-cracker
double cream	heavy whipping cream
gammon slice	ham steak
haricot beans	dry white beans
icing sugar	confectioners sugar
marrows	large zucchini, or squash
Martini	vermouth
pancake	crêpe
plain flour	all-purpose flour
potato chips	French fries
potato crisps	potato chips
prawns	shrimp
salt beef	corned beef
scone	baking powder biscuit
single cream	light cream
sorbet	sherbert
sprats	smelts
spring onion	scallion
sultana	raisin
treacle	molasses
tunny fish	tuna fish
wholemeal flour	whole-grain flour

MEASUREMENT CONVERSIONS
Solid Measures

(1 ounce = 28.352 metric grams, but for convenience it is usually calculated, as in this chart, 1 ounce = 30 grams)

½ ounce = 15 grams	3½ ounces = 100 grams
1 ounce = 30 grams	1 pound, 1½ ounces = 500 grams
2 ounces = 60 grams	2 pounds, 3 ounces = 1,000 grams
2½ ounces = 75 grams	(1 kilogram)

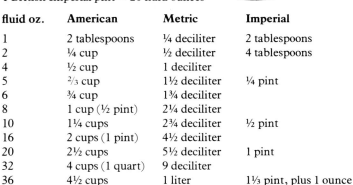

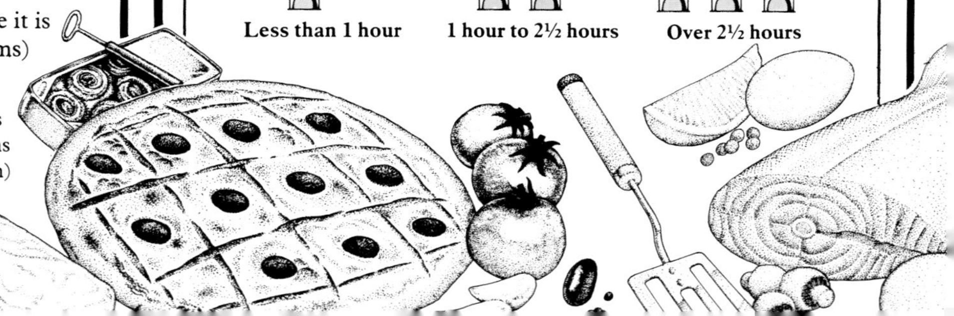

Liquid measures

1 American cup = 8 fluid ounces
1 British Imperial cup = 10 fluid ounces

1 pint = 16 fluid ounces (2 cups)
1 British Imperial pint = 20 fluid ounces

fluid oz.	American	Metric	Imperial
1	2 tablespoons	¼ deciliter	2 tablespoons
2	¼ cup	½ deciliter	4 tablespoons
4	½ cup	1 deciliter	
5	⅔ cup	1½ deciliter	¼ pint
6	¾ cup	1¾ deciliter	
8	1 cup (½ pint)	2¼ deciliter	
10	1¼ cups	2¾ deciliter	½ pint
16	2 cups (1 pint)	4½ deciliter	
20	2½ cups	5½ deciliter	1 pint
32	4 cups (1 quart)	9 deciliter	
36	4½ cups	1 liter	1⅓ pint, plus 1 ounce

Frequently-used measurements

	American	Metric	Imperial
butter	1 tablespoon	15 grams	½ ounce
	½ cup	25 grams	4 ounces
	1 cup	250 grams	1 pound
all-purpose flour	¼ cup	35 grams	1¼ ounces
	½ cup	75 grams	2½ ounces
	1 cup	142 grams	5 ounces
self-raising flour	¼ cup	30 grams	1 ounce
	½ cup	60 grams	2 ounces
	1 cup	120 grams	4 ounces
raisins	1 cup	156 grams	5½ ounces
rice	1 cup	240 grams	8 ounces
brown sugar	1 tablespoon	10 grams	⅓ ounce
	½ cup	90 grams	3 ounces
	1 cup	180 grams	6 ounces
super fine sugar	1 tablespoon	15 grams	½ ounce
	½ cup	120 grams	4 ounces
	1 cup	240 grams	8 ounces

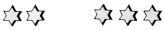This is the guide to the amount of skill needed for each recipe.

Easy   **Needs special care**   **Complicated**

This is an estimated guide to the dish's cost, which will, of course, vary with the season.

Inexpensive   **Reasonable**   **Expensive**

This is an indication of the amount of time needed for preparing and cooking the dish.

Less than 1 hour   **1 hour to 2½ hours**   **Over 2½ hours**

Parsley and Lemon Stuffing

This is a light, fragrant stuffing for a turkey. The lemon flavouring permeates the flesh of the turkey and the parsley gives an attractive appearance and flavour. This amount of stuffing is enough for an 8 to 9 pound turkey.

ABOUT 14 OUNCES [1¾ CUPS]
6 oz. [2 cups] dry breadcrumbs
    grated rind and juice of 2 lemons
4 tablespoons chopped fresh
    parsley
1 teaspoon grated orange rind
¼ teaspoon dried thyme
¼ teaspoon dried marjoram
6 oz. [¾ cup] butter, softened
3 eggs

In a medium-sized mixing bowl combine the breadcrumbs, lemon rind, parsley, orange rind, thyme, marjoram and butter. Stir in the lemon juice and eggs and blend well.

Use the stuffing for the rib cavity and the neck end cavity of the turkey.

Parsley Potatoes

An easy and delicious way to serve new potatoes, Parsley Potatoes may be served as an accompaniment to any meat or fish dish.

4-6 SERVINGS
2 lb. new potatoes, scrubbed
¼ teaspoon salt
2 oz. [¼ cup] butter
4 tablespoons chopped fresh
    parsley

Place the potatoes in a large saucepan and pour in enough water to cover. Add the salt and set the pan over high heat. Bring the water to the boil. Reduce the heat to low and simmer the potatoes for 15 to 20 minutes or until they are tender.

Remove the pan from the heat and drain the potatoes in a colander. Carefully peel the skins off the potatoes. Transfer the potatoes to a warmed serving dish and keep warm.

In a small saucepan, melt the butter over moderate heat. When the foam subsides, remove the pan from the heat. Stir in the parsley. Spoon the butter and parsley mixture over the potatoes. Using two large spoons, toss the potatoes to coat them with the butter and parsley mixture. Serve at once.

Parsley Potatoes are delicious new potatoes, coated in butter and parsley.

Parsley Sauce

A delicious green sauce, Parsley Sauce goes very well with fish or lighter meat dishes.

ABOUT 15 FLUID OUNCES [1⅞ CUPS]
10 tablespoons chopped fresh
    parsley
15 fl. oz. [1⅞ cups] béchamel sauce,
    hot
1 tablespoon single [light] cream
⅛ teaspoon cayenne pepper

Put enough water in a medium-sized saucepan to make a ½-inch layer in the bottom. Add the parsley. Place the pan over high heat and bring the water to the boil. Cover the pan, reduce the heat to low and simmer for 5 minutes.

Remove the pan from the heat and drain the parsley in a strainer, pressing out any excess moisture with the back of a wooden spoon.

Stir the parsley into the béchamel sauce. Add the cream and cayenne and blend well. Taste the sauce and add salt and pepper if necessary.

Pour the sauce into a warmed sauceboat and serve at once.

Parsnip

Parsnip is a root vegetable, carrot-like in shape, with a pale yellow exterior. It is one of the commonest winter vegetables grown in temperate climates — and also one of the least appreciated.

Parsnips are most usually added to stocks and soups but they make a delicious addition to casseroles and stews and taste excellent served as a vegetable accompaniment. Any recipes for CARROTS or KOHLRABI are suitable for parsnips.

To prepare parsnips for cooking, trim both ends and peel off the coarse outer skin. With a sharp knife, cut the parsnip in half, lengthways, and remove the hard centre core.

To cook parsnips, cut them into 2-inch lengths or thick slices and place them in a large saucepan. Add enough water just to cover and 1 teaspoon of salt. Bring the water to the boil over high heat. Reduce the heat to low, cover the pan and simmer the parsnips for 25 to 30 minutes or until they are tender. Remove the pan from the heat and transfer the parsnips to a colander to drain.

The parsnips are now ready to serve, or they may be added to a sauce, stew or casserole.

Parsnips, Glazed

A particularly delicious way to serve parsnips, Parsnips, Glazed goes especially well with grilled [broiled] or roast meat.

4 SERVINGS

2 oz. [¼ cup] butter, melted
12 small whole parsnips, cooked
2 oz. [⅓ cup] soft brown sugar

Preheat the oven to fairly hot 375°F (Gas Mark 5, 190°C).

Pour the butter into a medium-sized baking dish. Add the parsnips, sprinkle over the sugar and place the dish in the oven.

Bake, turning occasionally, for 10 to 15 minutes or until the parsnips are well glazed.

Remove the baking dish from the oven and transfer the parsnips to a warmed serving dish. Serve immediately.

Parsnips with Onions

Parsnips with Onions is a delicious vegetable accompaniment to grilled [broiled] fish dishes or cold meat.

4 SERVINGS

2 oz. [¼ cup] butter
2 medium-sized onions, thinly sliced
1 garlic clove, crushed
4 medium-sized parsnips, thickly sliced and cooked
1 tablespoon chopped fresh parsley

In a large frying-pan, melt the butter over moderate heat. When the foam subsides, add the onions and garlic and cook, stirring occasionally, for 5 to 7 minutes or until the onions are soft and translucent but not brown. Add the parsnips and cook, turning occasionally, for 5 to 8 minutes or until the parsnips are lightly and evenly browned and slightly crisp.

With a slotted spoon, transfer the parsnip and onion mixture to a warmed serving dish. Sprinkle over the parsley and serve at once.

Parsnips, Puréed

Parsnips, Puréed makes an excellent and very economical accompaniment to chops or grilled [broiled] steaks.

4 SERVINGS

6 large parsnips, cooked
1 oz. [2 tablespoons] butter
½ teaspoon salt
¼ teaspoon black pepper

1 tablespoon chopped fresh parsley

Using the back of a wooden spoon, gently rub the cooked parsnips through a wire strainer into a medium-sized saucepan. Discard any pulp remaining in the strainer. Alternatively, purée the parsnips in a food mill or electric blender and transfer the purée to the saucepan.

Add the butter, salt and pepper and place the pan over low heat. Gently cook the parsnip mixture, stirring frequently, for 2 to 3 minutes or until it is heated through and the butter has completely melted.

Remove the pan from the heat. Stir in the parsley and serve at once.

Parsnip Salad

The parsnip is a much more versatile vegetable than most people give it credit for — as this recipe proves. Parsnip Salad makes a delightful accompaniment to cold roast meats.

4 SERVINGS

6 medium-sized parsnips, sliced, cooked and cooled
8 oz. green beans, trimmed, cooked and cooled
2 spring onions [scallions], thinly sliced
6 fl. oz. [¾ cup] mayonnaise
6 large lettuce leaves, washed and shaken dry
¼ teaspoon paprika

Cut the parsnips into strips roughly the same size as the green beans and place the strips in a large mixing bowl. Add the green beans and spring onions [scallions]. Stir in the mayonnaise and, using two large spoons, toss until the vegetables are well coated.

Arrange the lettuce leaves decoratively on a large serving platter. Heap the parsnip mixture in the centre and sprinkle over the paprika.

Place the salad in the refrigerator to chill for 30 minutes before serving.

Parsnip and Tomato Soup

This warming, easy-to-make soup, flavoured with parsnips, tomatoes, garlic and thyme, tastes delicious served with croûtons and

A very versatile vegetable, the parsnip can be prepared in many different ways. Here are just two — Parsnips with Onions and Parsnip Salad.

poached eggs. For a richer soup, substitute single [light] cream for the milk used in this recipe.

6 SERVINGS

1 oz. [2 tablespoons] butter
2 medium-sized onions, thinly sliced
1 garlic clove, crushed
1 lb. parsnips, trimmed, peeled and chopped
3 tablespoons flour
1 teaspoon salt
½ teaspoon black pepper
½ teaspoon dried thyme
1½ pints [3¾ cups] chicken stock
5 fl. oz. [⅝ cup] milk
1 bay leaf
14 oz. canned peeled tomatoes

In a large saucepan, melt the butter over moderate heat. When the foam subsides, add the onions and fry, stirring occasion-

ally, for 5 to 7 minutes or until they are soft and translucent but not brown. Add the garlic and parsnips and fry, stirring occasionally, for 4 minutes.

Remove the pan from the heat and sprinkle over the flour, salt, pepper and thyme. Stir well with a wooden spoon to coat the vegetables with the flour and seasonings. Gradually add the chicken stock, stirring constantly and being careful to avoid lumps. Stir in the milk, bay leaf and tomatoes with the can juice.

Return the pan to the heat and bring the soup to the boil, stirring constantly. Reduce the heat to low, cover the pan and

simmer for 40 minutes, or until the parsnips are very tender. Remove the pan from the heat and remove and discard the bay leaf. Strain the soup into a large mixing bowl, rubbing the vegetables through the strainer with a wooden spoon until only a dry pulp is left. Discard the pulp in the strainer.

Alternatively, blend the soup in an electric blender.

Pour the soup back into the saucepan and return the pan to moderate heat. Cook the soup, stirring occasionally, for 2 to 3 minutes or until it is heated through.

Remove the pan from the heat. Pour the soup into a large, warmed tureen or individual soup bowls and serve immediately.

Partridge

Partridge, a small game bird found in many countries, is much prized for its succulent flesh. There are two main types, both edible: the grey or common partridge and the red-legged partridge. The latter is larger than the former but its flesh is considered to be less delicate.

In Britain, partridges are in season from 1st September to 1st February.

Partridge, in common with all game, is hung for varying periods (depending on the age of the bird, weather conditions, etc.) before it is plucked and cooked. Most shops selling game will clean and pluck the bird before selling it — and in addition will usually truss and lard a partridge which is going to be roasted.

Young partridges are considered to have particularly delicate flesh and are usually roasted, while older ones are most often used in casseroles or stews. One bird will feed one person.

Roast young partridges in an oven pre-heated to hot 425°F (Gas Mark 7, 220°C) for 20 to 25 minutes or until the flesh is tender when pierced with the point of a sharp knife, and the juices that run out are only faintly rosy.

Partridges Catalan-Style

An elegant and absolutely delicious dinner party dish, Partridges Catalan-Style may be served with puréed potatoes and buttered carrots.

2 SERVINGS

2 young partridges, trussed, larded and livers reserved
3 oz. [⅜ cup] butter
2 tablespoons chopped cooked ham
2 tablespoons flour
10 fl. oz. [1¼ cups] dry white wine
bouquet garni, consisting of 4 parsley sprigs, 1 thyme spray and 1 bay leaf tied together
pared rind of ½ small orange
1 tablespoon tomato purée
½ teaspoon salt
¼ teaspoon black pepper
6 garlic cloves, boiled in salted water for 10 minutes and drained

STUFFING
½ oz. [¼ cup] fresh breadcrumbs
2 tablespoons finely chopped cooked ham
½ tablespoon chopped fresh parsley
1 garlic clove, crushed
1 small egg, lightly beaten

First make the stuffing. Using a sharp knife, finely chop the reserved partridge livers and place them in a medium-sized mixing bowl. Add the remaining stuffing ingredients and mix well to blend.

Place the partridges on a flat surface and, with a teaspoon, gently and carefully spoon the stuffing mixture into the cavities. Close the cavities with a skewer or a trussing needle and thread.

In a large deep frying-pan, melt the butter over moderate heat. When the foam subsides, add the partridges to the pan and cook, carefully turning occasionally, for 6 to 8 minutes or until they are lightly and evenly browned. Using tongs or two large spoons, remove the partridges from the pan and set aside.

Add the chopped ham to the pan and cook, stirring frequently, for 2 minutes. Sprinkle over the flour and cook for a further 2 minutes, stirring constantly. Stir in the wine, then add the bouquet garni, orange rind, tomato purée, salt and pepper. Stir well to blend.

Bring the liquid to the boil over high heat. Reduce the heat to low and simmer for 8 minutes. Remove the pan from the heat and strain the liquid into a large flameproof casserole. Discard the contents of the strainer.

Add the partridges to the casserole and place it over low heat. Simmer the partridges, basting occasionally, for 10 minutes.

Stir in the garlic. Cover the casserole and cook for a further 20 to 25 minutes or until the partridges are tender when pierced with the point of a sharp knife.

Remove the pan from the heat and remove and discard the garlic cloves. Serve at once.

Partridges with Orange and Vermouth Sauce

A sophisticated dinner party dish, Partridges with Orange and Vermouth Sauce may be served with sautéed potatoes and buttered broccoli. A smooth red claret would be the perfect accompaniment.

4 SERVINGS

4 young partridges, halved
1 teaspoon salt
½ teaspoon black pepper
2 oz. [¼ cup] butter
1 small onion, chopped
6 fl. oz. [¾ cup] chicken stock
4 fl. oz. [½ cup] dry vermouth
4 fl. oz. [½ cup] fresh orange juice
5 fl. oz. double cream [⅝ cup heavy cream]
1 tablespoon chopped fresh chives
1 tablespoon beurre manié
2 oranges, peeled and thinly sliced

Sprinkle the partridges, inside and out,

with half the salt and pepper.

In a large saucepan, melt the butter over moderate heat. When the foam subsides, add the partridge halves and cook for 6 to 8 minutes or until they are lightly and evenly browned. Cover the pan and cook for a further 12 to 15 minutes on each side or until the partridges are tender when pierced with the point of a sharp knife.

Using tongs or two large spoons, transfer the partridge halves to a warmed serving dish. Keep warm while you make the sauce.

Pour off all but 1 tablespoon of fat from the pan. Add the onion and fry, stirring occasionally, for 5 to 7 minutes or until it

is soft and translucent but not brown.

Pour in the chicken stock and vermouth and add the remaining salt and pepper. Increase the heat to high and boil for 5 to 7 minutes or until the liquid has reduced by about one-third.

Reduce the heat to moderate and add the orange juice, cream and chives. Gradually stir in the beurre manié, a small piece at a time. Continue cooking, stirring constantly, for 2 to 3 minutes or until the sauce is smooth and thick and hot but not boiling.

Remove the pan from the heat and pour the sauce over the partridges. Garnish with the orange slices and serve immediately.

Partridge Pie

Partridge Pie is rich and satisfying and is best accompanied by bland vegetables such as Brussels sprouts, buttered carrots, cabbage or potatoes. A smooth Beaune wine would go beautifully with Partridge Pie.

6 SERVINGS

2 oz. [¼ cup] butter
1 lb. pie veal, cut into small cubes
4 oz. button mushrooms, wiped clean and sliced
4 oz. lean cooked ham, roughly chopped
4 partridges, trussed, larded, roasted and meat removed from

Partridges with Orange and Vermouth Sauce and Partridges Catalan-Style.

the bone and cut into small pieces
2 tablespoons prepared French mustard
2 tablespoons chopped fresh parsley
1 teaspoon salt
½ teaspoon black pepper
4 fl. oz. [½ cup] home-made chicken stock
4 fl. oz. [½ cup] medium sherry
PASTRY
6 oz. [1½ cups] flour
¼ teaspoon salt

1½ oz. [3 tablespoons] butter
1½ oz. cream cheese
2 to 3 tablespoons iced water
1 egg, lightly beaten

First make the pastry. Sift the flour and salt into a large mixing bowl. Add the butter and cream cheese and cut them into small pieces with a table knife. Using your fingertips, rub the butter and cream cheese into the flour until the mixture resembles fine breadcrumbs.

Add 2 tablespoons of the water and mix it in with the knife. Lightly knead the

A nourishing dish of partridges and vegetables, Partridge Pot Roast can be served with potatoes and peas.

dough, adding more water if it looks too dry. Shape the dough into a ball, wrap it in greaseproof or waxed paper and chill in the refrigerator for 30 minutes.

Meanwhile, make the filling. In a medium-sized frying-pan, melt the butter over moderate heat. When the foam subsides, add the veal and cook, stirring and turning occasionally, for 5 minutes or until the cubes are lightly and evenly browned. Add the mushrooms and ham pieces and cook, stirring occasionally, for 3 minutes. Remove the pan from the heat and transfer the mixture to a large mixing bowl.

Add the partridge meat, mustard, parsley, salt and pepper to the bowl and mix well. Spoon the partridge mixture into a medium-sized deep pie dish and

pour over the stock and sherry. Set aside.

Preheat the oven to moderate 350°F (Gas Mark 4, 180°C).

Remove the dough from the refrigerator. On a lightly floured board, roll out the dough to a circle about 1-inch larger than the top of the pie dish. With a knife, cut a ½-inch strip around the dough. Dampen the rim of the dish with water and press the dough strip on to the rim. With a pastry brush dipped in water, lightly moisten the strip.

Using the rolling pin, lift the dough on to the dish. With a knife, trim the dough and, with your fingers, crimp the edges to seal. Use the pastry trimmings to make leaves or a flower to decorate the top of the pie. With a sharp knife, cut a slit in the centre of the pie. With a pastry brush, brush the top of the dough with the beaten egg.

Place the pie in the oven and bake for 45 to 50 minutes or until the pastry is golden brown.

Remove the pie from the oven and serve immediately.

Partridge Pot Roast

A hearty, nourishing and delicious pot roast, Partridge Pot Roast may be served with mashed potatoes and buttered peas. Serve with a good red Rhône wine, such as Hermitage.

4-6 SERVINGS

2 oz. [¼ cup] butter
2 medium-sized onions, chopped
2 medium-sized carrots, scraped and sliced
6 streaky bacon slices, chopped
4 oz. mushrooms, wiped clean and sliced
4 partridges, trussed and larded
½ teaspoon salt
½ teaspoon black pepper
bouquet garni, consisting of 4 parsley sprigs, 1 thyme spray and 1 bay leaf tied together
1½ pints [3¾ cups] beef stock
4 fl. oz. [½ cup] red wine
1 tablespoon beurre manié
2 tablespoons chopped fresh parsley

In a large frying-pan, melt the butter over moderate heat. When the foam subsides, add the onions and carrots and fry, stirring occasionally, for 5 to 7 minutes or until the onions are soft and translucent but not brown.

Using a slotted spoon, transfer the vegetables to a large flameproof casserole. Set aside.

Add the bacon and mushrooms to the pan and fry, stirring frequently, for 5

minutes or until the bacon is crisp and has rendered most of its fat. With a slotted spoon transfer the bacon mixture to the casserole.

Place the partridges in the pan and cook, turning them occasionally, for 6 to 8 minutes or until they are lightly and evenly browned.

Remove the pan from the heat and transfer the partridges to the casserole. Add the salt, pepper and bouquet garni. Pour over the stock and wine. Place the casserole over high heat and bring the liquid to the boil. Reduce the heat to low, cover the casserole and cook, stirring occasionally, for 1 hour until the partridges are tender when pierced with the point of a sharp knife.

Remove the casserole from the heat. Using tongs or two large spoons, remove the partridges from the casserole. Cut them into 4 pieces and keep warm. Strain the cooking liquid and set the vegetables aside to keep warm. Remove and discard the bouquet garni.

Return the strained cooking liquid to the casserole. Return the casserole to high heat and boil, stirring occasionally, for 5 to 7 minutes, or until the cooking liquid has reduced by about one-third.

Reduce the heat to low. Gradually stir in the beurre manié, a small piece at a time, and continue cooking, stirring constantly, for 2 to 3 minutes or until the sauce is smooth and has thickened.

Replace the partridges and vegetables in the casserole and stir in the parsley. Cook for a further 2 to 3 minutes or until the pot roast is piping hot. Remove the casserole from the heat and serve immediately.

Partridges Stuffed with Mushrooms

A delicious dinner party dish, Partridges Stuffed with Mushrooms may be served with roast potatoes and buttered broccoli. A smooth claret would go excellently with this dish.

4 SERVINGS

2 oz. [¼ cup] butter
1 small onion, finely chopped
4 lean bacon slices, chopped
8 oz. mushrooms, wiped clean and sliced
½ teaspoon salt
¼ teaspoon black pepper
½ teaspoon paprika
1 tablespoon chopped fresh parsley
4 young partridges, trussed and larded
1 oz. [¼ cup] flour
15 fl. oz. [1⅞ cups] chicken stock

In a medium-sized frying-pan, melt 1 ounce [2 tablespoons] of the butter over moderate heat. When the foam subsides, add the onion and bacon and fry, stirring occasionally, for 5 to 7 minutes or until the onion is soft and translucent but not brown.

Add the mushrooms and cook, stirring occasionally, for 3 minutes. Remove the pan from the heat. Add the salt, pepper, paprika and parsley and mix well. Set aside.

Preheat the oven to hot 425°F (Gas Mark 7, 220°C). Using the remaining butter, generously grease a medium-sized roasting tin. Set aside.

Place the partridges on a flat working surface. Using a teaspoon, carefully stuff the mushroom mixture into the cavities. Close the cavities with a skewer or a trussing needle and thread. Place the partridges in the roasting tin. Place the roasting tin in the oven and roast for 20 to 25 minutes or until the partridges are tender when pierced with the point of a sharp knife.

Remove the roasting tin from the oven. Transfer the partridges to a warmed serving dish. Keep warm while you make the sauce.

Sprinkle the flour into the roasting tin and stir well with a wooden spoon. Place the tin over moderate heat and gradually add the stock, stirring constantly. Bring

Partridge Terrine is a rich mixture of chicken livers and partridges, and makes an excellent first course.

the sauce to the boil and cook, stirring constantly, for 5 to 8 minutes or until the sauce has thickened.

Remove the tin from the heat. Pour the sauce into a warmed sauceboat and serve at once, with the partridges.

Partridge Terrine

A rich, dense terrine made from alternate layers of chicken liver farce and thin strips of partridge, Partridge Terrine is best kept for a day or two before eating. Serve Partridge Terrine with a green salad and crusty bread for a light lunch or with toast triangles for a first course.

4-8 SERVINGS

1 oz. [2 tablespoons] plus 1 teaspoon butter
1 large onion, finely chopped
1 garlic clove, crushed
12 oz. chicken livers, chopped
3 oz. [1½ cups] fresh breadcrumbs
2 tablespoons chopped fresh parsley
½ teaspoon ground allspice
1 teaspoon salt

½ teaspoon black pepper
2 fl. oz. [¼ cup] brandy
1 egg, lightly beaten
3 partridges, trussed, larded, roasted and meat removed from the bones and cut into thin strips
6 streaky bacon slices

In a medium-sized frying-pan, melt 1 ounce [2 tablespoons] of the butter over moderate heat. When the foam subsides, add the onion and garlic and fry, stirring occasionally, for 5 to 7 minutes or until the onion is soft and translucent but not brown.

Using a slotted spoon, transfer the onion and garlic mixture to a large mixing bowl. Set aside.

Add the chicken livers to the pan and fry, stirring occasionally, for 3 to 4 minutes or until they are tender but still slightly pink inside.

Remove the pan from the heat. Using the slotted spoon, transfer the chicken livers to the bowl with the onion mixture. Add the breadcrumbs, parsley, allspice, salt, pepper and brandy and mix well. Stir in the egg and set the mixture aside.

Preheat the oven to moderate 350°F (Gas Mark 4, 180°C).

Using the teaspoon of butter, grease a 2-pint [1½-quart] terrine or ovenproof dish. Spread a layer of the chicken liver mixture on the bottom of the terrine.

Cover with a layer of partridge strips. Continue making layers in this way until all the ingredients have been used up, ending with the chicken liver mixture. Arrange the bacon in criss-cross fashion on top. Cover the terrine with aluminium foil. Place the terrine in a large roasting tin half filled with boiling water and place the tin in the oven. Bake for 1 to 1½ hours or until the mixture has shrunk slightly from the sides of the dish.

Remove the terrine from the oven and let it cool to room temperature. Place the terrine in the refrigerator to chill for at least 6 hours.

Unmould the terrine on to a serving dish. Cut into slices and serve.

Party Cake

        ⧓ ⧓ ⧓

Basically a plain cake, Party Cake is given a delicious flavour by adding whisky-soaked sultanas or raisins to the mixture. Serve it in thick wedges with freshly percolated coffee.

ONE 9-INCH CAKE
thinly pared rind of 2 lemons
8 oz. [1⅓ cups] sultanas or seedless raisins
4 fl. oz. [½ cup] whisky
6 oz. [¾ cup] plus 1 tablespoon butter, softened

A plain cake stuffed with whisky-soaked sultanas and candied peel, Party Cake is baked until deep golden, cooled and cut into thick wedges.

6 oz. [1½ cups] flour
1 teaspoon baking powder
6 oz. [¾ cup] castor sugar
4 eggs, separated
3 oz. [½ cup] chopped candied peel

Place the lemon rind and sultanas or seedless raisins in a medium-sized bowl and pour over the whisky. Set aside to marinate at room temperature for 12 hours or overnight.

Preheat the oven to moderate 350°F (Gas Mark 4, 180°C). Using half the tablespoon of butter, grease a 9-inch cake tin. Line the cake tin with greaseproof or waxed paper and grease with the remaining half tablespoon of butter.

Sift the flour and baking powder into a medium-sized mixing bowl. Set aside.

In a large mixing bowl, cream the remaining butter and the sugar together with a wooden spoon until the mixture is light and fluffy. Beat in the egg yolks, one at a time, adding a tablespoon of flour with each addition. Stir in the lemon rind, sultanas or raisins and whisky and another tablespoon of the flour. Stir in the candied peel.

Using a metal spoon, fold in the remaining flour.

In a medium-sized mixing bowl beat the egg whites with a wire whisk or rotary beater until they form stiff peaks. Using the metal spoon, gently fold the egg whites into the butter and flour mixture.

Spoon the batter into the prepared cake tin and place the tin in the centre of the oven. Bake for 1 hour, or until a skewer inserted into the centre of the cake comes out clean.

Remove the cake from the oven and leave it in the tin for 10 minutes. Turn the cake out on to a wire rack to cool completely before serving.

Paskha

RUSSIAN EASTER DESSERT

Easter is the main festival of the Russian Orthodox church, a time when families come together, when a great deal of food is consumed, when rejoicing is general. Paskha (pash-kah), a luscious dessert made from cream cheese, sour cream, almonds and fruit, is an integral part of the feasting. A special pyramid-shaped perforated mould, called a paskha mould, is traditionally used to make this dish, but a flower pot or colander with suitable perforations may be substituted. Paskha is usually decorated with nuts and crystallized [candied] fruit. Cottage cheese may be used instead of the cream cheese.

6-8 SERVINGS .

2 lb. cream cheese
4 oz. [½ cup] butter, softened
4 fl. oz. [½ cup] sour cream
4 oz. [½ cup] sugar
1 egg yolk
½ teaspoon vanilla essence
   very finely grated rind of
   1 lemon
3 tablespoons sultanas or seedless
   raisins
2 tablespoons raisins
2 tablespoons slivered almonds
1 tablespoon slivered almonds,
   toasted
1 tablespoon chopped glacé
   cherries

Place the cream cheese in a large wire strainer set over a small mixing bowl. Cover the cheese with a clean cloth and place a heavy weight on top. Leave the cheese to drain for at least 1½ hours.

Discard any liquid in the bowl. Transfer the cheese to a large mixing bowl. With a wooden spoon, beat the butter into the cheese, a little at a time, and continue beating until the mixture is well blended.

In a medium-sized mixing bowl, combine the sour cream, sugar and egg yolk with a fork or spoon, beating until the sugar has dissolved. Gradually add the sour cream mixture to the cream cheese mixture, beating constantly. Beat in the vanilla essence and grated lemon rind. Fold in the sultanas or seedless raisins, the raisins, almonds, toasted almonds and glacé cherries. Set aside.

Line a paskha mould, if you have one, or some similar perforated mould with cheesecloth or muslin. Spoon in the cream cheese mixture and smooth the top with a flat-bladed knife. Cover the mould with a clean, damp cloth and place a heavy weight on top. Place the mould, on a large plate, in the refrigerator to chill for 8 hours or overnight.

To serve, remove the weight and cloth from the mould. Place a serving dish, inverted, over the mould and reverse the two, giving the mould a sharp shake. The dessert should slide out easily. Remove and discard the cheesecloth or muslin. The paskha is now ready to decorate and serve.

Passion Fruit

Passion fruit, or GRANADILLA, is the fruit of a perennial plant native to Brazil but now cultivated widely in most tropical countries.

Passion fruit is small and oval in shape with a dark purple, wrinkled skin. It is generally eaten as a dessert fruit and used for making sweet drinks and ices.

Passion Fruit and Banana Cream

A light, cream dessert that can be made in a matter of minutes, Passion Fruit and Banana Cream should be made just before serving to prevent the bananas from turning brown.

4 SERVINGS

4 ripe bananas
4 passion fruit
5 fl. oz. single cream [⅝ cup light
   cream]

In a small mixing bowl, mash the bananas with a fork until they form a thick purée.

Cut two of the passion fruit in half and, using a teaspoon, scoop out the pulp. Combine the passion fruit pulp with the banana purée. Add the cream and mix well. Transfer the mixture to 4 individual dessert glasses.

Cut the remaining passion fruit in half and spoon the pulp from each half on to the top of each serving. Place the glasses in the refrigerator to chill for 30 minutes before serving.

Passion Fruit and Banana Cream — easy to prepare and really delicious.

Pasta

Pasta, a name that is almost synonymous with Italian cuisine, is a farinaceous product made from flour, water and sometimes eggs. The flour used is made from a hard or durum wheat with a high gluten content, which gives the dough its slightly brittle consistency.

Pasta is usually made commercially these days, although some types — most particularly EGG NOODLES, RAVIOLI and GNOCCHI — are still traditionally made at home. In the factories, machines are used to produce the different shapes and sizes of pasta sold to the public as the familiar CANNELLONI, FARFALLE, FETTUCCINE, FUSILLI, LASAGNE, MACARONI, MANICOTTI, NOODLES, RAVIOLI, TAGLIATELLI, TORTELLINI, VERMICELLI, ZITE. Spinach is sometimes added to the basic pasta dough — thus fettuccine verdi and lasagne verdi.

Pasta is always served with a sauce of some kind — even though it may be as simple as melted butter and grated cheese. In Italy pasta is served as the course before the main, usually meat, course of the meal, although in other parts of Europe and the United States pasta is more often served as a main course. The lighter, smaller pasta, such as vermicelli, is often used in soups, and heavier pasta, such as macaroni, is made into substantial sweet or savoury puddings.

A varied selection of different shapes and types of pasta.

Pastel de Choclo

MEAT AND CORN PIE

A Chilean national dish, Pastel de Choclo (pah-stell day chorc-loh) is usually made with corn kernels stripped from fresh corn ears. When corn is in season, six ears will provide enough kernels for this recipe.

4 SERVINGS

1 teaspoon butter
3 tablespoons vegetable oil
2 medium-sized onions, thinly sliced
1 red chilli, seeded and finely chopped
1 garlic clove, crushed
12 oz. minced [ground] beef
12 oz. minced [ground] pork
1 teaspoon salt
1 teaspoon ground cumin
½ teaspoon hot chilli powder
1 tablespoon flour
2 oz. [⅓ cup] black olives, stoned
3 oz. [½ cup] raisins, soaked in water for 15 minutes and drained

TOPPING

2 tablespoons vegetable oil
1 medium-sized onion, finely chopped
12 oz. canned sweetcorn kernels, drained and puréed in a food mill or electric blender
½ teaspoon salt

From Chile, Pastel de Choclo makes an appetizing supper dish.

Preheat the oven to fairly hot 375°F (Gas Mark 5, 190°C). Grease a 2-pint [1½-quart] baking dish with the butter. Set aside.

In a large frying-pan, heat the oil over moderate heat. When the oil is hot, add the onions, chilli and garlic and fry, stirring occasionally, for 5 to 7 minutes or until the onions are soft and translucent but not brown.

Add the beef and pork and fry, stirring frequently, for 6 to 8 minutes or until the meat is well browned. Stir in the salt, cumin, chilli powder and flour. Mix in the olives and the raisins. Remove the pan from the heat. Spoon the mixture into the prepared baking dish. Set aside.

To make the topping, in a small frying-pan, heat the oil over moderate heat. When the oil is hot, add the onion and fry, stirring occasionally, for 5 to 7 minutes or until it is soft and translucent but not brown. Add the puréed sweetcorn and salt and cook, stirring occasionally, for 5 minutes. Remove the pan from the heat. Spoon the corn mixture evenly over the meat mixture in the baking dish.

Place the dish in the oven and bake the pie for 20 to 25 minutes or until the top is golden brown.

Remove the dish from the oven and serve immediately.

Pasteurization

Pasteurization is the process of heating and cooling certain foods and liquids (notably milk) to destroy bacteria, without impairing the quality of the product. Pasteurization, named after its inventor Louis Pasteur, also helps to prolong the keeping qualities of certain products.

Pastilles

Pastilles are small gum or boiled sugar sweets [candies] usually flavoured with concentrated fruit juices or essences, and coloured according to their flavour. Pastilles made for medicinal purposes (mainly for the relief of chest and throat irritations) are often flavoured with menthol, eucalyptus or honey.

Pastilles Flavoured with Lemon

These little lemon-flavoured sweets [candies] are very easy and quick to make. They can be flavoured with any fruit essence, for example blackcurrant or orange, and coloured accordingly.

Little golden boiled sweets [candies], Pastilles Flavoured with Lemon are both quick and easy to make.

ABOUT 24 SWEETS [CANDIES]

6 oz. [¾ cup] castor sugar
2 oz. icing sugar [½ cup confectioners' sugar]
6 fl. oz. [¾ cup] water
½ teaspoon lemon essence
2 drops yellow food colouring
1 teaspoon vegetable oil

In a small saucepan, dissolve the castor sugar and icing [confectioners'] sugar in the water over low heat, stirring constantly. When the sugar has dissolved, stir in the lemon essence and yellow food colouring. Increase the heat to moderate and boil the mixture, without stirring, until it registers 265°F on a sugar thermometer, or until a little of the mixture dropped into cold water forms a hard ball.

Remove the pan from the heat and set aside to cool for 3 minutes.

Using the teaspoon of oil, lightly grease a marble slab or a hard smooth working surface.

Using a lightly oiled metal teaspoon, drop spoonfuls of the lemon mixture on to the marble slab or working surface, spacing them apart slightly.

Leave the sweets [candies] to cool and harden completely before serving.

Pastis

As well as being the name of a classic cake, pastis (pass-tees) is also a French aniseed-flavoured liqueur, very similar in both appearance and taste to the Greek OUZO. Pastis, like ouzo, is usually diluted with water which makes it cloudy.

Pastis is particularly popular in the South of France.

Pastis

RICH EGG AND BRANDY CAKE

A classic French cake, Pastis (pah-stee) is delicious served plain or with butter and jam.

ONE 2-POUND CAKE

½ oz. fresh yeast
6 oz. [¾ cup] plus ¼ teaspoon castor sugar
2 tablespoons lukewarm milk
1 lb. [4 cups] flour
⅛ teaspoon salt
4 eggs
1 oz. [2 tablespoons] plus 1 teaspoon butter, melted
3 tablespoons brandy

GLAZE

1 egg yolk, well beaten with 2 tablespoons milk
2 tablespoons soft brown sugar

Crumble the yeast into a small mixing bowl and mash in ¼ teaspoon of the sugar with a kitchen fork. Add the lukewarm milk and cream the milk and yeast together to form a smooth paste. Set the bowl aside in a warm, draught-free place for 15 to 20 minutes, or until the yeast mixture is puffed up and frothy.

Meanwhile, sift the flour and salt into a medium-sized, warmed mixing bowl. Stir in the remaining sugar and set aside.

In a small mixing bowl, beat the eggs, 1 ounce [2 tablespoons] of the melted butter and the brandy together with a kitchen fork until they are well blended.

Make a well in the centre of the flour mixture and pour in the yeast mixture and the egg and brandy mixture.

Using a spatula or your fingers, mix the liquids together, gradually drawing in the flour mixture. When all the flour mixture has been incorporated and the dough comes away from the sides of the bowl, turn the dough out on to a lightly floured working surface. Knead it vigorously for 10 minutes, or until it is smooth and elastic. Shape the dough into a ball.

Rinse, dry and lightly grease the mixing bowl. Place the dough in the bowl and sprinkle over a little flour. Cover the bowl with a clean, damp cloth and set it aside in a warm, draught-free place for 2 hours, or until the dough has risen slightly.

Using the remaining teaspoon of melted butter, grease a 2-pound loaf tin and set it aside.

Turn the risen dough out of the bowl on to a lightly floured working surface and knead it for 5 minutes.

Shape the dough into a loaf and place it in the prepared tin. Cover the tin with a clean, damp cloth and set it aside in a warm, draught-free place for 30 minutes.

Preheat the oven to hot 425°F (Gas Mark 7, 220°C).

Using a pastry brush, lightly brush the top of the dough with the egg yolk and milk mixture. Sprinkle over the sugar.

Place the tin in the centre of the oven and bake the cake for 10 minutes. Then reduce the oven temperature to fairly hot 375°F (Gas Mark 5, 190°C) and bake for a further 55 minutes to 1 hour or until the cake is golden on top.

To test if the cake is cooked, remove it from the oven and turn it out of the tin. If the cake sounds hollow when you rap the underside with your knuckles, it is cooked. If the cake is not cooked, return it to the oven and bake for a further 10 minutes.

Cool the cake completely on a wire rack before serving.

Pastourma

Pastourma is a black smoked bacon, highly flavoured with garlic, eaten in Greece and Turkey. The bacon is generally fried until crisp then eaten with accompaniments.

Pastrami

Pastrami is a highly spiced smoked beef very popular as a sandwich filling in the United States. It may be served hot or cold, although the tradition in America is to serve it warm, liberally spread with mustard, on rye bread.

Pastry

Pastry is an unleavened dough, generally made from shortening (fats), flour and liquid, which is rolled out and used to line flan and tart tins, or to envelope or cover sweet and savoury fillings. The seven basic pastries are PUFF, ROUGH PUFF, SHORTCRUST, RICH SHORTCRUST, HOT WATER CRUST, CHOUX, SUET and flaky. Pastry is also the term loosely applied to sweet baked pastry confections, for example DANISH PASTRIES and jam turnovers.

The basic ingredients used to make pastry are:

Flour In almost every kind of pastry dough, refined plain [all-purpose] white wheat flour is used. Self-raising flour is used only when a heavier ingredient such as suet is incorporated.

Salt In most doughs, salt is added in amounts varying from ⅛ teaspoon to 1 teaspoon.

Sugar Sugar is added to sweet pastry doughs.

Shortening All pastry dough includes a shortening (a general term which describes fats used in doughs) in proportions which vary according to the richness of the pastry — the more shortening, the richer the pastry. Generally, butter is used, but margarine, suet, lard, vegetable fat and oil or a combination of shortenings — such as butter and vegetable fat in SHORTCRUST PASTRY—are also used.

Liquid Liquid is added to the flour and shortening mixture to bind it and make it more pliable. Water is most commonly used, but other liquids such as eggs, milk, cream, sour cream and buttermilk may be used.

Flavourings Cheese, herbs, spices and essences may be added to the basic pastry dough.

Yeast In some types of doughs, such as that used for making DANISH PASTRIES, yeast is used.

The method by which the shortening is incorporated into the flour determines the texture of the finished pastry. In PUFF, ROUGH PUFF and flaky pastry, the shortening, generally butter, is added either in one large or several smaller pieces and rolled and folded into the flour and liquid mixture. The resulting texture is, as the names of the pastries imply, very light and flaky. For closer-textured pastries, such as SHORTCRUST, the shortening is cut into small pieces and rubbed into the flour with the fingertips until the mixture resembles fine or coarse breadcrumbs. For cooked and even closer-textured pastry doughs, such as CHOUX or HOT WATER CRUST, the shortening is melted with the liquid and then stirred or beaten into the flour. The eggs in choux pastry open out the texture.

The basic points to remember when making pastry dough are:

1. Unless the dough is made with yeast, or cooked, the ingredients and implements should be kept cool. For some pastry doughs, such as PUFF, the ingredients should also be chilled.

2. Again with the exception of yeast and cooked doughs, a minimum of handling is desirable. When possible, use a table knife or pastry blender to incorporate the shortening into the flour. When rubbing the shortening into the flour, use your fingertips and work quickly and lightly. The more you handle the dough, the stickier and less manageable it becomes.

3. When rolling out dough, place it on a lightly floured working surface and use a floured rolling pin. Make sure that the dough does not stick to the surface as it is rolled out. Roll the dough lightly away from you. Do not turn the dough over or it will absorb too much flour from the working surface. If the dough is sticky or contains a high proportion of shortening, chill it in the refrigerator before rolling it out to make the handling easier.

4. Generally speaking, pastry should be baked, or at least start its baking time, in a hot oven. Long, slow baking produces hard, flat-tasting pastry.

5. Closer-textured pastry doughs, such as SHORTCRUST and RICH SHORTCRUST, are more suitable for lining flans and pie dishes and for baking blind. All types of pastry doughs are suitable for covering pies and enveloping sweet or savoury fillings.

If you have a freezer, it is well worth your while to make extra dough and store it in the freezer. Wrap it in quantities that are suitable for use, for example 8 ounces [2 cups] and 1 pound [4 cups]. Remember to remove it from the freezer at least 30 minutes before using so that the dough can thaw out thoroughly.

Pastry pies, tarts and flan cases can also be frozen. For most successful results it is best to freeze the pastry dough uncooked. If the pie has a cooked filling, such as steak and kidney, this should be cooked and cooled before covering with the pastry dough. Make sure all pastry doughs are wrapped in special freezer packaging.

Note: in all our recipes for basic pastry doughs, the yield is based on the amount of flour used. In other words, if 8 ounces [2 cups] of flour are used, the yield will be given as 8 ounces [2 cups] of pastry dough.

Pastry Bag

Pastry Bag is another name for FORCING BAG.

Pastry Blender

A pastry blender is a useful implement which is used to cut fats into flour for pastry-making. It consists of strips of thick wire or sharp metal, shaped in a

semi-circle and joined at each end to a wooden or plastic handle.

The advantages of using a pastry blender rather than your fingertips to blend the fat into the flour are that it keeps the handling of the dough to a minimum, and is less messy.

Pastry Cake

This unusual very rich fruit cake, traditionally called Black Bun in Scotland, is covered in a crisp pastry. Pastry Cake is best made at least two weeks before serving as this improves the flavour — wrap it in aluminium foil and store it in a cool place.

ONE 7-INCH CAKE

PASTRY

12 oz. [3 cups] flour
¼ teaspoon salt
3 oz. [⅜ cup] butter
2 tablespoons sugar
2 small eggs, lightly beaten
4 to 6 tablespoons iced water

FILLING

8 oz. [2 cups] flour
1 teaspoon bicarbonate of soda
   [baking soda]
1½ teaspoons baking powder
4 oz. [⅔ cup] soft brown sugar
1 teaspoon mixed spice or ground
   allspice
½ teaspoon ground cinnamon
½ teaspoon ground ginger
¼ teaspoon ground mace
12 oz. [2 cups] sultanas or seedless
   raisins
12 oz. [2 cups] currants
4 oz. [⅔ cup] almonds, chopped
4 oz. [⅔ cup] walnuts, chopped
4 oz. [⅔ cup] chopped mixed
   candied peel
   grated rind and juice of 1 lemon
6 fl. oz. [¾ cup] milk
1 tablespoon brandy
1 egg, lightly beaten

First, make the pastry. Sift the flour and salt into a medium-sized mixing bowl. Add the butter and cut it into small pieces with a table knife. With your fingertips, rub the butter into the flour until the mixture resembles fine breadcrumbs. Mix in the sugar.

Add the beaten eggs with 4 tablespoons of the iced water and mix them into the flour mixture with the knife. Add more water if the dough is too dry.

Knead the dough gently and form it into a ball. Wrap the dough in greaseproof or waxed paper and place it in the refrigerator to chill for 30 minutes.

Divide the dough into two unequal pieces and set the smaller piece aside. On a lightly floured board, roll out the larger piece of dough to a circle about ½-inch thick. Carefully lift the dough on the rolling pin and place it over a 7-inch cake tin. Gently ease the dough into the tin to line the bottom and sides. Trim off any excess dough. Place the tin in the refrigerator to chill while you make the filling.

For Pastry Cake gently ease the dough into the tin then press the dough against the sides and bottom.

Spoon the filling into the pastry case. Press the filling flat with the back of the wooden spoon.

Preheat the oven to fairly hot 400°F (Gas Mark 6, 200°C).

Sift the flour, soda and baking powder into a large mixing bowl. Stir in the sugar, mixed spice or ground allspice, cinnamon, ginger, mace, sultanas or seedless raisins, currants, almonds, walnuts, mixed peel, and the lemon rind and juice. Pour in the milk and brandy. Using a wooden spoon, mix all the ingredients together until they are thoroughly combined.

Spoon the filling into the pastry case. Press the filling flat with the back of the spoon.

Set aside.

On a lightly floured board, roll out the smaller piece of dough into a circle large enough to cover the top of the tin. Dampen the edges of the dough already in the tin. Lift the dough circle on the

Using a wooden spoon, mix all the ingredients together until they are all thoroughly combined.

Dampen the edges of the dough in the tin. Lift the dough circle on to the tin and lay over the filling.

rolling pin and lay it over the filling. Press the edges together to seal them. Using a sharp knife, cut a fairly large cross in the centre of the dough. Using a pastry brush, brush the dough with the beaten egg.

Place the tin in the oven and bake for 15 minutes. Remove the tin from the oven and cover it with aluminium foil. Reduce the oven temperature to warm 325°F (Gas Mark 3, 170°C) and return the tin to the oven. Continue baking for 3½ hours, or until a skewer inserted into the centre of the cake comes out clean.

Remove the tin from the oven and carefully turn the cake out on to a wire rack to cool completely.

When the cake is cold, wrap it in aluminium foil and leave for at least 1 week before serving.

Pastry Cutter

There are two types of pastry cutter. The first is a small fluted wheel attached to a wooden handle, and it is used to cut rolled out dough.

The second type of pastry cutter (also known as a biscuit [cookie] cutter) is generally made of metal. It can be round, square, oval, patterned, plain or fluted. It is hollow, with sharp edges, and varies in size from $\frac{1}{2}$-inch to 7-inches in diameter. This type of pastry cutter is not only used to cut dough, but any substance that is rolled out or flat and needs to be cut into a uniform shape, for example marzipan and bread slices.

Made in various sizes, the biscuit [cookie] cutter is used to cut any substance rolled out flat.

A small fluted wheel attached to a wooden handle, this pastry cutter is used to cut rolled-out dough.

Pastry Glazes

Pastry is usually glazed with egg yolk, lightly beaten egg white, egg white and sugar or whole beaten egg. Of these, egg yolk usually produces the glossiest finish. Sweet pastry can be brushed lightly with water and then sprinkled with sugar for a pretty sparkling effect. Milk or a mixture of milk and sugar is also a successful glaze, although the result is not as shiny as egg yolk. Fruit pies are sometimes glazed with sweetened fruit juice.

An open-face fruit tart is glazed with jam. Choose a jam of the same colour as the fruit. Spread the glaze over the fruit in the tart after the tart has cooked but while the fruit is still warm. If the pastry case has been baked blind, glaze it with a jam glaze before putting in the fruit. The glaze prevents the fruit juices from seeping into the pastry and making it soggy.

Pasty

Pasties are semi-circular pastry cases, usually made from shortcrust pastry and filled with meat and vegetables or fruit. The most famous pasties are CORNISH PASTIES which are filled with chopped beef, potatoes and turnips.

Pâte

Pâte (pat) is the French word for pastry. The French make pastry in a different way from many other methods. The flour is sifted on to a large board, or marble slab. A well is made in the centre of the flour and into the well is placed the butter, and the egg or egg yolk and sugar if used. The sugar used is either icing [confectioners'] sugar, if a very soft dough is required, or castor sugar.

Using the fingertips of one hand, the butter, egg and sugar are first blended together. The flour is then gradually incorporated. As soon as all the flour is incorporated the fingers are cleaned and the dough is then lightly kneaded with the heel of the hand. As soon as the dough can be formed into a ball the kneading should stop, otherwise the dough will become sticky and hard to manage. For small quantities of dough, this blending movement should not be repeated more than about five times.

The dough is formed into a ball, wrapped in greaseproof or waxed paper and chilled in the refrigerator for at least 30 minutes, but preferably for 1 hour or longer, before it is used.

To roll out, place the dough on a lightly floured board or marble slab and roll out away from you with quick light strokes. Carefully lift the dough on the rolling pin and lay it over the pie or flan dish. This

To make Pâte the butter and eggs are placed in the centre of the flour.

Using the fingertips of one hand, the butter, egg and sugar are blended.

The flour is then gradually incorporated into the other ingredients.

The dough is formed into a ball and kneaded with the heel of the hand.

whole operation must be done as quickly as possible before the butter has a chance to soften. Once the butter has softened, the dough will stick to the board.

To bake the dough shell blind (for fruit tarts and flans), preheat the oven to fairly hot 375°F (Gas Mark 5, 190°C).

Prick the base of the shell all over with a fork. Line the shell with aluminium foil or greaseproof or waxed paper and fill it with dried beans. Place the shell in the oven and bake for 15 minutes. Remove the shell from the oven and remove the beans and the foil or paper. Return the shell to the oven and continue baking for a further 5 minutes or until the pastry is lightly browned.

The best-known pâtes are:
PATE SUCREE, a rich, sweet short pastry; Pâte Brisée, which is made with the same proportions of fat to flour as ordinary SHORTCRUST PASTRY — sometimes with the addition of an egg; sugar can be added if a sweet pastry is desired;
Pâte Moulée, a type of shortcrust pastry often used for raised pies;
PATE A PATE, similar to Pâte Moulée but slightly richer; excellent as a crust for PATES EN CROUTE.

Pâté

Pâtés (pa-tay) are made from minced [ground] liver, veal, pork or game or a mixture of them all. They are flavoured with herbs and liquor and either larded with pork fat or covered with strips of fatty bacon and baked in a terrine.

A successful pâté should contain as much fat meat as lean meat.

Pâtès may also be made from fish—cod's roe, salmon and kipper are particularly popular.

Most pâtés will keep for up to 10 days in a cool larder or refrigerator.

Originally a pâté was enclosed in pastry and could be served either hot or cold, but the words pâté and terrine are now used interchangeably, and both are nearly always served cold.

Pâté en Croûte I

STUFFED BONED DUCK WRAPPED IN PASTRY

☆ ☆ ☆ ① ① ① ✕ ✕ ✕

A rich, sophisticated dish of duck stuffed with veal and chicken livers and covered in pastry, Pâté en Croûte I (pa-tay on kroot) may be served cold with a crisp green salad.

6-8 SERVINGS

1 x 5 lb. duck, boned
1 oz. [2 tablespoons] plus 1 teaspoon butter
2 shallots, finely chopped
1 garlic clove, crushed

For Pâté en Croûte I, carefully slice off the thickest pieces of meat being careful not to pierce the skin.

Using a wooden spoon, mix two of the beaten eggs and the brandy into the mixture, blending thoroughly.

Place the stuffing in the centre of the duck. Fold the skin over the stuffing to enclose it completely.

Holding the skin firmly together, sew the duck up securely, using a trussing needle and string.

In a large frying-pan, fry the duck in the hot oil for 6 minutes, or until it is brown and crisp.

Lay the dough over the baking tin and place the duck in the centre. Fold and press the dough around the duck.

Lift the remaining dough on top of the duck. Trim the dough and crimp the two edges together to seal them.

Using the dough trimmings, make a decoration for the top of the dough case, and gently place in position.

Using a pastry brush, carefully brush the top and sides of the dough with the remaining beaten egg.

1 lb. lean veal, minced [ground]
8 oz. chicken livers, minced [ground]
8 streaky bacon slices, finely chopped
½ teaspoon salt
½ teaspoon black pepper
¼ teaspoon ground allspice
¼ teaspoon dried thyme
3 eggs, lightly beaten
3 tablespoons brandy
3 tablespoons vegetable oil
PASTRY
1½ lb. [6 cups] flour
1 teaspoon salt
1 lb. [2 cups] butter, cut into small pieces

4 egg yolks, lightly beaten
8 to 10 tablespoons water

First make the pastry. Sift the flour and salt on to a large marble slab. Make a well in the centre of the flour mixture and place the butter and egg yolks in the well. Using your fingertips mix the butter and egg yolks together, adding the water a little at a time and slowly drawing in the flour. Continue mixing in this way until all the flour is incorporated. Knead lightly until the dough forms a ball.

Cover the dough with greaseproof or waxed paper and chill in the refrigerator for 2 hours.

Meanwhile, lay the duck, skin side down, on a wooden board. With a sharp knife, carefully slice off the thickest pieces of meat, being careful not to pierce the skin. Chop the meat very finely and place it in a large mixing bowl. Set aside.

In a small frying-pan, melt 1 ounce [2 tablespoons] of the butter over moderate heat. When the foam subsides, add the shallots and garlic and fry, stirring occasionally, for 3 to 4 minutes or until the shallots are soft and translucent but not brown.

Remove the pan from the heat. Using a slotted spoon, transfer the shallot mixture to the chopped duck in the mixing bowl.

Add the veal, chicken livers, bacon,

salt, pepper, allspice and thyme and mix well.

Stir in two of the beaten eggs and the brandy.

Place the stuffing in the centre of the duck and form it into a loaf shape. Fold the duck skin over the stuffing to enclose it completely. Using a trussing needle and string, sew up the skin securely.

In a large frying-pan, heat the oil over moderate heat. When the oil is hot add the duck and fry it, turning occasionally, for 6 minutes or until it is brown and crisp.

Remove the pan from the heat and, using tongs or two large spoons, transfer the duck to kitchen paper towels. Set aside.

Using the remaining teaspoon of butter, lightly grease a large baking tin. Set aside.

Preheat the oven to moderate 350°F (Gas Mark 4, 180°C).

Remove the dough from the refrigerator. Break off one-third and set it aside. On a lightly floured surface, roll out the other two-thirds of the dough into a rectangle about ⅛-inch thick. Lift the dough on the rolling pin and lay it over the baking tin. Place the duck in the centre of the dough. Carefully fold the dough around it, pressing it into place so that it comes up the sides of the duck but leaves the top uncovered. Using a pastry brush, moisten the edges of the dough with a little of the remaining beaten egg.

On a lightly floured surface, roll out the remaining third of the dough. Lift the dough on the rolling pin and lay it on top of the duck. Trim it so that it overlaps the bottom dough by about ½-inch. Crimp the two edges together to seal. Use the dough trimmings to make a decoration for the top.

Using the pastry brush, brush the top and sides of the dough with the remaining beaten egg. Place the baking tin in the oven and bake for 2 hours. If the pastry starts to brown too much, cover with aluminium foil.

Remove the pâté from the oven and set it aside to cool to room temperature. Then chill it in the refrigerator until you are ready to serve it.

Pâté en Croûte II

VEAL AND PORK PATE WRAPPED IN PASTRY

A rich, delicious veal and pork pâté enclosed in pastry, Pâté en Croûte II (pa-tay on kroot) makes a superb dinner party dish accompanied by a crisp green salad. Served in small quantities it is also a magnificent first course.

6-8 SERVINGS

8 oz. lean veal, minced [ground]
4 oz. calf's liver, minced [ground]
8 oz. belly of pork, minced [ground]
2 oz. [⅔ cup] fine dry breadcrumbs
1 garlic clove, crushed
½ teaspoon dried thyme
¼ teaspoon grated nutmeg
1 teaspoon salt
½ teaspoon black pepper
1 tablespoon chopped fresh parsley
2 eggs, lightly beaten
2 tablespoons brandy
1 oz. [2 tablespoons] plus 1 teaspoon butter
4 oz. mushrooms, wiped clean and sliced
3 oz. lean cooked ham, cut into thin strips
6 oz. veal escalope, cut into thin strips
2 streaky bacon slices

PASTRY

12 oz. [3 cups] flour
½ teaspoon salt
8 oz. [1 cup] butter, cut into small pieces
2 egg yolks, lightly beaten
4 to 5 tablespoons water

First make the pastry. Sift the flour and salt on to a large marble slab. Make a well in the centre of the flour mixture and place the butter and egg yolks in the well. Using your fingertips, mix the butter and egg yolks together, adding the water a little at a time and slowly drawing in the flour. Continue mixing in this way until all the flour is incorporated. Knead lightly until the dough forms a ball.

Cover the dough with greaseproof or waxed paper and chill in the refrigerator for 2 hours.

Meanwhile, in a large mixing bowl, combine the veal, liver, pork, breadcrumbs, garlic, thyme, nutmeg, salt, pepper and parsley. Stir in the eggs and brandy and beat well to blend thoroughly. Set aside.

In a small frying-pan, melt 1 ounce [2 tablespoons] of the butter over moderate heat. When the foam subsides, add the mushrooms and fry, stirring occasionally, for 3 minutes. Remove the pan from the heat and, with a slotted spoon, transfer the mushrooms to a dish. Set aside.

Preheat the oven to moderate 350°F (Gas Mark 4, 180°C). Lightly grease a 2-pound loaf tin or terrine with the teaspoon of butter. Set aside.

A rich veal and pork pâté enveloped in golden pastry, Pâté en Croute II can be served as a dinner party dish, or as a first course.

Remove the dough from the refrigerator. Break off one-quarter of the dough and set it aside. On a lightly floured board, roll out the remaining three-quarters of the dough to an oblong about ¼-inch thick. Line the bottom and sides of the loaf tin or terrine with the dough, dampening the edges with water.

Place about one-half of the veal and liver mixture on the bottom of the dough-lined tin or terrine. Top with a layer of the ham, then a layer each of the veal

escalope and mushrooms.

Continue making layers in this way, finishing with a layer of the veal and liver mixture. Arrange the bacon slices on top. On a lightly floured surface, roll out the remaining dough to an oblong about $\frac{1}{4}$-inch thick. Lay it over the tin or terrine and trim off the excess dough. Crimp the edges of the dough together to seal. Roll out the trimmings and use them to make a decoration for the top.

Place the tin or terrine in the oven and bake for $1\frac{1}{2}$ hours, covering the top with aluminium foil if the pastry becomes brown too quickly.

Remove the pâté from the oven and serve at once, or set aside to cool completely before serving.

Pâté de Foie Gras

Pâté de foie gras (pa-tay de fwah grah) is a soft pâté, almost a paste, made from fattened goose livers, pork or veal and sometimes truffles. Reputed to have been invented in Alsace in the eighteenth century, pâté de foie gras was originally served enveloped in pastry.

The foie gras geese are bred and raised especially for making pâté de foie gras. Most of them are bred in the Perigord, Toulouse and Strasbourg areas of France. They are kept in a confined space at a constant temperature and fed a steady and very large diet of eggs, skimmed milk, oats and maize.

Pâte à Pâté
RICH FRENCH PASTRY

This is a rich pastry dough, often used instead of hot water crust pastry for raised pies such as Veal and Ham Pie. But since it is so rich, Pâte à Pâté (pat ah pa-tay) is mostly used for very special pies and for pâtés. The yield is based on the amount of flour used.

12 OUNCES [3 CUPS]

12 oz. [3 cups] flour
½ teaspoon salt
8 oz. [1 cup] butter, cut into small pieces
2 egg yolks, lightly beaten
4 to 5 tablespoons water

Sift the flour and salt on to a marble slab or board. Make a well in the centre of the flour mixture and place the butter and egg yolks in the well. Using your fingertips, mix the butter and egg yolks together, adding the water a little at a time and slowly drawing in the flour. Continue mixing in this way until all the flour is incorporated. Knead lightly until the dough forms a ball.

Cover the dough with greaseproof or waxed paper and chill in the refrigerator for 2 hours before using.

Pâte Sucrée
SWEET FRENCH PASTRY

This is a rich buttery pastry dough ideal for fruit tarts and flans. Pâte Sucrée (pat soo-cray) should be used when a very rich short pastry is required. The yield is based on the amount of flour used.

6 OZ. [1½ CUPS]

6 oz. [1½ cups] flour
3 oz. [⅜ cup] butter, at room temperature
3 oz. icing sugar [¾ cup confectioners' sugar], sifted
3 egg yolks

Sift the flour on to a marble slab. Make a well in the centre of the flour and place the butter, sugar and egg yolks in the well.

Using the fingertips of one hand, mix the butter, sugar and egg yolks together, slowly drawing in the flour. Continue mixing in this way until all the flour is incorporated. Knead lightly until the dough forms a ball.

Cover the dough with greaseproof or

An Australian dish from Queensland, Paterson Creek Stew should be served with a can of ice-cold beer.

waxed paper and chill in the refrigerator for 1 hour before using.

Paterson Creek Stew

Paterson Creek Stew is named after a town in Queensland, Australia. It is a delicately flavoured stew of veal, mushrooms and sour cream. Serve it with noodles and buttered French beans.

4 SERVINGS

2 oz. [¼ cup] butter
1 large onion, sliced
1 garlic clove, crushed
1 green pepper, white pith removed, seeded and chopped
2 lb. lean pie veal, cut into 1-inch cubes
½ teaspoon salt
¼ teaspoon freshly ground black pepper
1 teaspoon paprika
¼ teaspoon dried thyme
6 fl. oz. [¾ cup] water
2 large tomatoes, blanched, peeled and chopped or 8 oz. canned peeled tomatoes, drained and chopped
4 oz. mushrooms, wiped clean and sliced

5 fl. oz. [⅝ cup] sour cream
2 tablespoons chopped fresh
parsley
1 teaspoon finely grated lemon
rind

In a large saucepan, melt 1 ounce [2 table-spoons] of the butter over moderate heat. When the foam subsides, add the onion, garlic and green pepper and fry, stirring occasionally, for 5 to 7 minutes or until the onion is soft and translucent but not brown.

Add the veal cubes and fry, stirring and turning frequently, for 6 to 8 minutes or until they are lightly and evenly browned. Add the salt, pepper, paprika, thyme, water and tomatoes. Cover the pan, reduce the heat to low and simmer for 1 to 1½ hours or until the veal is tender when pierced with the point of a sharp knife.

Meanwhile, in a small frying-pan, melt the remaining butter over moderate heat. When the foam subsides, add the mush-rooms and cook, stirring occasionally, for 3 minutes.

Remove the pan from the heat and, using a slotted spoon, transfer the mush-rooms to the saucepan. Stir in the sour cream, parsley and lemon rind. Increase the heat to moderately high and cook, stirring occasionally, for 8 to 10 minutes or until the liquid has thickened slightly.

Remove the pan from the heat and

transfer the stew to a warmed serving dish. Serve immediately.

Pâtisserie

Pâtisserie (pah-tees-ree) is the French word for a confection made with pastry as well as the shop in which they are sold.

History records that pastries existed in classical Greece, but history also attributes the development and elevation of the art of pastry-making to the French, particularly during the Middle Ages. This ascendancy was confirmed by the great pâtissier, Antonin Carême who, during the nineteenth century, almost single-handedly revolutionized and modernized French pastry-making with the invention of such delights as MILLE-FEUILLE and croquembouche.

Today, pâtisseries are sold commercially all over France as well as being made by bevies of devoted cooks at home. They are usually eaten as a dessert or with coffee.

Patriotic Pudding

A sustaining banana-flavoured steamed pudding, Patriotic Pudding should be served with Crème à la Vanille. To obtain the correct consistency, use bananas which are very ripe and soft.

Serve Patriotic Pudding with a plain custard, such as Crème à la Vanille.

4-6 SERVINGS

4 oz. [½ cup] plus 2 teaspoons butter
6 oz. [1½ cups] flour
¼ teaspoon salt
1 teaspoon baking powder
4 oz. [½ cup] castor sugar
2 eggs
3 large bananas, peeled and
mashed
2 tablespoons milk
grated rind of 1 orange

Using 1 teaspoon of the butter, grease a 2-pint [1½-quart] pudding basin and set aside.

Sift the flour, salt and baking powder into a medium-sized mixing bowl. Set aside.

In another medium-sized mixing bowl, cream 4 ounces [½ cup] of the butter and the sugar together with a wooden spoon until the mixture is light and fluffy. Beat in the eggs, one at a time, adding a little of the flour mixture with each egg. Using a metal spoon, carefully fold in the remaining flour mixture. Mix in the mashed bananas, milk and orange rind. Spoon the mixture into the prepared pudding basin and set aside.

Cut out a circle of greaseproof or waxed paper about 4-inches wider in

Place the jelly [gelatin] in a large serving bowl and pour over the boiling water. Using a wooden spoon, stir briskly until the jelly [gelatin] has dissolved. Stir in the condensed milk and lemon rind and, using a wire whisk or rotary beater, beat until the mixture becomes light and frothy.

Place the bowl in the refrigerator and chill for 3 to 5 hours or until the pudding has set. Remove from the refrigerator and serve.

Paupiette

Paupiette (poh-pee-yet) is the French culinary term for a thin slice of meat, usually beef, spread with stuffing or forcemeat, then rolled up in a slice of bacon and secured with string or thread. Paupiettes are usually baked or braised.

Fillets of firm-fleshed white fish may be used instead of meat to make paupiettes.

Paupiettes de Boeuf à l'Hongroise

BEEF ROLLS, HUNGARIAN-STYLE

A delicious dinner party dish, Paupiettes de Boeuf à l'Hongroise (poh-pee-yet d' berf ah lang-wahz) is surprisingly easy to make. Serve with puréed potatoes and French beans for an elegant and filling meal.

4 SERVINGS

3 oz. [⅜ cup] butter
4 medium-sized onions, finely chopped
4 oz. lean veal, minced [ground]
2 tablespoons dry breadcrumbs
½ teaspoon salt
¼ teaspoon black pepper
2½ teaspoons paprika
½ teaspoon dried dill
8 slices silverside [brisket] of beef, about 6-inches by 6-inches, pounded thin
6 streaky bacon slices
8 fl. oz. [1 cup] dry white wine
2 tablespoons tomato purée
4 oz. button mushrooms, wiped clean and sliced
6 fl. oz. double cream [¾ cup heavy cream]

In a small frying-pan, melt 1 ounce [2 tablespoons] of the butter over moderate heat. When the foam subsides, add one of the chopped onions and cook, stirring occasionally, for 5 to 7 minutes or until it

---

diameter than the rim of the pudding basin. Grease the paper circle with the remaining teaspoon of butter. Cut out a circle of aluminium foil the same size as the circle of paper. Place the circle of paper against the circle of foil, buttered side away from the foil and, holding them firmly together, make a 1-inch pleat across the centre. Place the pleated circle, foil uppermost, over the pudding basin and tie it on securely with string.

Place the basin in a large saucepan and pour in enough boiling water to come two-thirds of the way up the sides of the basin. Cover the pan and place it over low heat. Steam the pudding for 1½ hours, adding more boiling water to the pan when necessary.

Remove the pan from the heat. Lift the pudding out of the pan. Remove and discard the paper, foil and string. Run a sharp knife around the edge of the pudding to loosen the sides. Place a serving dish, inverted, over the top of the pudding and reverse the two, giving the basin a good shake. The pudding should slide out easily. Serve immediately.

Patty

Patty, called *petit pâté* (peh-tee pa-tay) in France, is a small round pastry case, usually baked in a patty tin, filled with a savoury filling. It may be either open or closed. Patties are most often made with flaky or PUFF PASTRY, and may be filled with game, poultry, sausage meat, or shellfish, often with the addition of vegetables. In closed patties the filling is uncooked. In open patties the cooked filling is put in after the pastry case has been baked.

Paul's Lemon Pudding

Bachelors don't starve in between dinner invitations issued by kindly females who wish to save them from the quite dreadful fate of actually having to eat their own cooking! These days, in fact, they are quite likely to give their own dinner parties and most young men living or cooking on their own have at least one or two 'company' dishes that are quick and easy to prepare yet look attractive. Paul's Lemon Pudding is the pièce de résistance of one such bachelor. Serve with lots of whipped cream or a fresh fruit salad for a really delicious dessert.

4 SERVINGS

1 package lemon-flavoured jelly [gelatin]
10 fl. oz. [1¼ cups] boiling water
14 oz. canned condensed milk
1 teaspoon finely grated lemon rind

is soft and translucent but not brown. Remove the pan from the heat and transfer the onion to a medium-sized mixing bowl.

Add the veal, breadcrumbs, salt, pepper, $\frac{1}{2}$ teaspoon of paprika and the dill and beat well to blend. Set aside.

Preheat the oven to moderate 350°F (Gas Mark 4, 180°C).

Lay the beef slices out flat. Divide the veal mixture into 6 pieces and shape each piece into a thin cork-shape. Place one piece in the centre of each beef slice. Roll up the beef slices and wrap each roll in a bacon slice. Secure with trussing thread or string and set aside.

In a large flameproof casserole, melt the remaining butter over moderate heat. When the foam subsides, add the remaining onions to the pan and cook, stirring occasionally, for 5 to 7 minutes or until they are soft and translucent but not brown. Add the beef rolls to the pan and cook, stirring and turning occasionally, for 6 to 8 minutes or until they are lightly and evenly browned.

Pour in the wine, then stir in the tomato purée and the remaining paprika. Bring the liquid to the boil, stirring occasionally. Cover the casserole and transfer it to the oven. Braise the beef rolls for 1 hour, or until they are almost tender.

Remove the casserole from the oven and, using a slotted spoon, remove the rolls from the casserole. Remove and discard the thread or string and bacon slices.

Surprisingly easy to prepare, Paupiettes de Boeuf à l'Hongroise is beef slices rolled with a delicious stuffing and braised until tender.

Return the beef rolls to the casserole and place the casserole over moderate heat. Add the mushrooms and stir well to blend. Reduce the heat to low and simmer for 5 minutes, or until the meat is tender when pierced with the point of a sharp knife.

Stir in the cream and cook gently for a further 2 minutes or until the sauce is hot but not boiling. Remove the casserole from the heat and transfer the mixture to a warmed serving platter. Serve at once.

Paupiettes de Porc

PORK FILLETS STUFFED WITH APPLE PUREE

Succulent fillets of pork, stuffed with an apple purée, Paupiettes de Porc (poh-pee-yet de por) may be served with sautéed potatoes and a green vegetable.

4 SERVINGS

2 cooking apples, peeled, cored and sliced
2 tablespoons water
1 tablespoon sugar
½ teaspoon dried sage
½ teaspoon dried thyme
½ teaspoon salt
¼ teaspoon black pepper
1 small onion, finely chopped
2 tablespoons fresh breadcrumbs
8 slices of pork fillet, pounded thin, approximately 4-inches by 3-inches
8 streaky bacon slices
1 oz. [2 tablespoons] butter
10 fl. oz. [1¼ cups] cider
bouquet garni, consisting of 4 parsley sprigs, 1 thyme spray and 1 bay leaf tied together
1 oz. [2 tablespoons] beurre manié

In a saucepan, cook the apples, water and the sugar over low heat for 5 minutes, stirring occasionally. Cover the pan and continue cooking the apples for 15 to 20 minutes or until they are soft.

Remove the pan from the heat. With the back of a wooden spoon, mash the apples until they form a purée. Stir in the sage, thyme, salt, pepper, onion and breadcrumbs.

Lay the pork slices out flat. Spoon equal amounts of the apple mixture on to the pork slices. Roll up the meat.

Wrap each roll in a bacon slice and secure with thread. Set aside.

In a large saucepan, melt the butter over moderate heat. When the foam subsides, add the pork rolls and cook them, turning frequently, for 6 to 8 minutes or until they are evenly browned. Pour in the cider and add the bouquet garni. Increase the heat to moderately high and bring the cider to the boil.

Cover the pan, reduce the heat to low and simmer the paupiettes for 35 to 40 minutes, or until they are tender when pierced with the point of a sharp knife.

Remove the pan from the heat. Using a slotted spoon, transfer the paupiettes to a warmed serving dish. Remove and discard the thread and bacon. Keep the paupiettes warm while you finish the sauce.

Strain the cooking liquid and return it to the pan. Return the pan to moderate heat and bring the liquid to the boil. Add the beurre manié, a small piece at a time, stirring constantly with a wooden spoon until the sauce thickens slightly. Taste the sauce and add more salt and pepper if necessary. Remove the pan from the heat. Pour the sauce over the paupiettes and serve immediately.

Paupiettes de Sole à l'Indienne

FILLETS OF SOLE ROLLS IN CURRY CREAM SAUCE

A delicately spiced dish, Paupiettes de Sole à l'Indienne (poh-pee-yet d' sole ah lan-dee-en) should be served in a ring of buttered rice.

4 SERVINGS

8 sole fillets, skinned and cut in half lengthways
½ teaspoon salt
½ teaspoon white pepper
6 fl. oz. [¾ cup] fish stock
4 fl. oz. [½ cup] white wine
4 fl. oz. double cream [½ cup heavy cream]
2 tablespoons mild curry powder
1 tablespoon beurre manié
STUFFING
8 oz. whiting fillets, minced [ground]
1 egg, lightly beaten
4 tablespoons double [heavy] cream
2 tablespoons fresh white breadcrumbs
1 teaspoon salt
½ tablespoon white pepper

Preheat the oven to moderate 350°F (Gas Mark 4, 180°C).

Lay the sole fillets on a work surface and rub them all over with the salt and pepper. Set aside.

To make the stuffing, in a medium-sized mixing bowl, combine the whiting, egg, cream, breadcrumbs, and half the salt and pepper. With a wooden spoon mix the ingredients well together.

With a palette knife, spread a thin layer of the fish stuffing over each fillet. Roll up the fish fillets and tie them securely with thread.

Place the rolled fish fillets in a flame-proof baking dish and pour over the fish stock and wine. Place the dish over moderate heat and bring the liquid to the boil. Cover the dish and transfer it to the oven. Bake for 20 to 25 minutes or until

Served on a bed of buttery rice, Paupiettes de Sole à l'Indienne are tender fillets of sole, with a creamy curry sauce poured over before serving.

the fish flakes easily when tested with a fork.

Remove the dish from the oven. With a slotted spoon, transfer the fish rolls to a warmed serving dish. Remove the thread and keep warm while you finish the sauce.

Place the dish over moderate heat and boil the liquid for 5 minutes or until it is reduced by one-third. Reduce the heat to low and stir in the cream, curry powder and the remaining salt and pepper. Cook gently for a further 2 minutes.

Stir in the beurre manié, a small piece at a time, and continue cooking until the sauce thickens slightly.

Remove the dish from the heat. Pour the sauce over the fish and serve immediately.

Paupiettes de Veau
VEAL ROLLS STUFFED WITH CHICKEN
LIVERS AND MUSHROOMS

A really impressive dish, Paupiettes de Veau (poh-pee-yet d' voh) is a delicious way to serve veal. Paupiettes de Veau may be served with creamed potatoes and a crisp green salad.

                              6 SERVINGS
3 large veal escalopes, pounded thin
2 oz. [¼ cup] butter
1 medium-sized onion, finely chopped
8 oz. chicken livers
4 oz. mushrooms, wiped clean and finely chopped
4 tablespoons fresh white breadcrumbs
1 teaspoon dried basil
1 teaspoon salt
½ teaspoon black pepper
4 fl. oz. [½ cup] dry white wine
4 fl. oz. [½ cup] chicken stock
4 fl. oz. double cream [½ cup heavy cream] beaten with 1 egg yolk

Preheat the oven to moderate 350°F (Gas Mark 4, 180°C).

Place the veal escalopes on a chopping board and cut them into 2-inch by 4-inch strips. Set aside.

In a medium-sized frying-pan melt 1 ounce [2 tablespoons] of the butter over moderate heat. When the foam subsides, add the onion and cook, stirring occasionally, for 5 to 7 minutes or until it is soft and translucent but not brown. Add the chicken livers and mushrooms and cook, stirring frequently, for a further 5 minutes, or until the livers are well browned but still slightly pink inside.

Remove the pan from the heat and, with a slotted spoon, transfer the chicken liver mixture to a chopping board.

Chop the liver mixture very finely or mince [grind] it in a mincer [grinder]. Transfer the chopped or minced [ground] liver mixture to a medium-sized mixing bowl. Add the breadcrumbs, basil, salt and pepper. Mix the ingredients together until they are well blended.

Using a palette knife or spatula, spread a layer of the liver mixture over each veal strip. Roll up the strips and tie them securely with string.

In a medium-sized frying-pan, melt the remaining butter over moderate heat. When the foam subsides, add the veal rolls, a few at a time, and cook, turning frequently, for 6 to 8 minutes or until they are well browned. With a slotted spoon, transfer the veal rolls to a plate. Keep warm while you brown the remaining rolls in the same way.

Arrange the rolls in a medium-sized flameproof casserole and pour over the wine and stock. Cover the casserole and place it in the oven. Bake the paupiettes for 45 minutes or until they are tender.

Remove the casserole from the oven. With a slotted spoon, transfer the veal rolls to a warmed serving dish. Keep warm while you prepare the sauce.

Place the casserole over high heat and bring the liquid to the boil. Boil, stirring frequently, for 5 minutes, or until the liquid has reduced by half. Reduce the heat to low and gradually stir in the cream mixture. Cook, stirring constantly, for a further 2 minutes or until the sauce has thickened. Do not allow the sauce to boil or the egg will scramble.

Remove the casserole from the heat and pour the sauce over the veal rolls. Serve immediately.

Paupiettes de Veau is veal stuffed with chicken livers and mushrooms.

Pavlova

Pavlova is a famous meringue-based dessert, named after the Russian ballerina, Anna Pavlova. It was created in honour of her performance of the Dying Swan in Swan Lake which she danced while touring Australia, and the dessert is now considered to be traditionally Australian.

Pavlova should be crisp on the outside, but soft and creamy in the centre. Fresh, exotic fruits such as passion fruit, pineapples and Chinese gooseberries go beautifully with the soft meringue, but any fresh or canned fruit may be used, according to choice.

ONE 9-INCH CAKE

5 egg whites
10 oz. [1¼ cups] plus 1 tablespoon
    castor sugar
2 teaspoons cornflour [cornstarch],
    sifted
½ teaspoon vanilla essence
1 teaspoon malt vinegar
1 teaspoon orange-flavoured
    liqueur
10 fl. oz. double cream [1¼ cups
    heavy cream], stiffly whipped
1 lb. fresh or canned and drained
    fruit

To make Pavlova, draw a 9-inch circle on non-stick silicone paper (use a plate or board as guide).

Using a forcing bag with a 1-inch nozzle, pipe the remaining mixture around the edge of the circle.

When the meringue mixture is stiff, spread one-third over the circle to make a base about ¼-inch thick.

When the meringue case has cooked and cooled completely, transfer it to a serving plate.

Preheat the oven to cool 300°F (Gas Mark 2, 150°C). With a pencil draw a 9-inch circle (use a plate as a guide) on a piece of non-stick silicone paper and place this on a baking sheet. Set aside.

In a large mixing bowl, beat the egg whites with a wire whisk or rotary beater until they form stiff peaks. Beat in 4 ounces [½ cup] of the sugar and continue beating for 1 minute or until the mixture is very stiff and glossy. Using a metal spoon, fold in all but 1 tablespoon of the remaining sugar, the cornflour [cornstarch], vanilla essence and vinegar.

Spoon one-third of the mixture on to the circle of paper to make a base about ¼-inch thick. Fill a forcing bag, fitted with a 1-inch nozzle, with the remaining mixture and pipe it round the edge of the circle in decorative swirls, to form a case to hold the filling.

Place the baking sheet in the oven and bake for 1 hour. Turn off the oven and leave the meringue in the oven for a further 30 minutes, or until it is crisp on the outside but still soft in the centre.

Remove the baking sheet from the oven. Leave the meringue to cool completely. When it is cold, lift it off the baking sheet and carefully remove and discard the paper from the bottom.

Place the meringue case on a serving plate. Fold the orange-flavoured liqueur and the remaining tablespoon of sugar into the cream. Spoon the cream into the centre of the meringue case and pile the fruit on top of the cream. Serve at once.

Paysanne, à la

A la paysanne (ah lah pay-zahn), literally peasant-style in French, is a cooking term applied to meat and poultry braised with buttered vegetables and bacon. The vegetables, which usually include carrots, turnips, onions and celery, and bacon are served as a garnish to the finished dish.

Pea

The pea, or *pisum sativum*, originated in the Near East although it now grows extensively all over the world. There are two basic types, usually classified as edible-podded or shelling peas, depending on whether the outer casing may be eaten or not.

Garden peas, the most common form of shelling pea, may be bought fresh (when in season), canned or frozen. Peas are also dried and used whole or split in soups and stews.

To cook fresh garden peas, place 1 pound (weighed after shelling) in a large saucepan and pour over enough water just to cover. Add a little salt and, if you wish,

a sprig of mint. Place the pan over high heat and bring the water to the boil. Reduce the heat to low and simmer the peas for 10 to 12 minutes or until they are tender. Remove the pan from the heat and drain the peas in a colander. Add a little butter and serve.

Petits pois, the smallest and sweetest of the shelling peas, are cooked in the same way.

The MANGE-TOUT or snow pea is an edible-podded variety of pea and should be cooked in the same way as FRENCH BEANS.

Pea Soup with Ham

A warming winter soup, Pea Soup with Ham may be served on its own or with French bread for a sustaining lunch or supper. For the best results, make the soup the day before you intend to serve it.

4-6 SERVINGS
1 ham hock, soaked overnight and drained
5 pints [6¼ pints] water
    bouquet garni, consisting of 4 parsley sprigs, 1 thyme spray and 1 bay leaf tied together
1 teaspoon black pepper
1 oz. [2 tablespoons] butter
1 medium-sized onion, thinly sliced
1 garlic clove, crushed
2 small carrots, scraped and sliced
8 oz. [1 cup] split peas, soaked overnight and drained

Place the ham hock in a large saucepan and pour over 4 pints [5 pints] of the water. Add the bouquet garni and black pepper. Place the pan over moderate heat and bring the water to the boil, skimming off any scum that rises to the surface. Reduce the heat to low, cover the pan and simmer for 1½ to 2 hours or until the meat is tender and nearly falling off the bone.

Remove the pan from the heat. Using tongs or two large spoons, transfer the ham hock to a plate. Cover it with aluminium foil. Set aside.

Strain the cooking liquid into a large mixing bowl and set aside to cool to room temperature. Then place the bowl in the refrigerator and chill for 2 hours or until a layer of fat has formed on the top of the liquid. Remove and discard the layer of fat. Set the cooking liquid aside.

In a large saucepan, melt the butter

Tasty and nourishing, Pea Soup with Ham makes a wonderfully warming start to lunch or supper.

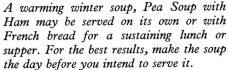

over moderate heat. When the foam subsides, add the onion, garlic and carrots and fry, stirring occasionally, for 5 to 7 minutes or until the onion is soft and translucent but not brown.

Add the split peas to the pan and cook, stirring constantly, for 5 minutes.

Add the cooking liquid and the remaining water and bring it to the boil over high heat, stirring occasionally. Cover the pan, reduce the heat to low and simmer for 2 hours or until the peas are tender. Remove the pan from the heat and set aside to cool for 15 minutes. Then purée the mixture in a food mill or electric blender. Return the puréed soup to the pan. Add more water if the soup is too thick for your taste. Set aside.

Cut the meat from the ham hock bone, discarding any fat. Chop the meat into small pieces.

Add the meat to the pan and return the pan to low heat. Simmer the soup for a further 10 minutes or until it is heated through.

Remove the pan from the heat and transfer the soup to a warmed tureen. Serve immediately.

Peach

The peach is the fruit of a small deciduous tree native to China, now cultivated extensively in temperate zones throughout the world. It is round and medium-sized, usually between 3- and 5-inches in diameter, and has a fine, slightly downy, yellow and pink skin.

Peaches are most often eaten as a dessert fruit, or as part of a salad or sundae; they are also a popular canning and preserving fruit. They may be cooked, usually poached gently in syrup, then added to flans, tarts and gâteaux. The classic dish PEACH MELBA contains poached fresh peaches as does PECHES CARDINAL.

To poach peaches, blanch, peel, halve and stone 1 pound of firm ripe peaches. In a large saucepan, dissolve 6 ounces [¾ cup] of sugar in 10 fluid ounces [1¼ cups] of water over moderate heat, stirring constantly. Add a vanilla pod to the syrup and bring to the boil. Boil the syrup for 5 minutes or until it has thickened. Reduce the heat to low and add the peach halves to the pan, cut sides down. Poach them gently for 3 to 5 minutes or until they are tender but still firm. With a slotted spoon, remove the peach halves from the syrup. They are now ready to serve. (The poaching syrup may be strained and served as a sauce with the peaches.)

Peach Brandy

Fruit-flavoured brandies make a delicious accompaniment to coffee or a superb ending to a good meal, and home-made ones can be just as good as those produced commercially. Apricots may be substituted for peaches in this recipe, if you prefer.

ABOUT 16 FLUID OUNCES [2 CUPS]

1½ lb. fresh peaches, sliced and stones reserved

6 oz. [¾ cup] sugar

16 fl. oz. [2 cups] brandy

½ teaspoon ground mixed spice or allspice

¼ teaspoon grated nutmeg

Place the peach slices in a large mixing bowl. Add the sugar, stirring with a long-handled spoon until the ingredients are well mixed.

Pour over the brandy and mix well.

Peaches in Brandy is a rich and luxurious conserve.

Pour 1 pint [2½ cups] of the syrup into a medium-sized saucepan. Discard the remaining syrup. Place the pan over moderately high heat and bring the syrup to the boil, stirring occasionally. Boil the syrup, without stirring, until it registers 220°F on a sugar thermometer, or until a teaspoon of the syrup dropped into cold water forms a soft ball when rolled between your fingertips.

Remove the pan from the heat and stir in the brandy. Combine the mixture thoroughly and pour it over the peaches in the preserving jars.

Seal the jars with their vacuum lids and store them in a cool, dry dark place for at least 4 months before using.

Peach Cobbler

An American deep-dish pie, Peach Cobbler is made with Baking Powder Biscuit dough and fresh peaches. An alternative way of making the crust is to drop spoonfuls of the dough on top of the fruit. In this case the brandy must be sprinkled over the fruit before it is covered with the dough. Cobblers may be served with a Hard Sauce or Brandy Butter, with a fruit sauce or vanilla ice-cream.

4-6 SERVINGS

10 peaches, blanched, peeled, stoned and sliced
2 oz. [¼ cup] sugar
½ teaspoon ground cinnamon
1 tablespoon butter, cut into pieces
  Baking Powder Biscuit dough
  made from 6 oz. [1½ cups]
  flour, etc.
2 tablespoons brandy

Preheat the oven to fairly hot 400°F (Gas Mark 6, 200°C).

In a 2-inch deep 8-inch square cake tin, combine the peach slices, sugar and cinnamon. Dot the top of the fruit with the butter.

On a lightly floured board, roll out the dough into an 8-inch square ¼-inch thick. Lift the dough on the rolling pin and lay it over the fruit. Trim the dough but do not press down the edges.

Put the tin in the centre of the oven and bake for 40 minutes or until the pastry is golden brown.

Remove the cobbler from the oven. Using a palette knife or spatula, carefully lift up the pastry crust. Sprinkle the brandy over the peaches. Replace the crust and serve immediately.

Add the mixed spice or allspice and nutmeg, stirring to blend.

Crack the peach stones with a hammer and extract the kernels. Discard the stones. Remove the skin from the kernels. Add the kernels to the bowl and stir well.

Pour the mixture into a large jug or crock and cork it tightly. Set the jug or crock aside and leave the mixture to infuse for 60 days.

Sterilize and dry 2 or 3 bottles. Uncork the jug and strain the liquid through a piece of cheesecloth into a clean jug. Squeeze out any peach pulp remaining in the cheesecloth to extract as much liquid as possible. Pour the liquid into the bottles.

Cork the bottles and set them aside for at least 1 week before serving.

Peaches in Brandy

Peaches in Brandy is a well-known and very luxurious conserve. The peaches should be stored in vacuum-sealed jars and left to mature for 4 to 6 months — remember that the longer you leave the peaches to mature the better they will taste — so do not be tempted to sample them too soon!

2-3 POUNDS

2 lb. small peaches
3 lb. [6 cups] sugar
2 pints [5 cups] water
1 pint [2½ cups] brandy

Place the peaches in a large heatproof mixing bowl and pour over enough boiling water to cover them completely. Set aside for 3 minutes.

With a slotted spoon, remove the peaches from the bowl. Discard the water. Skin the peaches, cut them in half and remove and discard the stones.

In a large saucepan, dissolve the sugar in the water over low heat, stirring constantly. Increase the heat to moderate and bring the syrup to the boil. Carefully lower the peach halves into the syrup and poach them for 1 minute.

Remove the pan from the heat. Using a slotted spoon, lift the peaches out of the syrup and place them in clean, dry preserving jars, filling the jars three-quarters full. Set aside.

Peach Flan

Sweet and melting Peach Flan is best made when peaches are plentiful. Serve the flan with single [light] cream or, if you like really sweet desserts, Brandy Butter.

4-6 SERVINGS

1 x 9-inch Flan Case made with shortcrust pastry, baked blind and cooled
4 large peaches, blanched, peeled, stoned and sliced
1 tablespoon peach brandy (optional)

TOPPING

2 tablespoons ground almonds
1 tablespoon chopped almonds
1 tablespoon chopped walnuts
3 tablespoons soft brown sugar
1 teaspoon grated orange rind
1 tablespoon butter, cut into small pieces

Place the flan case on a flameproof serving dish. Arrange the peach slices in the flan case. Sprinkle over the peach brandy, if you are using it. Set aside.

Eat this delicious and easy-to-make Peach Jam the way the French do — with warm croissants and butter for breakfast.

Preheat the grill [broiler] to high.

To make the topping, in a small mixing bowl, combine the ground and chopped almonds, the walnuts, sugar and orange rind.

Sprinkle the topping over the peach slices and dot the top with the butter pieces.

Place the dish under the grill [broiler] and grill [broil] for 4 minutes or until the topping is crisp and bubbling.

Remove the dish from under the grill [broiler] and serve immediately or allow to cool completely before serving.

Peach Jam

This easy to make Peach Jam keeps very well and tastes delicious spread on hot buttered Croissants or fresh white bread.

ABOUT 5 POUNDS

thinly pared rind of 2 lemons
1 medium-sized tart cooking apple, chopped
2 cloves
3 lb. peaches, stoned and coarsely sliced
10 fl. oz. [1¼ cups] water
3 lb. [6 cups] sugar
1 teaspoon ground allspice

Place the lemon rind, chopped apple and cloves in a muslin bag or a piece of cheesecloth. Tie the bag or cloth securely with string, leaving a long piece of string hanging from the bag. Place the bag in a preserving pan or large saucepan and tie the string to the handle of the pan.

Add the peaches and water to the pan. Place the pan over moderately high heat and bring the liquid to the boil, stirring constantly. Reduce the heat to moderate and cook, stirring frequently, for 6 to 8 minutes or until the peaches are just tender. Sprinkle over the allspice.

Stir in the sugar and cook the jam, stirring constantly, until the sugar has dissolved. Increase the heat to moderately high and boil the jam for 20 minutes, stirring frequently and skimming the scum off the surface with a metal spoon, or until setting point has been reached.

To test for setting point, remove the pan from the heat. Drop a teaspoonful of the jam on to a cold saucer. Allow the jam to cool and then push the edge with your fingertip. If the surface of the jam wrinkles, setting point has been reached. If setting point has not been reached, return the jam to the heat and continue boiling and stirring, testing it every few minutes.

Alternatively, if you use a sugar thermometer, setting point has been reached when the thermometer registers 220°F to 222°F.

Remove the pan from the heat. Using the back of a wooden spoon, squeeze the muslin or cheesecloth bag against the side of the pan to extract all the juices. Discard the bag. Let the jam stand for 5 minutes.

Using a jug or ladle, ladle the jam into clean, dry warmed jam jars. Lightly press a circle of greaseproof or waxed paper over the surface of the jam in each jar. Cover the jars with jam covers and secure with rubber bands. Label the jars and store them in a cool, dry dark place.

Dame Nellie Melba inspired this luscious Peach Melba, a combination of ice-cream, peaches and sauce.

Peach Melba

This dish is as superb as the singing of Dame Nellie Melba, for whom it was created. Serve Peach Melba as the perfect dessert for a special dinner.

4 SERVINGS

1 pint [2½ cups] vanilla ice-cream
2 large peaches, blanched, peeled, halved, stoned and poached
16 fl. oz. [2 cups] Melba Sauce

Place two scoops of ice-cream in each of 4 chilled sundae glasses or dessert dishes. Top each serving with a peach half. Pour equal quantities of melba sauce over the peaches.

Serve immediately.

Peach Pickle

A sour-sweet, fragrant preserve, Peach Pickle must be stored for at least 2 months before it is eaten. It will keep for up to 6 months. The pickle should be stored in clean, dry, vacuum-sealed glass jars. The net weight of the peaches after they have been peeled and stoned should be 4 pounds. Serve the pickle with cold pork or ham.

ABOUT 6 POUNDS

1 tablespoon cloves
1 tablespoon allspice berries, bruised

2-inch piece fresh root ginger, bruised
1 cinnamon stick
thinly pared rind of 1 orange
2 lb. [4 cups] sugar
1 pint [2½ cups] wine vinegar
5 lb. peaches, blanched, peeled, stoned and quartered

Tie the cloves, allspice berries, ginger, cinnamon and orange rind in a double thickness of cheesecloth. Set aside.

In a large saucepan, dissolve the sugar in the vinegar over low heat, stirring constantly. When the sugar has dissolved, increase the heat to moderate and bring the syrup to the boil. Boil for 5 minutes.

Add the peaches and the bag of spices. When the syrup comes to the boil again, reduce the heat to low and poach the peaches for 3 to 5 minutes or until they are tender.

Remove the pan from the heat. With a slotted spoon, remove the peaches from the pan and pack them into clean, warm dry jars. Set aside.

Return the pan to moderately high heat and boil the vinegar syrup for 10 minutes or until it has reduced by one-third.

Remove the pan from the heat and let the syrup cool for 2 minutes. Remove the bag of spices and discard it. Pour the vinegar syrup over the peaches until it covers them entirely and comes to the top of the jars. Allow the jars to stand for 2 minutes and then add more syrup if the level has subsided. If there is any vinegar syrup left, bottle and reserve it because a certain amount of evaporation might occur during storage. Examine the pickle every few weeks and top up the jars with the reserved vinegar syrup if necessary.

Wipe the jars clean with a damp cloth. Seal the jars with the vacuum-lids. Label the jars and store them in a cool, dry, dark place.

Peach Puffs

Tasty little pastries filled with peaches poached in white wine, Peach Puffs may be served hot with Crème à la Vanille as a dessert, or cold with tea or coffee. If you like, reserve the peach cooking liquid and thicken it with 2 teaspoons of arrowroot. It may then be served as a sauce.

8 PUFFS

10 fl. oz. [1¼ cups] dry white wine
1 tablespoon lemon juice
1 teaspoon ground allspice
2 tablespoons soft brown sugar
4 small fresh peaches, blanched, peeled, halved and stoned

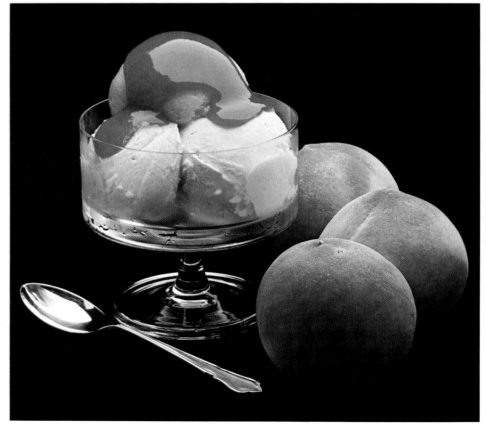

4 tablespoons sultanas or seedless
raisins
PASTRY
6 oz. [1½ cups] flour
¼ teaspoon salt
3 tablespoons castor sugar
4 oz. [½ cup] butter
3 to 4 tablespoons iced water
1 egg yolk, well beaten with 2
tablespoons milk

In a large saucepan, combine the wine,
lemon juice, allspice and sugar. Set the
pan over moderately low heat and cook
the mixture, stirring constantly, until the
sugar has dissolved.

Place the peaches, cut sides down, in
one layer on the bottom of the pan. Cover
the pan and poach the peaches for 3 to 5
minutes, or until they are just tender
when pierced with the point of a sharp
knife.

Remove the pan from the heat and set
the peaches aside to cool completely in
the cooking liquid.

While the peaches are cooling, make
the pastry. Sift the flour and salt into a
medium-sized mixing bowl. Stir in 1
tablespoon of the castor sugar.

Add the 4 ounces [½ cup] of butter to
the flour mixture and, with a table knife,
cut it into walnut-sized pieces. Add 3

*Versatile Peach Puffs may be served
with custard as a dessert, or as a
snack with coffee or tea.*

tablespoons of the water and, using the
knife, mix it quickly into the dough,
which should be lumpy. If the dough
looks too dry, add a little more of the
water.

Shape the dough into a ball and place
it on a lightly floured board or marble
slab. Using a floured rolling pin, roll out
the dough into an oblong. Fold the dough
in three and turn it so that the open ends
face you. Roll it out again into an oblong.
Repeat the folding and rolling process
twice more, reflouring the board or slab
if the dough sticks. Fold the dough in
three once more and wrap it in greaseproof or waxed paper. Chill the dough in
the refrigerator for 30 minutes.

Preheat the oven to fairly hot 400°F
(Gas Mark 6, 200°C).

Remove the dough from the refrigerator. If the dough looks streaky, roll it out
into an oblong and fold it in three once
again. Divide the dough in half. On a
lightly floured board or marble slab, roll
out one half of the dough into a large
circle approximately ⅛-inch thick. Using
a 3-inch round pastry cutter, cut out 8

circles. Roll out the remaining dough in
the same way. With a 4-inch round pastry
cutter, cut out another 8 circles. Discard
any leftover dough and set the circles
aside.

With a slotted spoon, remove the peach
halves from the cooking liquid and drain
them well on kitchen paper towels. Discard the cooking liquid.

Place the 3-inch dough circles on a
working surface. Put ½ tablespoon of the
sultanas or seedless raisins in the centre
of each circle. Place a peach half, cut side
down, in the centre of each dough circle.
The sultanas or raisins should fit inside
the cavities of the peach halves.

Place the 4-inch dough circles over the
peach halves and crimp the edges of the
dough circles together to seal them.

Carefully transfer the circles to a large
baking sheet, spacing them slightly apart.
With a pastry brush, brush the dough
with the egg yolk and milk mixture.
Sprinkle over the remaining castor sugar.

Place the baking sheet in the centre of
the oven and bake the pastries for 20 to
25 minutes, or until they are puffed up
and golden.

Remove the baking sheet from the
oven. Carefully transfer the pastries to a
wire rack. Serve them hot, or cool completely before serving.

Peanut

The peanut, sometimes known as the groundnut, is the seed of a leguminous plant native to South America. The plant forms a pod which buries itself in the ground (hence the name groundnut), each pod bearing approximately two nuts. The pods are broken open to extract the nuts, which are roasted to remove their dark skins. They are then salted or left plain.

Peanuts are cultivated in the United States, India, China and West Africa. In the United States, approximately half of the crop is used in the manufacture of peanut butter. Elsewhere, peanuts are grown mainly for their oil which is used in the production of cooking fats and oils.

Peanuts have a high protein content and, like other nuts, form an integral part of a vegetarian diet.

Peanut Biscuits [Cookies]

Rich, crunchy Peanut Biscuits [Cookies] taste even better sandwiched together with cream cheese.

ABOUT 26 BISCUITS [COOKIES]

8 oz. [2 cups] flour
1 tablespoon sugar
¼ teaspoon ground allspice

Peanut Butter Biscuits [Cookies] taste marvellous with a glass of milk.

4 oz. [½ cup] butter
1½ oz. [3 tablespoons] vegetable fat
4 to 5 tablespoons water
2 tablespoons finely chopped salted peanuts
3 tablespoons salted peanuts

Sift the flour, sugar and allspice into a medium-sized mixing bowl. Add the butter and vegetable fat and cut them into small pieces with a table knife. With your fingertips, rub the fats into the flour mixture until it resembles coarse breadcrumbs. Add 4 tablespoons of the water and the finely chopped peanuts and mix them into the flour mixture with the knife. With your hands, mix and knead the dough until it forms a ball. Add the remaining water if the dough is too dry.

Cover the dough and chill it in the refrigerator for 30 minutes.

Preheat the oven to fairly hot 375°F (Gas Mark 5, 190°C).

Remove the dough from the refrigerator and roll it out on a lightly floured surface to ¼-inch thick. Using a 2-inch round pastry cutter, cut the dough into approximately 26 circles and place them on two large baking sheets.

Divide the nuts among the dough circles, pressing them into the dough with your fingertips.

Place the baking sheets in the oven and bake for 15 minutes or until the pastry is lightly browned at the edges. Remove the baking sheets from the oven and allow the biscuits [cookies] to cool for 5 minutes. Transfer the biscuits [cookies] to a wire rack to cool completely before serving.

Peanut Butter

Home-made Peanut Butter is simple to make if you have an electric blender and far more delicious than the commercial variety. You can make either crunchy or smooth peanut butter, depending on how long you blend the nuts.

ABOUT 1 POUND

1 lb. roasted peanuts, weighed after shelling
1 teaspoon salt
2 fl. oz. [¼ cup] peanut oil

Place one-quarter of the peanuts in an electric blender and blend at high speed for 45 seconds for a crunchy texture, 60 seconds for a smooth texture.

Transfer the ground peanuts to a medium-sized mixing bowl. Set aside while you grind the remaining peanuts in the same way. When all the nuts have been ground, add the salt and oil and mix thoroughly. Place the peanut butter in screw-top jars and use as required.

Peanut Butter Biscuits [Cookies]

These economical biscuits [cookies] will quickly become firm favourites with the children and, if you offer them to the grownups, they won't be refused!

24 BISCUITS [COOKIES]

3 oz. [⅜ cup] plus 1 teaspoon butter
6 oz. [1½ cups] flour
3 tablespoons water
3 tablespoons crunchy peanut butter
2 tablespoons salted peanuts
1 teaspoon sugar

Preheat the oven to moderate 350°F (Gas Mark 4, 180°C).

Using the teaspoon of butter, grease a very large baking sheet. Set aside.

Sift the flour into a medium-sized mixing bowl. Add the remaining butter and cut it into small pieces with a table knife. With your fingertips, rub the butter into the flour until the mixture resembles fine breadcrumbs. Using the table knife, stir in the water and peanut butter. With your hands, mix and knead the dough until it forms a ball. Add a little more water if the dough appears to be too dry.

On a lightly floured surface, roll out the dough to a rectangle about 6-inches by 12-inches. Using the table knife, trim the edges. Carefully lift the dough on to the prepared baking sheet and cut it into 1½- by 2-inch rectangles. Do not separate the pieces of dough. Sprinkle the top of the dough with the salted peanuts and the sugar. Using the rolling pin, very gently roll the peanuts into the dough.

Place the baking sheet in the oven and bake the biscuits [cookies] for 15 to 20 minutes or until they are golden brown around the edges.

Remove the baking sheet from the oven. Transfer the biscuits [cookies] to a wire rack and leave them until they are completely cool. Break the biscuits

---

A spicy and colourful dish from West Africa, Peanut Butter and Chicken Stew may be served with rice.

[cookies] apart and either store them in a tin or serve immediately.

Peanut Butter and Chicken Stew

An interesting and unusual West African dish, Peanut Butter and Chicken Stew may be served with boiled rice and buttered spinach.

4 SERVINGS

2 tablespoons peanut oil
1 medium-sized onion, chopped
1 garlic clove, crushed
1 green pepper, white pith removed, seeded and chopped
1 x 3 lb. chicken, cut into serving pieces
8 oz. [1 cup] peanut butter
1 pint [2½ cups] chicken stock
1 teaspoon salt
1 teaspoon black pepper
1 teaspoon turmeric
1 tablespoon ground coriander
1 teaspoon ground cumin
½ teaspoon hot chilli powder
2 tomatoes, blanched, peeled and chopped
1 tablespoon chopped fresh parsley

In a large saucepan, heat the oil over moderate heat. When the oil is hot, add the onion, garlic and green pepper and fry, stirring occasionally, for 5 to 7 minutes or until the onion is soft and translucent but not brown.

Add the chicken pieces and cook, turning them occasionally, for 8 minutes or until they are evenly browned.

Meanwhile, in a small mixing bowl, combine the peanut butter, 4 fluid ounces [½ cup] of chicken stock, the salt, pepper, turmeric, coriander, cumin and chilli powder and stir until the mixture forms a smooth paste.

Add the paste to the chicken and cook, stirring constantly, for 5 minutes. Pour in the remaining chicken stock and add the tomatoes. Cover the pan, reduce the heat to low and simmer the stew for 45 minutes or until the chicken is tender. Uncover the pan for the last 15 minutes of the cooking time.

Remove the pan from the heat and transfer the mixture to a warmed serving dish. Sprinkle over the parsley and serve immediately.

Peanut Ice-Cream

Roasted peanuts are incorporated into lemon-flavoured ice-cream for this refreshing dessert.

4 SERVINGS

1 pint [2½ cups] milk
    pared rind of 1 lemon
1 egg yolk
1 tablespoon custard powder
3 tablespoons sugar
1½ teaspoons gelatine dissolved in 2 tablespoons hot water
½ teaspoon lemon essence
2 oz. [⅓ cup] roasted peanuts, chopped
1 egg white

Set the thermostat of the refrigerator to its coldest setting.

In a small saucepan, scald the milk with the lemon rind (bring to just under boiling point) over moderate heat. Remove the pan from the heat, cover it and leave the milk to infuse for 20 minutes.

In a medium-sized mixing bowl, beat the egg yolk, custard powder, sugar and 2 tablespoons of the scalded milk together with a wooden spoon. Strain the remaining milk on to the egg yolk mixture, stirring constantly. Pour the mixture back into the saucepan and return it to low heat. Cook, stirring constantly, for 5 minutes or until the custard starts to simmer and becomes thick enough to coat the back of the spoon.

Remove the pan from the heat and carefully stir in the dissolved gelatine and the lemon essence. Pour the custard into a bowl and set it aside to cool.

When the custard is cool, cover the bowl and place it in the refrigerator to chill for 1 hour.

When the custard is cold, pour it into a cold freezing tray and put it into the frozen food storage compartment of the refrigerator to freeze for 30 minutes.

Remove the tray from the storage compartment and spoon the ice-cream mixture into a chilled mixing bowl.

Sprinkle the nuts over the mixture and beat well with a wire whisk or rotary beater.

In a small mixing bowl, beat the egg white with a wire whisk or rotary beater until it forms stiff peaks. With a metal spoon, fold the egg white into the custard. Return the custard to the freezing tray and put it back into the storage compartment to freeze for 1 hour, or until the mixture is firm.

Remove the ice-cream from the frozen food storage compartment. Place it in the mixing bowl and beat it well.

Put the ice-cream mixture back in the freezing tray and into the frozen food storage compartment for another hour, or until it is firm. It is now ready to serve.

Pear

The pear is a hard fruit belonging to the genus *pyrus*. It is native to the temperate regions of Europe and Asia but is now also grown in Australia and the Americas.

There are thousands of varieties most of which, particularly the fine cultivated, dessert pears, have descended from the common pear, *pyrus communis*. Another species, the snow pear, *pyrus nivalis*, is grown solely for making PERRY or pear cider.

In shape, pears may be the traditional pear-shape, elongated or top-shaped. In colour, they vary from pale green to deep yellow, from russet to red and often the skins are dotted or marked with a flush. The skin of some varieties is fine and edible and in others coarse and rough. The flesh is gritty although in some of the finer dessert varieties the grittiness is barely noticeable and the flesh is soft and smooth.

The best-known dessert variety is the Williams [Bartlett] pear. Conference pears are very widely grown commercially and are versatile enough to be eaten uncooked or cooked in flans, pies and compôtes. The dessert pears of Europe include the fabulous Doyenné du Comice and the well-flavoured Beurré Hardy.

Pears do not keep very well—their storage time is therefore short and they tend to be expensive. Pears are also available bottled, canned and dried.

To poach pears, peel, halve and core 1½ pounds of firm pears. Make a syrup by dissolving 4 ounces [½ cup] of sugar in 10 fluid ounces [1¼ cups] of water over low heat. When the sugar has dissolved, increase the heat to moderate and bring the syrup to the boil. Boil the syrup for 3 minutes. Add the pears and reduce the heat to low. Cook them for 12 to 15 minutes or until they are soft but not pulpy. Allow the pears to cool in the syrup before serving.

Pears Baked with Cardamom

Pears baked in liqueur and cardamom, Pears Baked with Cardamom makes a light dessert after a rich main course.

4-6 SERVINGS

3 large pears, peeled, halved and cored
2 tablespoons soft brown sugar
4 fl. oz. [½ cup] orange-flavoured liqueur
2 teaspoons ground cardamom
8 fl. oz. double cream [1 cup heavy cream], stiffly whipped

Preheat the oven to moderate 350°F (Gas Mark 4, 180°C).

Using a sharp knife, cut the pears into slices. Arrange them in the bottom of a shallow ovenproof dish and sprinkle over the sugar. Pour the liqueur over the top, then sprinkle over the cardamom.

Place the dish in the oven and bake for 35 to 40 minutes or until the pear slices are tender. Remove the dish from the oven and transfer the pear mixture to individual serving dishes. Set aside to cool completely.

When the pears are cold, spoon equal amounts of the cream into each dish and serve at once.

Pear and Chicory [French or Belgian Endive] Salad

A refreshing first course, Pear and Chicory [French or Belgian Endive] Salad is simple and quick to prepare.

4 SERVINGS

4 fl. oz. [½ cup] French Dressing
1 teaspoon prepared French mustard
1 teaspoon sugar
8 oz. chicory [French or Belgian endive], cleaned and cut into 1-inch slices

2 large ripe pears, peeled, cored and thinly sliced
2 tablespoons chopped walnuts
2 tablespoons raisins
8 round lettuce leaves, washed and shaken dry

In a large mixing bowl, combine the French dressing, mustard and sugar, beating with a fork until the ingredients are well mixed.

Add the chicory [French or Belgian endive], pears, walnuts and raisins to the bowl. Using two spoons, toss the mixture until it is coated with the dressing.

Line 4 individual serving dishes with the lettuce leaves. Spoon equal quantities of the salad mixture on top of the lettuce and serve immediately.

Pear Chutney

Pear Chutney has a sharp, fruity flavour and goes well with any cold meat and cheese. Stored in a cool dry place, it will keep for several months.

ABOUT 4 POUNDS

3 lb. pears, peeled, cored and chopped
2 tart apples, peeled, cored and chopped
2 medium-sized onions, sliced
1 lb. [2⅔ cups] raisins
1 teaspoon hot chilli powder
2-inch piece fresh root ginger, peeled and finely chopped
1 garlic clove, crushed
1 teaspoon salt
½ teaspoon grated nutmeg
12 cloves
juice and grated rind of 2 oranges
1 lb. [2⅔ cups] soft brown sugar
1 pint [2½ cups] white vinegar

Place all the ingredients in a very large saucepan and stir well with a wooden spoon. Set the pan over high heat and bring the mixture to the boil, stirring occasionally.

Reduce the heat to low and, stirring occasionally, simmer the chutney for 3 hours or until it is thick.

Remove the pan from the heat. Ladle the chutney into clean, warmed jam jars. Place a disc of vinegar-resistant paper inside the lid of each jar and cover with jam-covers.

Label the jars and store them in a cool, dry place until ready to use.

Delicate, spicy Pears Baked with Cardamom makes a refreshing dessert served with cream.

Pear Condé

One of the great classic French desserts, Pear Condé is a delectable mixture of pears, rice, eggs and brandy. Serve it cold as a magnificent end to a special dinner-party meal.

6 SERVINGS

1 teaspoon vegetable oil
4 oz. [⅔ cup] round-grain rice, washed, soaked in cold water for 30 minutes and drained
1½ pints [3¾ cups] milk
10 oz. [1¼ cups] sugar
1 oz. [2 tablespoons] butter
⅛ teaspoon salt
1 teaspoon vanilla essence
6 egg yolks, lightly beaten
2 lb. firm pears, peeled, halved and cored
8 fl. oz. [1 cup] water
3 tablespoons brandy
4 glacé cherries, halved

Preheat the oven to cool 300°F (Gas Mark 2, 150°C). Lightly grease a 2-pint [1½-quart] soufflé dish with the oil. Set aside.

Place the rice in a large flameproof casserole and add the milk, 2 ounces [¼ cup] of the sugar, the butter, salt and vanilla essence. Place the casserole over moderate heat and bring the mixture to the boil, stirring constantly.

Cover the casserole and transfer it to the oven. Bake for 1 hour or until the rice is tender and all the liquid has been absorbed. Remove the casserole from the oven.

Stir the egg yolks into the rice mixture and place the casserole over low heat. Cook gently, stirring constantly, for 3 minutes. Remove the casserole from the heat and set it aside to cool.

With a sharp knife, cut about one-quarter of the pear halves into thin slices. Set aside.

When the rice mixture is cool, spoon about one-third of it into the soufflé dish. Place half the pear slices on top. Continue making layers until all the ingredients are used up, ending with a layer of the rice mixture. Cover the dish with aluminium foil and place it in the refrigerator to chill for 2 hours or until the rice mixture is firm.

Meanwhile, make the sauce. In a medium-sized saucepan, dissolve the remaining sugar in the water over mod-

erate heat, stirring constantly. Add the remaining pear halves. Reduce the heat to low and simmer for 12 to 15 minutes or until the pears are tender. Remove the pan from the heat.

With a slotted spoon, remove half of the pear halves from the pan and set them aside.

Purée the remaining pear halves with the syrup in a strainer or electric blender. Return the purée to the saucepan. Return the pan to high heat. Boil the sauce for 3 minutes.

Remove the pan from the heat and stir in the brandy. Pour the sauce into a bowl and set it aside to cool to room temperature. Then place it in the refrigerator to chill for 30 minutes.

Remove the soufflé dish from the refrigerator. Remove the aluminium foil. Place a serving dish, inverted, over the soufflé dish and reverse the two. The pudding should slide out easily. Arrange the reserved pear halves on the top and around the sides. Decorate with the cherries. Serve the sauce separately.

Pear Jam

A smooth-flavoured delicate preserve, Pear Jam should be made only with undamaged pears if a clear, bright jam with good keeping properties is to be made. If the pears are very firm, chop them into small pieces instead of quartering them.

ABOUT 10 POUNDS

7 lb. pears
1-inch piece fresh root ginger, peeled and bruised
thinly pared rind and juice of 3 lemons
2 pints [5 cups] water
5 lb. [10 cups] sugar

Peel, quarter and core the pears. Tie the pear peel and cores, the ginger and lemon rind in a large piece of cheesecloth.

Place the pears, cheesecloth bag and water in a preserving pan or large saucepan. Place the pan over high heat and bring the water to the boil. Reduce the heat to moderately low and simmer the pears for 30 minutes, or until they are soft. Remove the cheesecloth bag and, with the back of a wooden spoon, press it against the side of the pan to squeeze out as much juice as possible. Discard the bag. Add the sugar and stir until it has dissolved. Stir in the lemon juice.

Increase the heat to moderately high and bring the jam to the boil. Boil it for 15 to 20 minutes or until setting point is reached.

To test the jam for setting, remove the

pan from the heat and spoon a small amount of the jam on to a cold saucer. Allow it to cool. Setting point is reached when the surface sets and wrinkles when pushed with your finger. If setting point has not been reached, return the pan to the heat and continue boiling, testing frequently. Alternatively, use a sugar thermometer. When the temperature registers 220°F to 222°F, setting point has been reached.

When setting point is reached, remove the pan from the heat. With a slotted spoon, skim off the scum from the surface of the jam. Let the jam stand for 5 minutes. Pour the jam into clean, dry, warm jars. Put a circle of waxed paper on top of each jar. Wipe the outside and inside rims of the jars with a warm, damp cloth to remove any stickiness. Cover with jam covers and secure them with elastic bands.

Label the jars and store them in a cool, dry place.

Pears Paradiso

A delightful and easy-to-make dessert, Pears Paradiso may be served hot with chilled whipped cream.

4 SERVINGS

4 large firm pears, peeled, halved and cored
1 tablespoon lemon juice
2 tablespoons chopped candied peel
2 tablespoons chopped walnuts
2 tablespoons orange-flavoured liqueur
2 tablespoons sugar
5 fl. oz. [⅝ cup] orange juice

Preheat the oven to moderate 350°F (Gas Mark 4, 180°C).

Lay the pear halves, cut sides up, in a baking dish. Sprinkle over the lemon juice. Set aside.

In a small mixing bowl, combine the candied peel, walnuts and orange-flavoured liqueur. Spoon the mixture into the pear hollows. Set aside.

In a small saucepan, dissolve 1 tablespoon of the sugar in the orange juice stirring constantly over low heat. When the sugar has dissolved, increase the heat to moderate and bring the orange juice to the boil.

Remove the pan from the heat and pour the juice around the pears. Cover the baking dish and place it in the oven. Bake the pears for 1 hour, basting occasionally.

Preheat the grill [broiler] to high.

Remove the dish from the oven. Re-

A delectable mixture of pears, rice, eggs and brandy, Pear Condé makes a classic — and stunning — finale to a dinner party.

Pea

move the cover and sprinkle the remaining sugar over the top. Place the dish under the grill [broiler] and grill [broil] for 2 to 3 minutes or until the pears are golden brown.

Remove the pears from the grill [broiler] and serve immediately.

Pears Poached in Red Wine

Simple to make and absolutely delicious, Pears Poached in Red Wine may be served with whipped cream.

6 SERVINGS

- 6 large firm pears
- 6 oz. [¾ cup] sugar
- 4 fl. oz. [½ cup] water
- 2-inch piece cinnamon stick
   pared rind of 1 lemon
- 4 fl. oz. [½ cup] red wine

With a sharp knife, peel the pears.

Place the pears, sugar, water, cinnamon stick and lemon rind in a large saucepan. Place the pan over moderate heat, cover and cook the pears for 10 minutes. Add the wine, reduce the heat to very low and simmer, turning occasionally, for a further 20 to 25 minutes or until the pears are tender but still firm.

Using a slotted spoon, transfer the pears to a serving dish and set aside.

Increase the heat to high and boil the cooking liquid for 8 minutes or until it has thickened slightly.

Remove the pan from the heat and strain the liquid over the pears. Set the dish aside at room temperature until the pears are cool, then chill in the refrigerator for at least an hour before serving.

Pear Salad

Serve Pear Salad with cold ham or poultry. The dressing may be prepared in advance but the pears must be cut and peeled at the last minute. If Beurré Hardy pears are not available, Comice pears may be substituted.

4-6 SERVINGS

- 2 tablespoons cream cheese
- 2 tablespoons single [light] cream
- 2 tablespoons lemon juice
- 1 tablespoon apricot jam, strained
- 5 fl. oz. [⅝ cup] mayonnaise
- 1 cos [romaine] lettuce, outer leaves removed, washed and separated into leaves
- 4 large ripe Beurré Hardy pears, peeled, cored and cut into 6 slices
- 1 tablespoon capers

In a small mixing bowl, mash the cream

cheese with the cream, lemon juice and apricot jam. Beat in the mayonnaise. Taste the dressing and add some salt or sugar if necessary. Set aside.

Tear the lettuce leaves in half and arrange them on individual plates. Arrange the pear slices on top and pour the dressing over them. Scatter the capers over the dressing and serve immediately.

Pears Stuffed with Roquefort Cheese

   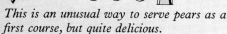

This is an unusual way to serve pears as a first course, but quite delicious.

4 SERVINGS

- 2 large ripe Comice or other dessert pears, peeled, halved and cored
- 1 teaspoon lemon juice
- 1½ oz. [3 tablespoons] unsalted butter, softened
- 3 oz. Roquefort cheese, crumbled
- 4 perfect round lettuce leaves

Using a pastry brush, brush the pears inside and out with the lemon juice. (This

will prevent the pears from browning.)

In a small mixing bowl, combine the butter and cheese together, mashing them with a fork until they are well blended.

Spoon the mixture into the pear halves. Place a lettuce leaf on 4 plates and arrange the pears on top. Chill in the refrigerator for 30 minutes before serving.

Pear Tart Bourdaloue

Pears cooked in a sweet spicy syrup and arranged on a creamy custard base, Pear Tart Bourdaloue makes a decorative dessert to serve at a dinner party. Pears discolour very quickly once they are peeled,

so if this worries you, add a few drops of red colouring to the syrup or, if you prefer, poach the pears in red wine and use a red jam glaze.

ONE 9-INCH TART

1 x 9-inch Flan Case, made with rich shortcrust pastry, baked blind and cooled

6 oz. [¾ cup] sugar
2 tablespoons lemon juice
1 cinnamon stick
16 fl. oz. [2 cups] water
4 large pears, peeled, halved and cored
4 fl. oz. [½ cup] Apricot Glaze, warm

12 fl. oz. [1½ cups] Crème Pâtissière
2 oz. [½ cup] slivered almonds, toasted

Pear Tart Bourdaloue and Pear Salad are two tasty pear dishes.

Place the flan case on a serving platter and set aside.

Place the sugar, lemon juice, cinnamon stick and water in a large saucepan. Set the pan over low heat and cook, stirring constantly with a wooden spoon, until the sugar has dissolved. Increase the heat to high and bring the syrup to the boil. Remove the cinnamon stick. Add the pear halves to the syrup, reduce the heat to low and simmer the pears for 12 minutes or until they are just tender. Remove the pan from the heat and leave the pears to cool in the pan. When the pears are cool, with a slotted spoon, lift them out of the syrup and place them on a rack to drain. Discard the syrup.

Using a pastry brush, brush the inside of the flan case with a little apricot glaze.

Spoon the crème pâtissière into the flan case, smoothing it over with a flat-bladed knife. Set aside.

Transfer the pears to a chopping board and, using a sharp knife, slice the pear halves, lengthways, into thin slices.

Arrange the slices decoratively on top of the crème pâtissière, narrow ends toward the centre, in a circle. Spread the slices out so that they overlap one another slightly.

Sprinkle the almonds over the pears. Using a spoon, lightly glaze the top of the tart with the remaining apricot glaze.

Serve immediately.

You'll find it difficult to limit yourself to just one of these rich, coffee-flavoured Pecan Bars with your afternoon tea or coffee!

Pearl Barley

Pearl barley is BARLEY husked and polished. It is mainly used to thicken soups and stews.

Pease Pudding

Once a popular dish in England, Pease Pudding seems recently to have fallen into some disfavour. A pity because it makes a hearty, healthy accompaniment to the cheaper meat dishes, such as boiled beef, that it was intended to stretch out. Traditionally Pease Pudding was cooked in a cheesecloth bag in the same pot as the meat with which it was to be served.

6-8 SERVINGS

1 lb. green split peas, washed, soaked in cold water for 3 hours and drained
1 medium-sized onion, finely chopped
1 teaspoon salt
1 oz. [2 tablespoons] butter
½ teaspoon Worcestershire sauce
1 teaspoon black pepper

Place the peas and onion in a medium-sized saucepan. Pour over enough water just to cover and add ½ teaspoon of the salt. Place the pan over moderately high heat and bring the water to the boil. Reduce the heat to low, cover the pan and simmer the peas, stirring occasionally, for 2 hours or until they are very soft.

Remove the pan from the heat and drain the peas and onion, discarding the cooking liquid. Using the back of a wooden spoon, rub the pea mixture through a strainer into a medium-sized mixing bowl. Discard any dry pulp remaining in the strainer. Alternatively, purée the pea mixture in a food mill or electric blender and place it in a bowl.

Stir in the butter, Worcestershire sauce, the remaining salt and the pepper and beat well to blend. Serve at once.

Pecan

One of the most popular of the dessert nuts, the pecan is native to the southern part of the United States and is cultivated and used widely throughout that country. It is slim and oval in shape, with a brittle, reddish-brown shell which is removed before the nut is eaten or used in cooking.

The pecan is a popular ingredient in many American pies and flans and may be used in the same way as the WALNUT.

Pecan Bars

Rich, sweet pastry bars with a pecan topping, Pecan Bars are an excellent addition to the tea table.

ABOUT 28 BARS

4 oz. [½ cup] plus 2 teaspoons butter
8 oz. [1 cup] sugar
1 egg
6 oz. [1½ cups] flour, sifted
4 teaspoons coffee essence
8 oz. [2 cups] pecans, coarsely chopped
3 egg whites

Preheat the oven to moderate 350°F (Gas Mark 4, 180°C). With the 2 teaspoons of butter, grease a 7- by 11-inch baking tin.

In a small mixing bowl, cream the remaining butter with 2 ounces [¼ cup] of the sugar until the mixture is light and creamy. Beat in the egg. Add the flour, a little at a time and beat well to blend. When all the flour has been incorporated, mix in the coffee essence. Turn the dough into the prepared tin, spreading it out evenly with the back of a spoon or with your hands.

Place the tin in the oven and bake the dough for 15 minutes.

A traditional American favourite, Pecan Pie is a rich mixture of pecans, syrup and brown sugar baked in a pastry case.

Meanwhile, in a medium-sized saucepan, combine the pecans, the remaining sugar and the egg whites. Place the pan over low heat and, stirring constantly, cook the mixture until all the sugar has dissolved. When the sugar has dissolved, increase the heat to moderate and continue cooking, stirring frequently, for 6 to 8 minutes or until the mixture leaves the sides of the pan.

Remove the baking tin from the oven. Spread the pecan mixture over the pastry with a table knife. Return the baking tin to the oven and continue baking for 15 minutes.

Remove the tin from the oven and let the pastry cool. When the pastry is cool cut it into bars 3-inches long by 1-inch wide.

Pecan Loaf

Teabreads are not only easy to make — they make delicious accompaniments to coffees and teas and tasty offerings for hungry children! Pecan Loaf is no exception and is marvellous spread with butter or cream cheese.

ONE 1-POUND LOAF

2 oz. [¼ cup] plus 1 teaspoon butter, softened
4 oz. [⅔ cup] soft brown sugar
3 eggs
3 fl. oz. [⅜ cup] corn syrup
8 oz. [2 cups] flour
2 teaspoons baking powder
¼ teaspoon salt
6 oz. [1½ cups] pecans, chopped

Preheat the oven to moderate 350°F (Gas Mark 4, 180°C). With the teaspoon of butter, lightly grease a 1-pound loaf tin. Set aside.

In a large mixing bowl, cream the remaining butter and the sugar together with a wooden spoon until the mixture is light and fluffy. Add the eggs, one by one, beating well between each addition. Add the syrup and beat briskly until the mixture is completely smooth and well blended.

Sift the flour, baking powder and salt into a medium-sized mixing bowl. Gradually add the flour mixture to the syrup mixture, beating constantly. Fold in the pecans.

Spoon the batter into the prepared loaf tin and place the tin in the oven. Bake for 1 hour or until a skewer inserted into the centre of the loaf comes out clean.

Remove the tin from the oven and allow the loaf to cool in the tin for a few minutes. Then run a sharp knife around the edges of the loaf and carefully turn it out on to a wire rack to cool completely before serving.

Pecan Pie

A delectable pie, one of the glories of American cuisine, Pecan Pie is so rich that it is best served in small wedges. Serve it as a dessert or with coffee or tea. N.B. Do not use Golden Syrup.

6-8 SERVINGS

1 x 9-inch Flan Case made with shortcrust pastry
2 oz [½ cup] whole pecans
3 eggs
8 fl. oz. [1 cup] corn syrup
3 oz. [½ cup] soft brown sugar
½ teaspoon vanilla essence
¼ teaspoon salt

Preheat the oven to fairly hot 375°F (Gas Mark 5, 190°C). Place the flan case in the oven and bake blind for 10 minutes. Remove the flan case from the oven and remove the foil or paper and beans. Set the flan case aside for 10 minutes.

Increase the oven temperature to hot 425°F (Gas Mark 7, 220°C).

When the flan case has cooled, arrange the pecans, in concentric circles, on the bottom. Set aside.

In a medium-sized mixing bowl, beat the eggs with a wire whisk or rotary beater until they are light and frothy. Beat in the syrup, then the sugar, and continue beating until it has dissolved. Add the vanilla essence and salt and beat the mixture until it is smooth.

Carefully pour the mixture into the flan case, taking care not to disturb the pecan circles — the pecans will rise to the top but will keep their pattern.

Place the pie in the oven and bake for 10 minutes. Reduce the oven temperature to moderate 350°F (Gas Mark 4, 180°C)

and continue to bake the pie for a further 30 minutes.

Remove the pie from the oven and set it aside to cool completely before serving. As the pie cools, the filling will set and become firm.

Pecan and Sour Cream Flan

A delicious variation on a traditional American favourite, Pecan and Sour Cream Flan makes a delicious and rich dessert.

4-6 SERVINGS

4 oz. cream cheese
8 fl. oz. [1 cup] sour cream

3 oz. [$\frac{3}{8}$ cup] sugar
2 eggs, lightly beaten
    finely grated rind of 1 lemon
$\frac{1}{4}$ teaspoon ground allspice
$\frac{1}{8}$ teaspoon ground cardamom
2 oz. [$\frac{1}{2}$ cup] pecans, chopped
1 x 9-inch Flan Case made with
    rich shortcrust pastry, baked
    blind and cooled
2 oz. [$\frac{1}{2}$ cup] whole pecans

Preheat the oven to moderate 350°F (Gas Mark 4, 180°C).

In a large mixing bowl, beat the cream cheese and sour cream together with a wooden spoon until they are well blended. Add the sugar and eggs, beating con-

An elegant dessert cake with just a hint of coffee, Pecan Torte makes a satisfying end to a meal.

stantly. Add the lemon rind, allspice, cardamom and chopped pecans and beat well to blend.

Spoon the mixture into the flan case, spreading it out evenly with a flat-bladed knife. Place the flan in the oven and bake for 30 minutes or until the filling is set and firm.

Remove the flan from the oven and arrange the whole pecans decoratively over the filling. Allow to cool completely before serving.

Pecan Torte

A rich, unusual cake which makes a super dessert, Pecan Torte may be made with sherry or rum instead of brandy. The whipped cream may be replaced by a coffee buttercream.

ONE 8-INCH CAKE

6 egg yolks
6 oz. [¾ cup] sugar
1 tablespoon coffee essence
1 teaspoon ground cinnamon
1½ oz. [¾ cup] fine fresh breadcrumbs
4 oz. [1 cup] pecans, ground
6 egg whites
8 fl. oz. [1 cup] brandy
10 fl. oz. double cream [1¼ cups heavy cream], whipped until stiff with 1 tablespoon sugar
12 pecan halves

Preheat the oven to moderate 350°F (Gas Mark 4, 180°C).

In a medium-sized mixing bowl, whisk the egg yolks and sugar with a wire whisk or rotary beater until the mixture is light and fluffy.

Mix in the coffee essence, cinnamon, breadcrumbs and ground pecans.

In another medium-sized mixing bowl, beat the egg whites with a wire whisk or rotary beater until they form stiff peaks.

Using a large metal spoon, fold the egg whites into the egg yolk mixture lightly but thoroughly.

Pour the mixture into an 8-inch round cake tin. Set the tin on a baking sheet and place it in the centre of the oven. Bake for 45 minutes. Reduce the heat to very cool 275°F (Gas Mark 1, 140°C) and cook for a further 30 minutes, or until a skewer inserted into the centre of the cake comes out clean.

Remove the tin from the oven and place it on a plate. Pour the brandy slowly over the hot cake. When all the brandy has been absorbed, allow the cake to cool completely.

When the cake is cool, remove it from the cake tin. Place the cake on a serving dish. With a flat-bladed knife, cover the top and sides of the cake with the whipped cream.

Decorate the cake with the pecan halves and serve.

Pečaná Husa se Zelím

ROAST GOOSE WITH SAUERKRAUT STUFFING

A Czechoslovakian dish for high days and holidays, Pečaná Husa se Zelím (petchennah hoose seh zel-eem) may be served with potato dumplings and a cucumber salad.

6-8 SERVINGS

1 x 8 to 9 lb. goose, oven ready
1 lemon, quartered
1 teaspoon salt
½ teaspoon freshly ground black pepper

STUFFING

2 lb. canned sauerkraut, drained
1 oz. [2 tablespoons] butter
1 large onion, thinly sliced
3 medium-sized cooking apples, peeled, cored and chopped
1 large potato, grated
grated rind of 1 orange
1 teaspoon salt
½ teaspoon freshly ground black pepper
1 teaspoon caraway seeds
¼ teaspoon ground allspice
¼ teaspoon grated nutmeg

Preheat the oven to very hot 450°F (Gas Mark 8, 230°C).

Prick the goose all over with a fork. Rub the skin of the goose with three of the lemon quarters and discard them. Squeeze the juice of the remaining lemon quarter into the cavity of the goose and discard it. Rub the salt and pepper all over the skin and set the goose aside.

To make the stuffing, squeeze out the excess moisture from the sauerkraut and set aside.

In a large frying-pan, melt the butter over moderate heat. When the foam subsides, add the onion and cook, stirring frequently, for 5 to 7 minutes or until it is soft and translucent but not brown. Add the apples and potato to the pan and cook, stirring constantly, for 5 minutes. Remove the pan from the heat and transfer the mixture to a large mixing bowl. Stir in the sauerkraut, orange rind, salt, pepper, caraway seeds, allspice and nutmeg and mix well to blend.

With a metal spoon, spoon the stuffing into the goose cavity and secure the opening with a trussing needle and thread, or with a skewer.

Place the goose, on its breast, on a rack in a roasting tin. Place the tin in the oven and roast the goose for 15 minutes. Reduce the oven temperature to moderate 350°F (Gas Mark 4, 180°C) and continue roasting for 2½ to 3 hours, removing the fat frequently from the tin with a basting bulb or spoon. Turn the goose on to its back halfway through the roasting period. To test if the goose is cooked, pierce the thigh with the point of a sharp knife. If the juices that run out are clear, the goose is cooked.

Remove the goose from the oven. Remove and discard the trussing thread or skewer. Place the goose on a carving board and serve immediately.

Pêches Cardinal
FRESH PEACHES WITH RASPBERRY PUREE

A classic French dessert, Pêches Cardinal (pehsh kar-din-ahl) has a fine fresh taste and is best made when both peaches and raspberries are in season. The syrup may be stored in a screw-top jar and kept for poaching other fruit.

4 SERVINGS

10 oz. [1¼ cups] sugar
1½ pints [3¾ cups] water
 1 vanilla pod
 4 large peaches, blanched, peeled, halved and stones removed
 8 fl. oz. [1 cup] Melba Sauce, chilled
 1 tablespoon kirsch
 5 fl. oz. [⅝ cup] Crème Chantilly, chilled
12 fresh raspberries, chilled
 2 tablespoons flaked almonds, toasted

In a large saucepan, dissolve the sugar in the water over low heat, stirring constantly. When the sugar has dissolved, add the vanilla pod, increase the heat to moderate and bring the syrup to the boil. Reduce the heat to low and simmer the syrup for 3 minutes. Remove the vanilla pod. Carefully place the peach halves, cut sides up, in the syrup and simmer them for 3 to 5 minutes or until they are just tender.

Remove the pan from the heat and set the peaches aside to cool in the syrup. When they are cool, transfer the peaches and the syrup to a large shallow mixing bowl. Put the bowl in the refrigerator and chill the peaches for 1 hour or until they are very cold.

In a small mixing bowl, combine the melba sauce and kirsch. Using a slotted spoon, transfer the peach halves to chilled individual glass dishes. Discard the syrup or reserve it for future use.

Pour the melba sauce and kirsch mixture over the peaches.

Spoon the crème chantilly into a forcing bag fitted with a ½-inch star nozzle.

Pipe stars of crème chantilly around the edges of the peach halves. Decorate the cream with the raspberries and scatter the almonds over the peaches.

Serve immediately.

Pêches aux Macarons
PEACHES WITH MACAROON CREAM FILLING

A simple but rich dessert, Pêches aux Macarons (pehsh oh mah-kar-ohn) may also be served in a pre-cooked flan case.

6 SERVINGS

 6 peaches, blanched, peeled, halved and the stones removed
 6 tablespoons redcurrant jelly dissolved in 1 tablespoon peach brandy

FILLING
10 fl. oz. [1¼ cups] milk
 1 vanilla pod
 2 eggs
 2 egg yolks
 2 oz. [¼ cup] sugar
 1 tablespoon flour
 1 oz. [2 tablespoons] butter
 6 oz. [¾ cup] crushed macaroons
 ¼ teaspoon almond essence

First make the filling. In a medium-sized saucepan, scald the milk with the vanilla pod over moderate heat (bring to just below boiling point). Remove the pan from the heat. Set aside to cool slightly. Remove and discard the vanilla pod.

In a medium-sized mixing bowl, beat the eggs, egg yolks and sugar together with a wooden spoon until the mixture is pale and thick. Stir in the flour.

Gradually pour the cooled milk into the egg mixture, stirring constantly. Return the custard to the pan and bring to just under boiling point, stirring constantly.

Remove the pan from the heat and beat the thickened custard until it is smooth. Beat in the butter, macaroons and almond essence. Spoon the custard mixture into a bowl and set aside to cool. When the mixture is cool, cover the bowl and put it in the refrigerator for 30 minutes.

Place the peach halves in the refrigerator and chill them for 30 minutes.

Arrange the peach halves, cut sides up, on a chilled serving dish and spoon equal quantities of the filling into them. Pour equal amounts of the redcurrant jelly mixture over each filled peach.

Serve immediately.

Pêches au Massepain
PEACHES WITH MARZIPAN

A lovely ending to a dinner party, Pêches au Massepain (pehsh oh mah-spahn) may be prepared ahead but must be assembled just before serving.

4 SERVINGS

 2 teaspoons cornflour [cornstarch]
 8 oz. Marzipan I
 8 oz. [1 cup] sugar
12 fl. oz. [1½ cups] water
 1 teaspoon grated lemon rind
 4 peaches, blanched, peeled, halved and stones removed
 6 fl. oz. [¾ cup] Apricot Glaze
 5 fl. oz. [⅝ cup] Crème Chantilly
 2 tablespoons chopped pistachio nuts

Preheat the oven to moderate 350°F (Gas Mark 4, 180°C).

Sprinkle the cornflour [cornstarch] over the working surface and roll out the marzipan into a rectangle about ¼-inch thick. With a 3-inch round pastry cutter, cut the marzipan into 8 circles. Line 8 patty tins with the marzipan circles.

Place the patty tins in the oven and bake the marzipan for 15 minutes.

Meanwhile, in a medium-sized saucepan dissolve the sugar in the water over low heat, stirring constantly. Add the lemon rind, increase the heat to moderate and bring the syrup to the boil. Add the peach halves, cut sides up. Reduce the heat to low and simmer them for 3 to 5 minutes or until they are just tender. Remove the pan from the heat. Using a slotted spoon, remove the peach halves from the pan and place them on a plate to drain and cool. Discard the syrup or reserve it for future use.

Remove the patty tins from the oven and allow the marzipan cases to cool completely in the tins.

Remove the marzipan cases from the patty tins and arrange them on a serving dish. Place a peach half, rounded side down, in each case. Spoon the apricot glaze over the peach halves.

Spoon the crème chantilly into a forcing bag fitted with a ½-inch star nozzle. Pipe swirls of cream over the peach halves. Sprinkle the cream with the pistachio nuts and serve immediately.

Pêches Rafraîchies aux Mûres
PEACH AND BLACKBERRY DESSERT

Serve Pêches Rafraîchies aux Mûres (pehsh rah-fray-shee oh meur) on their own or with whipped cream for a super dinner party dessert.

4 SERVINGS

 6 oz. [¾ cup] sugar
10 fl. oz. [1¼ cups] water
 4 large peaches, blanched, peeled, halved and stoned
 8 oz. blackberries
 2 tablespoons kirsch
DECORATION
12 large blackberries

Two delicious French desserts made from fresh peaches, Pêches au Massepain and Pêches Cardinal may be served with cream.

In a medium-sized saucepan, dissolve the sugar in the water over low heat, stirring constantly. When the sugar has dissolved, increase the heat to moderate and boil the syrup for 3 minutes, without stirring.

Add the peach halves to the pan, cut sides down, and poach them for 3 to 5 minutes, or until they are just tender.

Remove the pan from the heat. Using a slotted spoon, transfer the peach halves to 4 individual serving glasses, allowing 2 peach halves for each glass. Set aside.

Pour off all but 2 fluid ounces [¼ cup] of the poaching syrup from the pan. Stir the blackberries and kirsch into the reserved syrup and return the pan to moderately low heat. Cook the blackberries, stirring constantly, for 5 minutes, or until they are beginning to pulp.

Remove the pan from the heat. Strain the mixture into a small mixing bowl. Using the back of a wooden spoon, rub the blackberries through the strainer into the bowl. Discard any dry pulp remaining in the strainer.

Spoon equal amounts of the blackberry purée over the peaches. Decorate each glass with three of the whole blackberries.

Place the glasses in the refrigerator and chill the dessert for 1 hour before serving.

Pectin

Pectin is a complex carbohydrate found in many fruits and vegetables which, when boiled with sugar in the presence of acid, causes the liquid released from fruit or vegetables to become jelly-like.

Pectin is found in comparatively large quantities in cooking apples, quinces, black- and redcurrants, damsons, some plums and citrus fruit — thus these fruits make the most successful jams and jellies.

As the skins and pips, particularly of citrus fruit, apples and quinces, contain much of the pectin, these are sometimes tied in a cheesecloth bag and added to other fruit jams to give them a firm set.

Peebles Crab Bake

A simple, though slightly extravagant dish, Peebles Crab Bake is an adaptation of a traditional Scottish recipe. Serve with grilled [broiled] *tomatoes and a crisp green salad.*

4-6 SERVINGS

2 oz. [¼ cup] plus 1 teaspoon unsalted butter, melted
1 lb. canned crabmeat, shell and cartilage removed
2 oz. [½ cup] medium oatmeal
juice of 1 lemon
1 tablespoon white wine vinegar
2 teaspoons prepared French mustard
½ teaspoon salt
¼ teaspoon black pepper
2 eggs, well beaten
8 slices of brown bread, crusts removed
2 tablespoons chopped fresh parsley

Preheat the oven to fairly hot 400°F (Gas Mark 6, 200°C). With the teaspoon of butter, lightly grease a 9-inch pie dish. Set aside.

In a large mixing bowl, combine the crabmeat, oatmeal, remaining butter, the lemon juice, vinegar, mustard, salt and pepper, beating until all the ingredients are thoroughly blended. Set aside.

Place the eggs on a plate and dip in the bread slices, one by one. Line the pie dish with the bread slices, pressing the edges together to seal them.

An adaption of a traditional Scottish recipe, Peebles Crab Bake makes an elegant supper dish.

Exotic and spicy, Peleponnesian Lamb with Noodles makes an excitingly different dinner party dish.

Spoon the crabmeat mixture over the bread.

Place the dish in the oven and bake for 15 to 20 minutes, or until the filling is golden brown.

Remove the dish from the oven. Sprinkle over the parsley and serve at once.

Peking Duck

A traditional Chinese dish, Peking Duck is famous for its flavour and texture and the unusual way it is eaten (it is served wrapped in a pancake).

The duck is stuffed with spices and pastes, hung by its beak for over 10 hours, then glazed with malt sugar or honey mixed with vinegar or soy sauce and sometimes a little red colouring. The next day it is cooked quickly over hot coals until the skin is crisp.

The rich brown skin is separated from the flesh, cut into squares and served on one platter and the flesh is cut into pieces and served on another. The skin, flesh and chopped shallots or spring onions [scallions] are then wrapped in a pancake, which is first spread with a sweet sauce.

Peleponnesian Lamb with Noodles

A simple dish of lamb grilled [broiled] on skewers, flavoured with cumin and pine nuts, Peleponnesian Lamb with Noodles makes an excellent dish to serve at a dinner party.

4-6 SERVINGS

3 lb. boned leg of lamb, cut into 1-inch cubes
2 tablespoons olive oil
2 teaspoons red wine vinegar
1 tablespoon fresh lemon juice
1 teaspoon cumin seeds, crushed
1½ teaspoons salt
⅛ teaspoon black pepper
3 tablespoons pine nuts, crushed
1 lb. noodles
3 oz. [⅜ cup] butter, cut into small pieces

Preheat the grill [broiler] to moderate.

Thread the lamb cubes on to 8 or 12 skewers. Set aside.

In a small mixing bowl, combine the oil, vinegar, lemon juice, cumin seeds, ½ teaspoon of the salt, the pepper and half of the nuts. Using the pastry brush, brush the lamb cubes with half of the oil mixture. Place the skewers under the grill [broiler] and grill [broil], turning and brushing frequently with the remaining oil mixture, for 15 to 20 minutes or until the lamb is cooked through and tender.

Meanwhile, half fill a large saucepan with cold water. Add the remaining salt and set the pan over high heat. Bring the water to the boil. Reduce the heat to moderate, add the noodles and, stirring once or twice with a fork, cook them for 6 to 8 minutes or until they are 'al dente' or just tender.

Remove the pan from the heat and drain the noodles in a colander. Place the noodles on a large warmed serving platter. Add the butter and, using two large spoons, toss the noodles until the butter has melted and they are thoroughly coated. Set aside and keep warm.

Remove the skewers from the grill [broiler]. Slide the lamb cubes on to the bed of noodles. Sprinkle over the remaining nuts.

Serve at once.

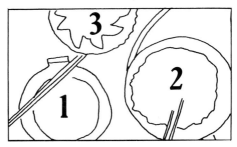

Three marvellous examples of an exotic cuisine, Penang Beef, Penang Cabbage and Penang Curry Puffs are all easy and quick to make (the Chinese stir-fry method of cooking are particularly popular in Malaysia) and quite fabulous to eat.

Penang Beef

A Malaysian-Chinese dish with a strong taste of ginger, Penang Beef should be served with plain boiled rice as part of a Malaysian meal.

4 SERVINGS

3 tablespoons dark soy sauce
2 garlic cloves, crushed
2 teaspoons cornflour [cornstarch]
1 teaspoon sugar
1½ lb. rump steak, thinly sliced and cut into strips
4 tablespoons vegetable oil
3-inch piece fresh root ginger, peeled and finely shredded
8 oz. bean sprouts

In a large mixing bowl, combine the soy sauce, garlic, cornflour [cornstarch] and sugar. Mix in the beef strips. Cover the bowl and set aside for 30 minutes, stirring occasionally.

In a large frying-pan, heat the oil over moderate heat. When the oil is hot, add the ginger and fry, stirring constantly, for 4 to 5 minutes or until the ginger is lightly browned.

Increase the heat to moderately high and add the beef mixture. Fry the beef, stirring constantly, for 5 minutes.

Add the bean sprouts and continue frying, stirring constantly, for a further 3 minutes.

Remove the pan from the heat. Spoon the mixture into a warmed serving dish and serve immediately.

Penang Cabbage

A Malaysian cabbage and prawn or shrimp dish, Penang Cabbage is quickly cooked. The finely shredded cabbage must be fried

only until it is just cooked but still crisp. If you do not like pungent food remove the seeds from the chillis.

4 SERVINGS

3 tablespoons vegetable oil
8 oz. prawns or shrimps, shelled
2 medium-sized onions, thinly sliced
1-inch piece fresh root ginger, peeled and shredded
2 red or green chillis, finely chopped
1 medium-sized white cabbage, coarse outer leaves removed, washed and finely shredded
1 teaspoon salt
½-inch slice creamed coconut dissolved in 1½ tablespoons hot water

In a large frying-pan, heat the oil over moderate heat. When the oil is hot, add the prawns or shrimps and fry them, stirring occasionally, for 4 to 5 minutes or until they are pink and firm. With a slotted spoon, transfer the prawns or shrimps to a plate and set aside. Keep warm.

Add the onions, ginger and chillis to the pan and fry them, stirring occasionally, for 5 to 7 minutes or until the onions are soft and translucent but not brown.

Stir in the cabbage and fry it, stirring constantly, for 2 minutes. Stir in the salt and the coconut mixture and cook, stirring frequently, for a further 5 minutes. Stir in the prawns or shrimps.

Remove the pan from the heat. Spoon the mixture into a warmed serving dish. Serve immediately.

Penang Chicken

A delightful hot-sour-sweet dish, Penang Chicken is easy to make. Serve it with rice as part of a Malaysian meal.

4 SERVINGS

4 tablespoons vegetable oil
3 medium-sized onions, finely chopped
2 garlic cloves, crushed
2 red or green chillis, finely chopped
1 tablespoon soft brown sugar
8 chicken pieces, or 1 x 3 lb. chicken cut into 8 serving pieces
3 tablespoons dark soy sauce
3 tablespoons wine vinegar
2 tablespoons water
½ teaspoon salt

In a large saucepan or deep frying-pan, heat the oil over moderate heat. When the oil is hot, add the onions, garlic and

chillis and fry, stirring occasionally, for 6 minutes. Stir in the sugar and continue cooking, stirring occasionally, for 4 minutes.

Add the chicken pieces and fry them, turning them over frequently, for 8 minutes or until they are evenly browned.

Stir in the soy sauce, vinegar, water and salt. Bring the mixture to the boil. Cover the pan, reduce the heat to low and cook the chicken for 15 minutes.

Uncover the pan, increase the heat to moderately low and continue cooking for a further 25 minutes or until the chicken is tender when pierced with the point of a sharp knife.

Remove the pan from the heat. Spoon the chicken and sauce into a warmed serving dish. Serve immediately.

Penang Curry Puffs

These curry puffs are baked, but they may also be deep-fried, which is the traditional way of cooking them. Serve Penang Curry Puffs warm with a fresh Mint or Tamarind Chutney.

20 PUFFS

PASTRY
12 oz. [3 cups] flour
½ teaspoon salt
3 oz. [⅜ cup] butter
3 to 4 tablespoons iced water
FILLING
2 tablespoons vegetable oil
1 onion, finely chopped
½-inch piece fresh root ginger, peeled and finely chopped
1 garlic clove, crushed
2 red or green chillis, finely chopped
1 teaspoon hot chilli powder
½ teaspoon turmeric
½ teaspoon ground coriander
½ teaspoon salt
8 oz. lean minced [ground] beef
1 tomato, blanched, peeled and chopped
2 oz. green peas, weighed after shelling, cooked and drained
2 tablespoons lime or lemon juice

First make the pastry. Sift the flour and salt into a medium-sized mixing bowl. Add the butter and, with a table knife, cut it into small pieces. Using your fingertips, rub the butter into the flour until the mixture resembles fine breadcrumbs.

Add 3 tablespoons of the iced water and, using the knife, mix it into the flour mixture. With your hands, mix and knead the dough until it is smooth. Add more water if the dough is too dry. Pat the dough into a ball, wrap it in greaseproof or waxed paper and place it in the refrigerator to chill for 30 minutes.

Meanwhile, make the filling. In a medium-sized frying-pan, heat the oil over moderate heat. When the oil is hot, add the onion, ginger, garlic and chillis and fry, stirring occasionally, for 5 to 7 minutes or until the onion is soft and translucent but not brown.

Stir in the chilli powder, turmeric, coriander and salt and cook, stirring occasionally, for 3 minutes.

Add the beef and fry, stirring frequently, for 6 to 8 minutes or until it is lightly browned.

Add the tomato, peas and lime or lemon juice, and cook, stirring occasionally, for 5 minutes. Remove the pan from the heat. Taste the mixture and add more salt if necessary. Set aside.

Preheat the oven to fairly hot 375°F (Gas Mark 5, 190°C).

Remove the dough from the refrigerator. On a lightly floured board, roll out the dough into a circle about ⅛-inch

thick. With a 4-inch round pastry cutter, cut the dough into 20 circles.

Place 2 teaspoonfuls of the meat mixture slightly to the side on each dough circle. Dampen the edges of the dough with water. Fold one-half of the circle over to make a semi-circle. Press the edges together to seal them.

Place the semi-circles on a baking sheet. Put the baking sheet in the oven and bake the puffs for 30 to 35 minutes or until they are golden brown.

Remove the baking sheet from the oven. Transfer the curry puffs to a wire rack to cool slightly.

Serve warm.

Pennsylvania Dutch Chicken Corn Soup

The gentle people who, many years ago, went to the United States seeking religious toleration and the freedom to pursue their simple Old Testament way of life have given their name to one of the most distinctive cuisines of the Americas. The Pennsylvania Dutch are farming folk and

their food reflects this — lots of plain but hearty fare with the emphasis on fresh fruits and vegetables and good succulent meat. This adaptation of the classic Pennsylvania Dutch Chicken Corn Soup is no exception — a meal in itself and guaranteed to keep the chills well away. It need be served only with lots of home-made bread.

4-6 SERVINGS

3 tablespoons vegetable oil
2 medium-sized onions, thinly sliced
4 celery stalks, trimmed and sliced
3 pints [7½ cups] home-made chicken stock
10 black peppercorns, coarsely crushed
1 x 3 lb. chicken, roasted, the flesh removed from the bone, skinned and cut into small pieces
4 oz. large thick egg noodles
14 oz. canned sweetcorn, drained
1 teaspoon chopped fresh sage or ½ teaspoon dried sage
1 teaspoon chopped fresh savoury or ½ teaspoon dried savoury
½ teaspoon salt
½ teaspoon saffron threads soaked in 1 tablespoon hot water

Warming Pennsylvania Dutch Chicken Corn Soup is a meal in itself.

Pennsylvania Dutch Mixed Chow-Chow is an old fashioned pickle made with a variety of vegetables. It is excellent served with cold meat.

In a large saucepan, heat the oil over moderate heat. When the oil is hot, add the onions and cook, stirring occasionally, for 5 to 7 minutes or until they are soft and translucent but not brown. Add the celery and cook, stirring occasionally, for a further 5 minutes.

Pour in the chicken stock and add the peppercorns. Bring the liquid to the boil over moderately high heat. Reduce the heat to low and simmer for 20 minutes.

Add the chicken, noodles, sweetcorn, sage, savory, salt and saffron and stir well to mix. Increase the heat to moderately high and bring the mixture to the boil. Reduce the heat to low and simmer the soup for 15 to 20 minutes or until the noodles are just tender. Taste the soup and add more salt if necessary.

Remove the pan from the heat and serve at once.

Pennsylvania Dutch Mixed Chow-Chow

The Pennsylvania Dutch are famous for their pickles and preserves and perhaps the most famous single pickle in the cuisine is Chow-Chow. There are almost as many versions as there are Pennsylvania Dutch housewives but basically it consists of various types of vegetables, always cooked separately then stored in a pickling solution containing vinegar, sugar, mustard and mustard seed. The result is a marvellous pickle to serve with any type of cold meat.

ABOUT 3½ POUNDS

12 oz. red or white kidney beans, soaked overnight in cold water and drained

4 green or red peppers, white pith removed, seeded and cut into 2-inch pieces

1½ teaspoons salt

1 medium-sized cauliflower, trimmed and broken into small flowerets

1 lb. French beans, trimmed and cut into 2-inch lengths

1 lb. canned sweetcorn, drained

2 pints [5 cups] wine vinegar

6 oz. [1 cup] soft brown sugar

5 tablespoons dry mustard

3 tablespoons mustard seed

1 teaspoon turmeric

Place the kidney beans in a medium-sized saucepan and add enough water just to cover. Place the pan over high heat and bring the liquid to the boil. Cover the pan, reduce the heat to low and simmer the beans for 1 to 1½ hours or until they are just tender.

Meanwhile, place the green or red peppers in a small saucepan. Pour over enough water just to cover and add ½ teaspoon of the salt. Place the pan over high heat and bring the water to the boil. Reduce the heat to moderate and cook the peppers for 10 minutes or until they are tender but still firm. Remove the pan from the heat and drain the peppers in a colander. Set aside.

Place the cauliflower flowerets in a medium-sized saucepan. Pour over enough water just to cover and add ½ teaspoon of salt. Place the pan over moderately high heat and bring the water to the boil. Reduce the heat to moderate and cook the cauliflower for 8 to 12 minutes or until the flowerets are tender but still firm. Remove the pan from the heat and drain the flowerets in a colander. Set aside.

Place the French beans in a large saucepan. Pour over enough water just to cover and add the remaining salt. Place the pan over high heat and bring the water to the boil. Reduce the heat to moderate and boil the beans for 5 to 8 minutes or until they are just tender. Remove the pan from the heat and drain the beans in a colander. Set aside.

When the kidney beans are cooked, remove the pan from the heat and drain the beans in a colander. Transfer them to a large mixing bowl and add the peppers, cauliflower flowerets, beans and corn, stirring well to blend. Set aside.

Place the vinegar, sugar, mustard, mustard seed and turmeric in a large saucepan and place the pan over low heat. Cook, stirring constantly, until the sugar has dissolved. Increase the heat to high and bring the mixture to the boil. Reduce the heat to moderately low and add the vegetables to the pan. Cook the mixture, stirring occasionally so that all the vegetables are well basted, for 5 minutes.

Remove the pan from the heat and ladle the pickle into clean, warmed preserving jars. Seal the jars and label them. Store in a cool, dry place until ready to use.

Pennsylvania Dutch Poultry Stuffing

This authentic Pennsylvania Dutch recipe for poultry stuffing is a mixture of mashed potatoes, parsley and croûtons. Its bland taste particularly complements the flavour of chicken and is excellent for those who dislike the strong sage taste of traditional English poultry stuffing. This recipe yields just enough stuffing for one 4- to 5-pound chicken.

ABOUT 1¼ POUNDS

- 3 medium-sized cooked potatoes, mashed
- 2 eggs, beaten
- 1 teaspoon salt
- ¼ teaspoon black pepper
- ¼ teaspoon dried thyme
- ¼ teaspoon paprika
- 3 tablespoons chopped fresh parsley
- 2 oz. [¼ cup] butter
- 1 small onion, finely chopped
- 1 celery stalk, trimmed and finely chopped
- 4 thick slices of bread, crusts removed and cut into ½-inch cubes

In a medium-sized mixing bowl combine the mashed potatoes and beaten eggs together.

Add the salt, pepper, thyme, paprika and parsley and mix well to blend. Set aside.

In a medium-sized frying-pan, melt the butter over moderate heat. When the foam subsides, add the onion and celery and cook, stirring occasionally, for 5 to 7 minutes or until the onion is soft and translucent but not brown.

Add the bread cubes to the pan and cook, turning frequently, for 3 to 4 minutes or until the bread is evenly browned.

Remove the pan from the heat. Transfer the onion and bread mixture to the mashed potato mixture and mix well.

The stuffing is now ready to use.

Peperonata

RED PEPPER AND TOMATO STEW

Peperonata (pep-'roh-nah-tah) is a stew of red peppers and tomatoes, which may be served as an accompaniment to roast or grilled [broiled] meat. Peperonata is equally good hot or cold and will keep for several days if stored in a screw-top jar with a tablespoon of olive oil on top.

4-6 SERVINGS

- 1 oz. [2 tablespoons] butter
- 2 tablespoons olive oil
- 1 large onion, thinly sliced
- 1 garlic clove, crushed

Peperonata is a colourful Italian stew, made with peppers, tomatoes and garlic. Serve it with meat, or on its own as a light vegetarian meal.

- 1 lb. red peppers, white pith removed, seeded and cut into strips
- 1 lb. tomatoes, blanched, peeled and chopped
- ½ teaspoon salt
- ¼ teaspoon black pepper
- 1 bay leaf

In a large saucepan, heat the butter with the oil over moderate heat. When the foam subsides, add the onion and garlic and fry, stirring occasionally, for 5 to 7 minutes or until the onion is soft and translucent but not brown.

Add the red peppers. Cover the pan, reduce the heat to low and cook for 15 minutes. Add the tomatoes, salt, pepper and bay leaf and simmer, uncovered, for a further 20 minutes.

If there is too much liquid in the pan, increase the heat to moderately high and cook for 5 minutes or until the mixture is thick and some liquid has evaporated.

Remove the pan from the heat and remove and discard the bay leaf. Serve at once, if you are serving the peperonata hot.

Peperoni alla Bagna Cauda

SWEET PEPPERS WITH GARLIC AND
ANCHOVY SAUCE

*Bagna Cauda is a traditional Italian dip,
almost always eaten hot. With the addition
of peppers and other vegetables, it becomes
an informal light meal, somewhat like
Fondue. Serve with lots of red wine and
Italian bread.*

4-6 SERVINGS

2 lb. red or green peppers, white
   pith removed, seeded and cut
   into $\frac{1}{2}$-inch wide strips
6 medium-sized tomatoes,
   quartered and seeded
3 celery stalks, trimmed, halved
   lengthways and chopped into
   3-inch lengths
SAUCE
3 oz. [$\frac{3}{8}$ cup] butter
3 tablespoons olive oil
4 garlic cloves, crushed
6 anchovy fillets, chopped
$\frac{1}{2}$ teaspoon salt

Arrange the peppers, tomatoes and celery
on a serving dish and set aside.

To make the sauce, in a small frying-
pan, melt the butter with the oil over
moderate heat. When the foam subsides,
reduce the heat to low. Add the garlic and
anchovies and cook, stirring constantly,
for 8 to 10 minutes, or until the anchovies
have dissolved into a pulp. Stir in the
salt. Remove the pan from the heat and
transfer the sauce to a small, warmed
serving dish.

Serve immediately, with the vegetables.

Peperoni Ripieni

PEPPERS STUFFED WITH TOMATOES, TUNA,
ANCHOVIES AND OLIVES

*Peperoni Ripieni (pep-eh-rony ree-pee-
yeni) is a popular Italian dish of stuffed
peppers. It may be served as a rather filling
first course, or as a light lunch with sautéed
potatoes and a green salad.*

4 SERVINGS

4 large red, green or yellow peppers
4 tablespoons olive oil
1 medium-sized onion, thinly sliced
2 garlic cloves, crushed
28 oz. canned peeled tomatoes
1 tablespoon tomato purée
$\frac{1}{2}$ teaspoon dried basil
$\frac{1}{2}$ teaspoon dried oregano
$\frac{1}{2}$ teaspoon salt
$\frac{1}{4}$ teaspoon black pepper
1 tablespoon chopped fresh parsley
12 oz. canned tuna, drained and
   flaked
4 anchovy fillets, chopped
6 black olives, stoned and chopped
2 teaspoons capers
1 oz. [$\frac{1}{4}$ cup] Parmesan cheese,
   grated

With a sharp knife, slice off 1-inch from
the wider end of each pepper. Carefully
remove and discard the white pith and
seeds. Set the peppers aside. Remove and
discard the stems from the sliced tops and
chop the flesh into small dice. Set aside.

In a large frying-pan, heat 2 table-

Peppers stuffed with a succulent mixture of tomatoes, tuna fish, anchovy, black olives and herbs, Peperoni Ripieni makes a tasty light meal.

spoons of the oil over moderate heat. When it is hot, add the onion, garlic and pepper dice and fry, stirring occasionally, for 5 to 7 minutes, or until the onion is soft and translucent but not brown.

Add the tomatoes with the can juice, the tomato purée, basil, oregano, salt and pepper. Cover the pan and cook, stirring occasionally, for 20 to 30 minutes or until the mixture has thickened.

Stir in the parsley, tuna, anchovy fillets, olives and capers and cook for a further 5 minutes.

Preheat the oven to warm 325°F (Gas Mark 3, 170°C).

Remove the pan from the heat and spoon the tomato sauce into the peppers, filling them to within about ½-inch of the top.

With a pastry brush, brush a baking tin with 1 tablespoon of the remaining oil. Place the peppers in the baking tin and put the tin in the oven. Bake the peppers for 45 minutes, basting occasionally with the remaining oil. After 45 minutes, sprinkle the tops of the peppers with the grated cheese and cook for a further 15 minutes or until the cheese is brown and bubbly.

Remove the baking tin from the oven and serve the peppers immediately.

Peperoni e Zucchini
PEPPERS AND COURGETTES [ZUCCHINI] IN TOMATO SAUCE

An Italian dish of peppers and courgettes [zucchini], Peperoni e Zucchini (pep-per-oh-nee ay soo-kee-nee) may be served with grilled [broiled] or roast meat.

4 SERVINGS

2 tablespoons olive oil
1 medium-sized onion, sliced
1 garlic clove, crushed
1½ lb. courgettes [zucchini], trimmed and sliced
2 large green or red peppers, white pith removed, seeded and sliced
14 oz. canned peeled tomatoes
½ teaspoon black pepper
1 tablespoon fresh basil or 1½ teaspoons dried basil
1 bay leaf
6 anchovy fillets, chopped
2 oz. [½ cup] Parmesan cheese, grated

In a large frying-pan, heat the oil over

moderate heat. When the oil is hot, add the onion, garlic, courgettes [zucchini] and peppers and fry, stirring occasionally, for 5 to 7 minutes or until the onion is soft and translucent but not brown.

Stir in the tomatoes with the can juice, the pepper, basil and bay leaf. Reduce the heat to low and simmer for 30 minutes or until the sauce has thickened and the vegetables are cooked. Remove the pan from the heat and remove and discard the bay leaf.

Preheat the grill [broiler] to high.

Spoon the mixture into a baking dish and scatter the chopped anchovy fillets over the top. Sprinkle over the grated cheese. Place the dish under the grill [broiler] and grill [broil] for 3 to 5 minutes or until the top is brown and bubbly. Remove the dish from under the grill [broiler] and serve immediately.

Pepper
Pepper, both black and white, comes from a climbing vine native to India. The fruit of the vine, called peppercorns, are green when unripe and turn red when they ripen.

To make black peppercorns, unripe peppercorns are dried in the sun — the skin then turns black and wrinkled. To make white peppercorns, ripe red peppercorns are soaked in water and the outer hulls removed.

Peppercorns bought whole and ground coarsely in a pepper mill taste fresher and have more flavour than the pre-ground commercial powder sold as pepper.

Pepper and Corned Beef Hash

An adaptation of a West African dish, Pepper and Corned Beef Hash is quick and

simple to prepare. Serve it as a light supper with a crisp green salad.

4-6 SERVINGS

1 oz. [2 tablespoons] butter
1 tablespoon vegetable oil
1 medium-sized onion, chopped
1 garlic clove, crushed
3 green peppers, white pith removed, seeded and chopped
3 medium-sized cooked potatoes, diced
2 tomatoes, blanched, peeled and chopped
½ teaspoon salt
¼ teaspoon black pepper
⅛ teaspoon cayenne pepper
1 tablespoon chopped fresh parsley
28 oz. canned corned beef, flaked

In a large frying-pan, melt the butter with the oil over moderate heat. When the foam subsides, add the onion, garlic and green peppers and fry, stirring occasionally, for 5 to 7 minutes or until the onion is soft and translucent but not brown.

Add the diced potatoes and cook, stirring frequently, for 4 minutes. Add the tomatoes, salt, pepper, cayenne, parsley and corned beef. Cook for a further 5 minutes or until the mixture is hot.

Remove the pan from the heat and spoon the mixture on to a serving dish. Serve immediately.

Pepper Sauce

This delicious, pungent Pepper Sauce may be served with shellfish or used as a dip for fresh vegetables. The sauce requires no cooking, but an electric blender is essential to obtain the correct consistency. It keeps well if stored in a screw-top jar.

ABOUT 26 FLUID OUNCES [3¼ CUPS]

1 large green pepper, white pith removed, seeded and chopped
1 large red pepper, white pith removed, seeded and chopped
4 green chillis, chopped
1 onion, finely chopped
2 tomatoes, blanched, peeled and chopped
1 teaspoon salt
½ teaspoon black pepper

In a medium-sized mixing bowl, combine all the ingredients thoroughly. Spoon half of the mixture into an electric blender and blend at high speed for 30 seconds.

Pour the sauce into another medium-sized mixing bowl and set it aside while you blend the remaining mixture. Add the remaining sauce to the bowl and place it in the refrigerator to chill for 30 minutes before serving.

Peppers

Peppers come from the CAPISCUM family of plants and are native to South America, although they are now extensively cultivated throughout the world.

The most common pepper is sweet or bell pepper, *capiscum annum*, a medium-sized, bell-shaped vegetable with a slightly sweet, mild taste. Sweet peppers are used unripe (green) or ripe (red or yellow). Red pepper, or PIMIENTO as it is sometimes called, is sometimes dried and ground to make the spice PAPRIKA.

Sweet or bell peppers may be cooked and served on their own or as an ingredient in stews, casseroles or salads. They are very rich in Vitamin C.

CHILLI peppers are small and elongated, red or green and very pungent. Native to Central and South America, they are an essential ingredient in curries and many Latin American dishes. The seeds of the chilli pepper are especially hot and should be removed if a milder flavour is required.

If you are not used to handling chillis, be very careful with their preparation. Do not touch your face or eyes while you are chopping them. If you have sensitive skin, wear rubber gloves because their volatile oils can make your eyes burn and your skin itch. Always wash your hands thoroughly in hot soapy water after handling chillis.

Several varieties of small pungent peppers are also dried and either ground or flaked for use as condiments. CAYENNE pepper and RED PEPPER FLAKES are both made from peppers.

A colourful selection of various types of peppers: green and red peppers, or bell peppers, pimientos and fresh and dried red and green chillis.

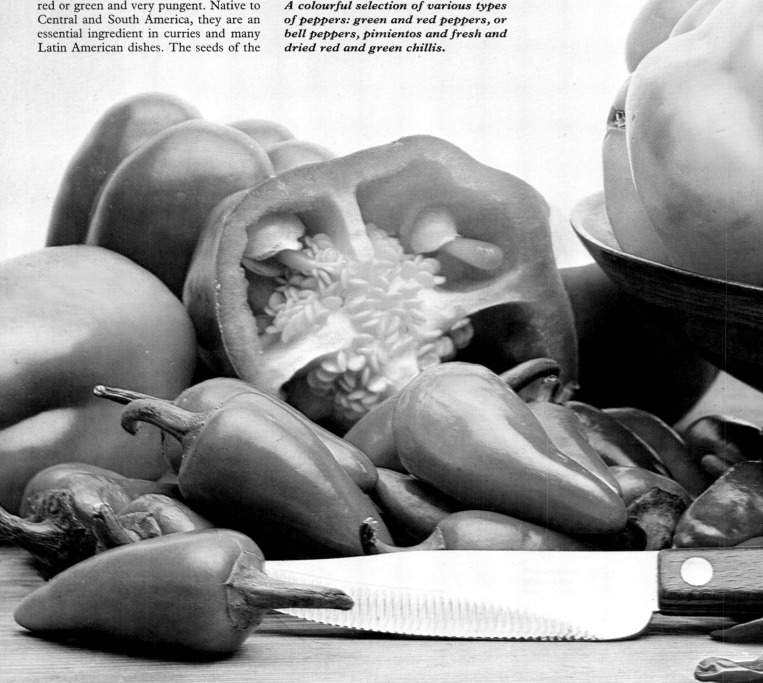

Peppers Preserved in Vinegar

These preserved peppers are excellent served as part of an hors d'oeuvre or antipasto. To serve them, wash in cold water, dry and sprinkle them with a little olive oil. They will keep, unopened, for several months.

ABOUT 4 POUNDS

6 large red peppers, white pith removed, seeded and halved lengthways
1 pint 12 fl. oz. [4 cups] white wine vinegar
½ teaspoon salt
6 black peppercorns
   bouquet garni, consisting of 4 parsley sprigs, 1 thyme spray and 1 bay leaf tied together
4 tablespoons olive oil

Preheat the grill [broiler] to high.

Place the peppers, skin sides up, on the grill [broiler] rack and grill [broil] for 5 to 8 minutes or until the skin of the peppers is black and charred. Remove the peppers from the grill [broiler] and, with your fingertips, rub off the charred skin.

Cut the peppers into 2-inch slices and pack them into four 1-pound sterilized preserving jars. Set aside.

In a medium-sized saucepan, combine the vinegar, salt, peppercorns and bouquet garni. Place the pan over moderate heat and bring the vinegar to the boil. Boil for 5 minutes, then remove the pan from the heat. Strain equal amounts of the vinegar into each jar and set aside, uncovered, at room temperature until it has cooled.

When the vinegar is cool, pour 1 tablespoon of the olive oil on top of each jar. Cover tightly and store in a cool, dark place.

Peppers Stuffed with Lamb and Rice

An adaptation of a Middle-Eastern dish, Peppers Stuffed with Lamb and Rice is delicious served with a green salad, lots of crusty bread and red wine.

4 SERVINGS

4 large red or green peppers
1 tablespoon plus 1 teaspoon vegetable oil
1 small onion, chopped
1 garlic clove, crushed
8 oz. minced [ground] lamb

Two exciting ways to use peppers — Peppers Stuffed with Lamb and Rice and Peppers Preserved in Vinegar.

14 oz. canned peeled tomatoes
1 teaspoon salt
½ teaspoon black pepper
1 teaspoon coriander seeds, crushed
5 oz. [2 cups] cooked long-grain rice
1 teaspoon chopped mint leaves or ½ teaspoon dried mint

With a sharp knife, slice off and discard 1-inch from the wider end of each pepper. Carefully remove and discard the white pith and seeds from the inside of each pepper. Set the peppers aside.

Preheat the oven to fairly hot 375°F (Gas Mark 5, 190°C).

In a medium-sized saucepan, heat the 1 tablespoon of oil over moderate heat. When the oil is hot, add the onion and garlic and fry, stirring occasionally, for 5 to 7 minutes or until the onion is soft and translucent but not brown. Add the minced [ground] lamb and cook, stirring constantly, for 6 to 8 minutes or until the lamb is well browned. Add the tomatoes with the can juice, the salt, pepper and coriander seeds. Cover the pan, reduce the heat to low and simmer for 30 minutes. Add the rice and mint and cook, stirring occasionally, for a further 5 minutes. Remove the pan from the heat.

Using a pastry brush, brush a medium-sized baking dish with the remaining oil. Spoon equal amounts of the lamb mixture into each pepper. Stand the peppers upright in the baking dish and place the dish in the centre of the oven.

Bake for 40 minutes or until the peppers are tender. Remove the peppers from the oven and serve immediately.

Peppermint

Peppermint is a herb belonging to a genus of strong-scented plants of the *labiatae* family. See information on MINT.

Peppermint and Chocolate Ice-cream

This fresh-tasting ice-cream makes a super dessert, served with Krumkaker or Nut Waffles. For a richer ice-cream, substitute single [light] cream for the milk, and add one or two tablespoons of Crème de Menthe to the cooked custard.

Smooth, tingling peppermint ice-cream with crunchy pieces of dark chocolate, Peppermint and Chocolate Ice-cream is delicious served with wafers.

ABOUT 1 PINT [2½ CUPS]

1 pint [2½ cups] milk
1 vanilla pod, split in half
1 egg yolk
1 tablespoon custard powder
3 tablespoons sugar
1½ teaspoons gelatine, dissolved in
 2 tablespoons hot water
½ teaspoon peppermint essence
1 egg white
4 oz. dark [semi-sweet] cooking
 chocolate, coarsely grated

Set the thermostat of the refrigerator to its coldest setting.

In a small saucepan, scald the milk with the vanilla pod (bring to just below boiling point) over moderate heat. Remove the pan from the heat, cover it and leave the milk to infuse for 20 minutes.

In a medium-sized mixing bowl, beat the egg yolk, custard powder, sugar and 2 tablespoons of the scalded milk with a wire whisk or rotary beater until the mixture is thoroughly combined. Strain the remaining milk on to the egg yolk mixture, whisking constantly. Pour the mixture back into the saucepan and place the pan over low heat. Cook the mixture, stirring constantly, for 5 minutes or until the custard is thick enough to coat the back of the spoon.

Remove the pan from the heat and stir in the dissolved gelatine and the peppermint essence. Set the mixture aside to cool completely, stirring occasionally.

When the mixture is completely cold, cover the pan and place it in the refrigerator to chill for 1 hour.

Remove the pan from the refrigerator and pour the mixture into a chilled freezer tray. Place the tray in the frozen food storage compartment of the refrigerator and freeze the mixture for 30 minutes.

Remove the tray from the storage compartment and turn the mixture into a chilled medium-sized mixing bowl. Using a wire whisk or rotary beater, whisk the mixture for 1 minute, or until it is smooth.

In a small mixing bowl, beat the egg white with the wire whisk or rotary beater until it forms stiff peaks. With a metal spoon, fold the egg white into the peppermint mixture. Spoon the mixture back into the freezer tray. Return the tray to the frozen food storage compartment and freeze for 1 hour, or until the mixture is firm.

Remove the ice-cream from the storage compartment and turn it out into a chilled mixing bowl. Using the wire whisk or rotary beater, beat the mixture for 1 minute, or until it is smooth. With a

wooden spoon, beat in the grated chocolate. Spoon the mixture back into the freezer tray and return it to the frozen food storage compartment. Freeze the ice-cream for 1 hour, or until it is firm.

While the ice-cream is freezing for the last time, place 4 sundae glasses or individual serving glasses in the refrigerator to chill.

Remove the ice-cream and glasses from the refrigerator. Spoon the ice-cream into the glasses and serve immediately.

Peppermint Clouds

 ①

Light-as-air little sponge cakes made with no fat, Peppermint Clouds are flavoured with peppermint essence. They can be sandwiched together with chocolate buttercream, cream or just left plain.

ABOUT 36 CAKES

8 oz. [1 cup] castor sugar
3 teaspoons butter
4 eggs
6 drops peppermint essence
6 oz. [1½ cups] flour, sifted

Peppermint Clouds are just the thing to serve with a hot cup of tea!

Preheat the oven to moderate 350°F (Gas Mark 4, 180°C).

Spread the sugar evenly on a large baking sheet. Place the baking sheet in the oven and bake the sugar for 5 minutes. Remove the baking sheet from the oven.

Increase the oven temperature to fairly hot 400°F (Gas Mark 6, 200°C). Using the butter, grease three large baking sheets and set them aside.

Place the sugar and eggs in a medium-sized mixing bowl. Using a wire whisk or rotary beater, whisk the eggs and sugar together until they are very pale. Stir in the peppermint essence. Using a metal spoon, gently but thoroughly fold in the flour.

Drop tablespoons of the mixture on to the baking sheets, well spaced apart. Place the baking sheets in the oven and bake for 15 to 20 minutes or until the cakes have risen and are light golden brown.

Remove the baking sheets from the oven. Using a palette knife or spatula, transfer the cakes to a wire rack to cool completely.

Easy to make Peppermint Creams may be cut into decorative shapes and served with after-dinner coffee.

When the cakes are cold, fill with the desired filling or leave plain and serve.

Peppermint Creams

A delightful and easy-to-make sweet [candy], Peppermint Creams are the perfect accompaniment to after-dinner coffee. If you wish a very strong peppermint taste, the amount of peppermint essence may be increased. The shape of the creams may also be varied by using heart-shaped or diamond-shaped pastry cutters.

ABOUT 1 POUND

1 lb. icing sugar [4 cups confectioners' sugar], **sifted**
1 teaspoon lemon juice
1 egg white
4 drops peppermint essence

In a large mixing bowl, combine all of the ingredients together with a wooden spoon, beating until they are well mixed.

Generously sprinkle a large board or slab with icing [confectioners'] sugar and turn the peppermint mixture out on to it. Using a rolling pin sprinkled with icing [confectioners'] sugar, roll out the mixture to ¼-inch thick. Using ½-inch round pastry cutter, cut the mixture into circles.

Place the circles on a large baking sheet or aluminium foil and set aside for at least 24 hours before serving.

Peppermint Fondants

Peppermint Fondants are little green and white sweets [candies], which look very attractive piled in a small silver dish and served with after-dinner coffee. Stored in an airtight tin, the sweets [candies] will keep for up to two weeks.

ABOUT 1 POUND

1 lb. [2 cups] sugar
7 fl. oz. [⅞ cup] water
⅛ teaspoon cream of tartar
½ teaspoon peppermint essence
2 drops green food colouring

In a medium-sized, heavy-based saucepan, dissolve the sugar in the water over low heat, stirring constantly. When the sugar has dissolved, increase the heat to high and bring the mixture to the boil, without stirring. As soon as the mixture is boiling, sprinkle over the cream of tartar and continue boiling, without stirring, until the temperature registers 238°F to 240°F on a sugar thermometer, or until a teaspoon of the mixture dropped

For Peppermint Fondants, test the consistency of the sugar syrup by dropping a teaspoon of it into cold water.

Start working the cooled fondant with a sugar scraper or spatula until it turns white and opaque.

Knead the fondant thoroughly with your hands to make it completely smooth and pliable.

Divide the fondant in half and set one half aside. Sprinkle the other half with the green food colouring.

Knead the green food colouring evenly into the fondant, and then cut the green and white fondant into shapes.

into a small bowl of cold water forms a soft ball when rolled between your fingers.

Remove the pan from the heat and stir in the peppermint essence, blending it in thoroughly.

Pour the fondant on to a marble slab or hard, cold working surface, which has been sprinkled with a little cold water. Do not scrape out any of the fondant which remains in the bottom of the pan. Sprinkle the surface of the fondant on the marble slab or working surface with a few drops of cold water and set it aside to cool for 3 minutes.

Using a metal spatula or a sugar scraper, start working the fondant by bringing the mixture in from the edges to the centre.

When the fondant 'turns', or goes white and opaque, knead it with your hands until it is smooth. Divide the fondant in half. Sprinkle the green food colouring over one half of the fondant and knead it in until the fondant is evenly coloured. Break off small pieces of the green fondant and roll them into balls. Place the balls on a flat surface and flatten them with the palms of your hands to make disc-shapes.

Wash off all the green food colouring from your hands and shape the white fondant into discs or cut into shapes.

Set the fondants aside for 1 hour, and then pile them into a serving dish and serve, or store in an airtight tin until needed.

Pepperoni

A hot, spicy Italian pork sausage flavoured with chilli, pepperoni is often used in PIZZAS. It can also be sliced very thinly and eaten as part of an antipasto.

Pepperoni sausage is very popular in the United States. Since it is difficult to buy in the United Kingdom, Spanish chorizo or Hungarian smoked sausage may be used instead.

Pepperoni Pizza

Pepperoni Pizza is spicy and hot and very popular in the United States. It needs only a crisp green salad and some Italian red wine to make it into a satisfying meal. If you cannot obtain pepperoni use either Spanish chorizo or Hungarian smoked sausage. Serve one pizza for each person if you are hungry, half if you are not.

2-4 SERVINGS

½ oz. fresh yeast
¼ teaspoon sugar
4 fl. oz. [½ cup] plus 3 teaspoons lukewarm water
8 oz. [2 cups] flour
1 teaspoon salt
1 teaspoon olive oil
FILLING
3 tablespoons olive oil
1 small onion, sliced
1 garlic clove, crushed
14 oz. canned peeled tomatoes
½ teaspoon salt
½ teaspoon black pepper
1 tablespoon tomato purée
½ teaspoon dried basil
½ teaspoon dried oregano
1 bay leaf
6 oz. Mozzarella cheese, sliced
1 tablespoon chopped fresh parsley
1 pepperoni sausage, cut into thin slices

Put the yeast and sugar in a small bowl, add 3 teaspoons of water and cream the water and yeast together. Set the bowl aside in a warm, draught-free place for 15 to 20 minutes or until the mixture is puffed up and frothy.

Sift the flour and salt into a warmed, large mixing bowl. Make a well in the centre and pour in the yeast and the remaining water.

Using your fingers or a spatula, gradually draw the flour into the liquids. Continue mixing until all the flour is incorporated and the dough comes away from the sides of the bowl.

Turn the dough out on to a lightly floured board or marble slab and knead it for about 10 minutes, reflouring the surface if the dough becomes sticky. The dough should be elastic and smooth.

Rinse, thoroughly dry and lightly grease the large mixing bowl. Shape the dough into a ball and return it to the bowl. Dust the top of the dough with a little flour and cover the bowl with a clean, damp cloth. Set the bowl in a warm, draught-free place and leave it for 45 minutes to 1 hour or until the dough has risen and almost doubled in bulk.

Meanwhile, make the filling. In a medium-sized saucepan, heat 2 tablespoons of the olive oil over moderate heat. When the oil is hot, add the onion and garlic and fry, stirring occasionally,

Sizzling hot, spicy Pepperoni Pizza makes an authentic Italian meal served with a green salad and red wine.

for 5 to 7 minutes or until the onion is soft and translucent but not brown.

Add the tomatoes with the can juice, the salt, pepper, tomato purée, half the basil and oregano and the bay leaf, stirring well. Cover the pan, reduce the heat to low and simmer, stirring occasionally, for 20 to 30 minutes or until the sauce is thick.

Remove the pan from the heat and remove and discard the bay leaf. Set aside.

Preheat the oven to very hot 450°F (Gas Mark 8, 230°C). With 1 teaspoon of the olive oil, lightly grease a large baking sheet and set aside. Turn the risen dough out of the bowl on to a floured surface and knead it for 3 minutes.

Cut the dough in half. With a lightly floured rolling pin, roll out each dough half into a circle about ¼-inch thick. Carefully arrange the dough circles, well apart, on the prepared baking sheet. Spoon the tomato sauce over them and arrange the Mozzarella slices on top.

Sprinkle with the parsley, the remaining basil and oregano and place the pepperoni slices on top.

Sprinkle with the remaining table-spoon of olive oil, place the pizzas in the centre of the oven and cook for 15 to 20 minutes or until the dough is cooked and the cheese has melted. Remove from the oven and serve immediately.

Perch

Perch is one of the most prolific of the freshwater fish. There are two main types — the common perch, which is found throughout Europe and Asia and the yellow and white perch, which is found along the eastern coast of North America. Both are greatly prized for their delicate flavour.

Although perch are usually quite small (weighing between one ½ and 3 pounds) larger ones are occasionally found — there is one on record weighing 150 pounds — and it wasn't a fisherman's tale!

Perch may be recognized by its rich green-brown skin with dark cross bands and pale belly, its dominant dorsal fin and its heavy, overlapping scales.

The best way to cook perch is to grill [broil] it. Make three deep cuts on both sides of the fish, brush it with melted butter and season with a little salt and pepper. Place it under a grill [broiler] preheated to high and grill [broil] for 5 minutes on each side. Larger perch may

Simple and quick to prepare, Perch with Oregano is delicious.

be baked with butter in an oven pre-heated to fairly hot 375°F (Gas Mark 5, 190°C) for 10 to 15 minutes.

The tiny fish, or perchettes, may be coated in seasoned flour and deep-fried in oil for 4 minutes or until they are crisp and golden brown.

Perch with Oregano

Quick and easy-to-prepare, Perch with

Oregano may be served with boiled peas and sautéed potatoes.

4-6 SERVINGS

2 lb. perch, filleted
1 oz. [2 tablespoons] butter
2 teaspoons dried oregano
1 teaspoon salt
¼ teaspoon red pepper flakes
1 tablespoon chopped fresh parsley
4 lemon slices

Preheat the grill [broiler] to high.

Lay the fillets in the grill [broiler] pan.

In a small saucepan, melt the butter over moderate heat. When the foam subsides, stir in the oregano, salt and pepper flakes and remove the pan from the heat.

Pour the butter mixture over the fillets and place the pan under the grill [broiler]. Grill [broil] the fillets for 5 minutes. Using a fish slice or spatula, turn the fillets over and continue cooking them for a further 5 minutes. Remove the pan from under the grill [broiler].

Using a fish slice or spatula, transfer the fillets to a warmed serving dish. Pour the cooking liquid over the fillets, sprinkle over the parsley and garnish with the lemon slices. Serve immediately.

Perciatelli con Piselli is an unusual dish of pasta with green pea sauce.

Perciatelli con Piselli
PASTA WITH GREEN PEA SAUCE

Perciatelli is a long, hollow pasta which resembles macaroni (if it is unavailable macaroni may be used as a substitute). The sauce, only really good when made with fresh green peas, may be served with most boiled pasta. Perciatelli con Piselli (pehr-chee-yah-tell-ee con piz-ell-ee) may be served as a supper dish or, in smaller quantities, as a first course to an Italian meal.

4 SERVINGS

2 tablespoons olive oil
1 medium-sized onion, chopped
4 slices bacon, chopped
1 teaspoon chopped fresh basil or
    ½ teaspoon dried basil
¼ teaspoon chopped fresh dill or
    ⅛ teaspoon dried dill
1 teaspoon salt
½ teaspoon black pepper
1½ lb. fresh green peas, weighed
    after shelling
8 fl. oz. [1 cup] water
4 fl. oz. single·cream [½ cup light
    cream]
12 oz. perciatelli, cooked, drained
    and kept warm in a colander
    over a pan of hot water
1 oz. [2 tablespoons] butter

2 oz. [½ cup] Parmesan cheese,
    grated

In a medium-sized saucepan, heat the oil over moderate heat. When the oil is hot, add the onion and the bacon and fry, stirring occasionally, for 5 to 7 minutes or until the onion is soft and translucent but not brown and the bacon is crisp.

Add the basil, dill, salt, pepper and peas. Pour in the water and bring to the boil. Reduce the heat to low and simmer the mixture for 10 to 12 minutes or until the peas are tender.

Remove the pan from the heat. Purée the contents of the pan through a food mill or in an electric blender.

Return the puréed sauce to the pan and stir in the cream. Place the pan over low heat and, stirring occasionally, simmer the sauce for 2 minutes or until it is hot. Taste the sauce and add more salt and pepper if necessary. Pour the sauce into a warmed serving bowl. Set aside and keep warm.

In a large saucepan, combine the perciatelli and the butter. Place the pan over low heat and toss the pasta in the butter.

Place the buttered perciatelli in a warmed serving dish.

Serve immediately with the sauce and cheese handed round separately.

Perdices Estofadas

PARTRIDGES WITH WHITE WINE AND
VEGETABLES

*Ideal for a dinner party, Perdices Estofadas
(pair-dees-es esto-fah-dahs) is a very
colourful Spanish dish and need be accompanied only by a green salad.*

4 SERVINGS

4 partridges, trussed and larded
1 teaspoon salt
½ teaspoon black pepper
2 oz. [¼ cup] butter
4 slices lean bacon, chopped
4 fl. oz. [½ cup] dry white wine
8 fl. oz. [1 cup] water
3 garlic cloves, crushed
  bouquet garni, consisting of 4
  parsley sprigs, 1 thyme spray
  and 1 bay leaf tied together
¼ teaspoon grated nutmeg
2 teaspoons grated lemon rind
12 small onions, blanched
12 small new potatoes, scraped
6 small carrots, scraped and cut
  into quarters lengthways
2 oz. green peas, weighed after
  shelling
4 small courgettes [zucchini],
  trimmed and sliced

Sprinkle the partridges with half of the
salt and half of the pepper.

In a large flameproof casserole, melt
the butter over moderate heat. When the
foam subsides, add the partridges and
cook for 5 to 8 minutes or until they are
lightly and evenly browned. Using tongs
or two forks, remove the partridges from
the casserole and place them on a plate.
Keep warm.

Add the bacon to the pan, increase the
heat to moderately high and fry for 5
minutes or until it is crisp and brown.
Remove the casserole from the heat.
Using a slotted spoon, remove the bacon
pieces and drain them on kitchen paper
towels. Set aside. Pour the cooking liquid
out of the casserole.

Pour the wine and water into the
casserole and return it to moderate heat.
Stir in the garlic, bouquet garni, nutmeg
and lemon rind. Return the partridges to
the casserole and bring the liquid to the
boil. Add the onions, potatoes and carrots
and reduce the heat to low. Simmer the
partridges and vegetables for 15 minutes.
Add the peas, courgettes [zucchini] and
bacon and cook for a further 15 minutes
or until the partridges are well cooked.

---

*Perdices Estofadas, partridges cas-
seroled with wine and vegetables,
makes a superb dinner party dish.*

Remove the casserole from the heat,
remove and discard the bouquet garni,
trussing string and lard, and serve at once.

Perdrix aux Choux

PARTRIDGES COOKED WITH CABBAGE

*This is a simplified version of the classic
French dish, Perdrix aux Choux (pehr-
dreeks oh shoo). Pheasant, grouse and
guinea-fowl may also be prepared and
cooked in a similar manner. Do not discard
the leftover cooking liquid as it may be
used as stock to make soup.*

4 SERVINGS

1 medium-sized firm white
  cabbage, coarse outer leaves
  removed, washed and shredded
6 oz. lean bacon, in one piece, diced
3 oz. [⅜ cup] butter
4 partridges, trussed and larded
2 small onions, sliced
2 carrots, scraped and sliced
8 oz. pork sausages
  bouquet garni, consisting of 4
  parsley sprigs, 1 thyme spray
  and 1 bay leaf tied together
1½ teaspoons salt
½ teaspoon black pepper
2 pints [5 cups] home-made beef
  stock

Preheat the oven to warm 325°F (Gas
Mark 3, 170°C).

Place the cabbage and bacon in a large
saucepan half-filled with water. Place the
pan over high heat and bring it to the
boil. Stirring frequently, boil the cabbage
for 5 minutes or until it is bright in
colour and has softened slightly.

Remove the pan from the heat and
drain the cabbage and bacon in a colander.
Set aside.

In a large frying-pan, melt the butter
over moderate heat. When the foam subsides, add the partridges, two at a time.
Reduce the heat to moderately low and
cook the birds, turning them frequently,
for 10 minutes, or until they are well
browned. Using tongs or two large
spoons, remove the birds and set them
aside on a plate. Brown the remaining
birds in the same way. Set aside.

Add the onions and carrots to the pan.
Increase the heat to moderate and cook
them, stirring occasionally, for 5 to 7
minutes or until the onions are soft and
translucent but not brown. Using a
slotted spoon, transfer the vegetables to
a plate. Set aside.

Add the sausages to the pan and fry
them, turning frequently, for 3 minutes
or until they are browned all over. Remove
the pan from the heat and set aside.

Place half of the cabbage and bacon in
a large ovenproof casserole. Cover with
the onions and carrots and place the
partridges on top. Add the bouquet garni
to the casserole and sprinkle over the salt
and pepper. Arrange the sausages around
the sides of the casserole and top with the
remaining cabbage and bacon. Pour the
stock into the casserole. Cover the
casserole and place it in the oven. Bake
for 1½ hours or until the partridges are
tender.

Remove the casserole from the oven
and remove and discard the bouquet
garni. Spoon the cabbage and bacon on
to a large warmed serving dish. Remove
the partridges, discard the trussing string
and lard and place them on top of the
cabbage. Garnish with the carrots and
onions. Slice the sausages thickly and
arrange them around the partridges. Pour
a little of the cooking liquid over the
partridges. Discard the remainder of the
cooking liquid or reserve it for further use.

Serve immediately.

Périgourdine, à la

*A la Périgourdine (ah lah pay-ree-goor-
deen) is the name given to dishes garnished with truffles or, in some cases, a
mixture of truffles and foie gras.*

Periwinkle

Periwinkle is the common name of small
edible sea snails belonging to the *lit-
torindae* family.

There are 80 species but the Common
Periwinkle is the largest in size and the
one found in the greatest numbers
around the coasts of Northern Europe
and Northeastern North America.

Periwinkles are known as *vignot* in
France, where they are sold cooked on the
streets or made into soup.

To cook periwinkles, first wash them in
plenty of water. Soak them for 10 minutes
and wash them again to remove any sand.
Drain the periwinkles and cook them in
plenty of boiling salted water for 20
minutes.

Pernod

Pernod is another name for PASTIS, an aniseed-flavoured liqueur very popular in France. It is very similar to the Greek liqueur OUZO.

Pernod and Chocolate Cream

A delectable cold dessert, perfect for those who like the taste of Pernod, Pernod and Chocolate Cream may be served on its own or with crisp plain biscuits [cookies], such as Langues de Chats.

4 SERVINGS

8 fl. oz. [1 cup] milk
10 fl. oz. double cream [1¼ cups heavy cream]
2 oz. dark [semi-sweet] cooking chocolate, broken into small pieces

---

Pernod, an aniseed-flavoured liqueur, makes a really different dessert used in Pernod and Chocolate Cream.

2 tablespoons castor sugar
1 tablespoon arrowroot dissolved in 2 tablespoons milk
3 tablespoons Pernod

In a medium-sized saucepan, scald the milk and cream (bring to just below boiling point) over moderate heat, stirring occasionally. Remove the pan from the heat and set aside.

Place the chocolate pieces in a medium-sized heatproof mixing bowl set in a large saucepan half-filled with hot water. Set the pan over moderately low heat and cook, stirring occasionally with a wooden spoon, for 3 to 4 minutes, or until the chocolate has melted and is smooth.

Remove the pan from the heat. Beat in the sugar and the dissolved arrowroot with the wooden spoon. Gradually add the hot cream and milk mixture, stirring constantly. Stir in the Pernod.

Return the pan to the heat and cook the custard, stirring constantly, for 10 minutes, or until it is smooth and thick.

Remove the pan from the heat. Lift the bowl out of the pan and set the custard aside to cool completely, stirring occasionally.

When the custard is cool, pour it into 4 individual serving glasses. Place the glasses in the refrigerator and chill the dessert for at least 1 or 2 hours before serving.

Perry

Perry is an alcoholic beverage made from the fermented juice of sour pears. Sour pears are astringent because of the tannin they contain, which makes them unfit for eating.

Perry is produced commercially in Germany, Great Britain and in parts of France.

Persian Fried Rice

Persian Fried Rice, or chelo as it is called in Iran, is a dish of rice, parboiled and then cooked in butter so that a crust forms on the bottom. Traditionally it is served with a

raw egg yolk on top, together with grilled [broiled] meat or poultry.

4-6 SERVINGS

12 oz. [2 cups] long-grain rice, washed, soaked in cold water for 30 minutes and drained
3 teaspoons salt
2 tablespoons water
4 oz. [½ cup] butter, melted

Half fill a large saucepan with water. Add the rice and 2 teaspoons of the salt. Set the pan over high heat and bring the water to the boil. Reduce the heat to moderate and boil for 10 minutes, stirring occasionally to prevent the rice from sticking. Remove the pan from the heat and drain the rice in a colander. Set aside.

In the same saucepan, combine the water with half of the butter. Gradually stir in the rice and the remaining salt, heaping the rice up slightly in the middle. Place a piece of aluminium foil over the top of the pan and place the lid on top. Set the pan over low heat and cook for 30 to 35 minutes or until the rice has absorbed all the liquid and a golden brown crust has formed on the bottom of the pan.

Spoon the rice on to a warmed serving platter. Sprinkle over the remaining butter. Scrape out the crust and arrange the pieces around the rice. Serve immediately.

Persian Onion and Aubergine [Eggplant] Omelet

An unusual supper dish, Persian Onion and Aubergine [Eggplant] Omelet is adapted from an Iranian recipe. Serve with a tomato salad.

2-3 SERVINGS

3 tablespoons vegetable oil
1 medium-sized onion, finely chopped
1 medium-sized aubergine [eggplant], cut into ¾-inch cubes and dégorged
½ teaspoon turmeric
¼ teaspoon ground cumin
¾ teaspoon salt
½ teaspoon black pepper
4 eggs
1½ tablespoons cold water
1 tablespoon butter

In a medium-sized frying-pan, heat the oil over moderate heat. When the oil is hot, add the onion and fry, stirring occasionally, for 8 to 10 minutes or until it is golden brown.

Add the aubergine [eggplant] cubes and cook them, stirring constantly, for 3 minutes. Stir in the turmeric, cumin, ½ teaspoon of the salt and ¼ teaspoon of the pepper. Reduce the heat to low and simmer the aubergine [eggplant] mixture for 10 minutes or until the aubergine [eggplant] cubes are tender when pierced with the point of a sharp knife. Remove the pan from the heat and set aside.

In a medium-sized mixing bowl, beat the eggs, the remaining salt and pepper and the water together with a fork. Add the aubergine [eggplant] mixture and beat until the ingredients are well mixed. Set aside.

In a medium-sized omelet pan, melt the butter over moderate heat. When the foam subsides, pour in the egg mixture. Stir the eggs, then leave them for a few seconds until the bottom sets. Reduce the heat to low. Using a palette knife or spatula, lift the edge of the omelet and, at the same time, tilt the pan away from you so that the liquid egg escapes from the top and runs into the pan. Put the pan down flat over the heat and leave until the omelet begins to set.

Invert a medium-sized plate over the omelet pan and reverse the two. The omelet should fall on to the plate. Slide the omelet back into the pan, so that the browned side is uppermost, and continue cooking for 1 minute or until the omelet is completely set.

Slide the omelet on to a heated serving dish. Cut into wedges and serve immediately.

Persian Yogurt Soup

This soup is based on a traditional recipe from Iran where yogurt plays a large part in the national cuisine.

4-6 SERVINGS

1 tablespoon butter
1 small onion, chopped
1 tablespoon flour
1½ pints [2½ cups] water
4 oz. [⅔ cup] walnuts, chopped
½ teaspoon ground fenugreek
⅛ teaspoon dried dill
1½ teaspoons salt
½ teaspoon black pepper
1 teaspoon sugar
1 pint [2½ cups] yogurt
1 teaspoon chopped fresh mint

In a medium-sized frying-pan, melt the butter over moderate heat. When the foam subsides, add the onion and cook, stirring occasionally, for 5 to 7 minutes or until it is soft and translucent but not brown. Stir in the flour and cook the mixture for 1 minute. Gradually add the water, stirring constantly until it is completely blended. Stir in the walnuts, fenugreek, dill, salt, pepper and sugar. Increase the heat to moderately high and, stirring constantly, bring the soup to the boil.

Reduce the heat to low and simmer the soup for 15 minutes or until it has thickened slightly.

Remove the pan from the heat and allow the soup to cool for 5 minutes. Stir in the yogurt. Return the pan to the heat and heat the soup to just below boiling point, stirring frequently.

Remove the pan from the heat and pour the soup into a warmed tureen.

Sprinkle over the mint and serve immediately.

Persillade

Persillade (pehr-see-lahd) is the French culinary term for chopped fresh parsley, or a mixture of chopped parsley and garlic, when it is added to a dish at the end of the cooking time. Cooked or leftover meat which has been sautéed in butter with a persillade is called *à la persillade*.

Persimmon

Persimmon is the name given to the fruit and tree of the *genus diospyrus*. It is grown on a small scale in the United States and some Mediterranean countries and an oriental version, called *kaki*, is widely cultivated in Japan and China.

The persimmon resembles a tomato in appearance, is about 3-inches in diameter and yellow to red in colour. The native American persimmon, *diospyrus virginiana*, is smaller in size, more flattened in shape and dark red in colour.

The persimmon is astringent before it is fully ripe and, as it ripens, it loses this astringency and develops a full, sweet flavour. Persimmons are most usually eaten raw as a dessert fruit although they may be cooked, puréed and added to puddings and ice-creams. They are also sometimes made into jams and jellies.

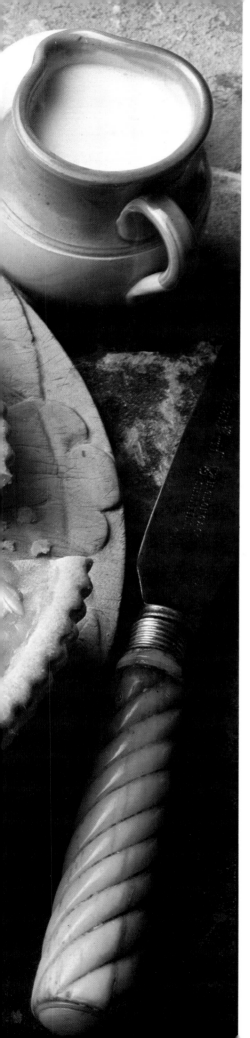

Perth Tart

An extremely rich tart made with marzipan and fruits topped with a rich cream, Perth Tart should be cut into small wedges and served as a dessert, or on its own with freshly percolated coffee.

ONE 9-INCH TART

1 x 9-inch Flan Case, made from rich shortcrust pastry, with trimmings reserved, baked blind and cooled
8 oz. Marzipan I
2 oz. [⅓ cup] almonds, slivered
2 tablespoons sultanas or seedless raisins
2 tablespoons currants
2 tablespoons candied lemon peel, chopped
grated rind of 1 lemon
12 fl. oz. [1½ cups] Crème Pâtissière
2 oz. icing sugar [½ cup confectioners' sugar]
1 tablespoon water
⅛ teaspoon lemon essence

Place the flan case on a baking sheet and set aside.

Roll the marzipan out into an 8-inch circle and carefully lift it into the flan case. Sprinkle with half of the almonds, the sultanas or seedless raisins, currants, peel and lemon rind. Pour over the crème pâtissière, smoothing it over with a flat-bladed knife.

Roll out the dough trimmings. Cut out 6 crescent-shaped pieces, approximately 2-inches by ¾-inch, and one 2-inch circle. Arrange the dough crescents, convex edges outwards, in a circle on top of the crème pâtissière and place the circle in the centre. Place the baking sheet in the refrigerator and chill the tart for 15 minutes.

Preheat the oven to moderate 350°F (Gas Mark 4, 180°C).

Place the baking sheet in the oven and bake the tart for 20 to 25 minutes, or until the pastry trimmings are golden brown and crisp.

Remove the sheet from the oven and set the tart aside to cool completely.

To make the icing, place the icing [confectioners'] sugar in a small mixing bowl. Using a wooden spoon, gradually stir in the water, beating until the icing is thin and of a dropping consistency. Beat in the lemon essence.

When the tart is cold, drop equal

Perth Tart is made with pastry, marzipan, fruit, almonds and Crème Pâtissière. Serve this very rich tart as a superb dessert.

amounts of the icing over the pastry crescents and circle. Sprinkle with the remaining almonds. Set the tart aside for 30 minutes to allow the icing to harden slightly before serving.

Perth Treacle Loaf

The Scots are famous for their teabreads — and rightly so. They come in a multitude of forms, all of them delicious, and are a traditional part of high tea ritual. This is a typical teabread, made with treacle and rolled oats and with a taste of ginger. Serve warm or cold, with lots of butter.

ONE 1½-POUND LOAF

4 oz. [½ cup] plus 1 teaspoon butter, melted
4 fl. oz. [½ cup] black treacle or molasses
2 large eggs
8 oz. [2 cups] flour
1½ teaspoons baking powder
1½ teaspoons ground ginger
½ teaspoon ground allspice
¼ teaspoon ground cinnamon
¼ teaspoon salt
4 oz. [1 cup] rolled oats
5 fl. oz. [⅝ cup] sour cream
4 tablespoons sultanas or seedless raisins
2 tablespoons chopped walnuts

Preheat the oven to moderate 350°F (Gas Mark 4, 180°C).

With the teaspoon of butter, lightly grease a 1½-pound loaf tin and set aside.

In a medium-sized mixing bowl, combine the remaining butter, treacle or molasses and eggs together, beating with a fork until they are well blended. Set aside.

Sift the flour and baking powder into a large mixing bowl. Add the ginger, allspice, cinnamon, salt and rolled oats and stir until they are well mixed.

Gradually add the butter mixture to the flour mixture, beating constantly until all the ingredients are well blended. Stir in the sour cream, then fold in the sultanas or raisins and walnuts.

Spoon the batter into the prepared loaf tin and place the tin in the oven. Bake the loaf for 1 hour or until a skewer inserted into the centre comes out clean.

Remove the tin from the oven and set the loaf aside to cool in the tin for 10 minutes. Run a sharp knife around the edge of the loaf and turn it out on to a wire rack.

Set the loaf aside to cool slightly, and then transfer it to a decorative serving plate. Serve warm or cold, cut into thick slices.

Peruvian Chowder

Shrimps and corn form the basis of this thick, warming soup or chupe (choo-pay), an adaptation of one of the great soups of Peru. Serve with brown bread as a light lunch or supper, or as a first course.

4-6 SERVINGS

2 fl. oz. [¼ cup] olive oil
2 medium-sized onions, thinly
   sliced
1 garlic clove, crushed
1 chilli, chopped
1 green pepper, white pith
   removed, seeded and chopped
2 tomatoes, blanched, peeled and
   chopped
3 oz. [½ cup] long-grain rice,
   washed, soaked in cold water for
   30 minutes and drained
16 fl. oz. [2 cups] water
1 lb. shrimps, shelled
8 oz. canned sweetcorn
1 pint [2½ cups] milk
8 fl. oz. double cream [1 cup heavy
   cream]
1 tablespoon chopped fresh parsley

In a large saucepan, heat the oil over moderate heat. When the oil is hot, add the onions, garlic, chilli and green pepper and cook, stirring occasionally, for 5 to 7 minutes or until the onions are soft and translucent but not brown.

Stir in the tomatoes and rice and cook, stirring frequently, for 2 minutes. Pour in 12 fluid ounces [1½ cups] of the water and bring the liquid to the boil. Reduce the heat to low, cover the pan and simmer the mixture for 15 to 20 minutes or until the rice is tender and fluffy.

Stir in the sweetcorn with the can liquid and shrimps and mix well. Pour over the remaining water and the milk and bring the liquid to the boil, stirring constantly. Reduce the heat to low and simmer the soup for 5 to 10 minutes or until the shrimps are cooked through.

Stir in the cream and simmer for a further 2 minutes or until the soup is hot but not boiling. Remove the pan from the heat and transfer the soup to a warmed tureen. Sprinkle over the parsley and serve at once.

Peruvian Pork Stew

An adaptation of a popular Peruvian recipe, Peruvian Pork Stew incorporates the basic staples of the country such as sweet potatoes, corn and tomatoes in a nourishing meat stew. Serve with bread and salad and some lager for a really appetizing meal.

4 SERVINGS

2 fl. oz. [¼ cup] vegetable oil
2 lb. pork fillets, cut into 2-inch
   pieces
2 medium-sized onions, thinly
   sliced
1 garlic clove, crushed
2 dried red chillis, chopped
1½ teaspoons cumin seeds, crushed
14 oz. canned sweetcorn, drained
14 oz. canned peeled tomatoes
6 fl. oz. [¾ cup] orange juice
1 teaspoon grated orange rind
½ teaspoon salt
¼ teaspoon black pepper
1 lb. sweet potatoes, boiled for 15
   minutes, peeled and cubed

In a large flameproof casserole or saucepan, heat the oil over moderate heat. When the oil is hot, add the pork fillets and cook, stirring and turning occasionally, for 5 to 8 minutes or until they are lightly and evenly browned. With a slotted spoon, transfer the pork to a plate and set aside.

Add the onions, garlic, chillis and cumin seeds to the casserole or pan and cook, stirring occasionally, for 5 to 7 minutes or until the onions are soft and translucent but not brown.

Stir in the sweetcorn and tomatoes with the can juice and cook for a further 2 minutes. Pour in the orange juice, then add the orange rind, salt and pepper and stir well to blend. Bring the mixture to the boil, stirring occasionally.

Return the pork to the casserole or pan and reduce the heat to low. Cover and simmer the pork mixture for 45 minutes or until the pork is nearly tender.

Stir in the sweet potatoes, re-cover the casserole or pan and simmer for a further 15 minutes or until the pork is cooked through and is tender when pierced with the point of a sharp knife.

Remove the casserole or pan from the heat and serve at once.

Peruvian Seviche

PICKLED FISH

Seviches (s'veh-cheh) are found all over Latin America and this version belongs to Peru, where it is almost a national dish. Serve as a first course, with lots of brown bread, or with salad and white wine as a light lunch.

4-6 SERVINGS

2 lb. sole fillets, skinned and cut
   into 3-inch pieces
5 fl. oz. [⅝ cup] lime juice
1 green pepper, white pith
   removed, seeded and finely
   chopped
1 red pepper, white pith removed,
   seeded and finely chopped
1 large onion, finely chopped
1 garlic clove, crushed
2 red or green chillis, finely
   chopped
½ teaspoon salt
¼ teaspoon black pepper

4 fl. oz. [½ cup] wine vinegar
1 small red or white onion, thinly
   sliced and pushed out into rings

Place the sole pieces in a large, shallow
dish and pour over the lime juice. Set the
dish aside and marinate the sole, basting
occasionally, for 4 hours. Remove the fish
pieces from the dish and pat them dry

with kitchen paper towels. Set aside.
Reserve the marinating liquid.

In a large, shallow serving bowl, combine the green and red peppers, the
chopped onion, garlic clove, chillis, salt,
pepper, vinegar and reserved marinade.

Carefully add the fish to the mixture
and stir to coat well. Place the mixture in
the refrigerator and chill for 1 hour.

*Two savoury dishes from Peru —
Peruvian Chowder, a thick, warming
soup, and Peruvian Pork Stew, a
colourful, hearty main dish.*

Remove the bowl from the refrigerator
and arrange the onion rings on top of the
fish. Serve at once.

Petite Marmite
BEEF CONSOMME WITH CHICKEN AND VEGETABLES

Petite Marmite (peh-teet mahr-meet) is a classic French consommé made from chicken, beef and vegetables. It is traditionally cooked in an earthenware pot, called a marmite, but a flameproof casserole may be used instead. Traditionally, cabbage balls, Croûtons, Parmesan cheese and rounds of beef marrow are served separately with the soup.

4-6 SERVINGS

1 chicken carcass
1 lb. topside [top round] of beef, excess fat removed and cut into ½-inch pieces
3 pints [7½ cups] cold beef consommé
2 carrots, scraped, blanched and cut into julienne strips
1 turnip, peeled, blanched and cut into julienne strips
2 leeks, white part only, trimmed, washed, blanched and cut into julienne strips
1 onion, finely chopped
2 celery stalks, trimmed and cut into julienne strips
½ small white cabbage, coarse outer leaves removed, washed and finely shredded
6 oz. cooked chicken breast, cut into julienne strips

Place the chicken carcass and beef in a marmite or large flameproof casserole. Pour over the consommé. Set the casserole over high heat and bring the consommé to the boil. Boil for 5 minutes, skimming off any scum from the surface with a slotted spoon. Add the carrots, turnip, leeks, onion, celery and cabbage to the casserole.

Reduce the heat to low, cover the pan and simmer, skimming the soup occasionally to remove any scum, for 2 to 2½ hours, or until the beef is very tender. Stir in the chicken strips.

Remove the pan from the heat. Using tongs or two large spoons, remove and discard the chicken carcass.

Ladle the soup into individual soup bowls and serve at once.

Petits Chaussons au Roquefort
PASTRY TURNOVERS WITH ROQUEFORT CHEESE

Small pastry turnovers, Petits Chaussons au Roquefort (peh-tee shoh-sawn oh rohk-for) are stuffed with a tangy mixture of Roquefort cheese, cream and chives. They make appetizing titbits to eat with drinks.

ABOUT 24 TURNOVERS

PASTRY
1 lb. [4 cups] flour
½ teaspoon salt
6 oz. [¾ cup] plus 1 teaspoon butter
6 oz. [¾ cup] vegetable fat
6 tablespoons iced water
1 egg, lightly beaten
FILLING
8 oz. Roquefort or any good blue cheese
4 oz. [½ cup] butter, softened
2 small egg yolks
2 tablespoons kirsch or brandy
1 teaspoon black pepper
2 tablespoons chopped fresh chives
5 tablespoons single [light] cream

First make the pastry. Sift the flour and salt into a large mixing bowl. Add the 6 ounces [¾ cup] of butter and the vegetable fat and cut them into small pieces with a table knife. Add the water and mix quickly to a dough, which should be lumpy.

On a lightly floured surface, roll out the dough into an oblong. Fold it in three and turn it so that the open edges are facing you. Roll out again, fold in three and turn. Repeat the rolling and folding once more. Wrap the dough in greaseproof or waxed paper and place it in the refrigerator to chill for 30 minutes.

Meanwhile make the filling. Crumble the cheese into a medium-sized mixing bowl. Add the butter and, with a wooden spoon, beat the cheese and butter together until they are well combined. Add the egg yolks, kirsch or brandy, pepper and chives and mix thoroughly. Gradually beat in the cream, being careful not to thin the mixture too much. Set aside.

Preheat the oven to hot 425°F (Gas Mark 7, 220°C). With the remaining teaspoon of butter, grease a large baking sheet. Set aside.

Remove the dough from the refrigerator. If it looks streaky, roll it out into an oblong and fold it in three once again. On a lightly floured surface, roll out the dough to an oblong about ½-inch thick. With a sharp knife, or pastry cutter, cut the dough into 24 squares.

Using a teaspoon, place a small amount of the Roquefort filling in the centre of each dough square. With a small pastry brush or your fingertip, moisten the edges of the dough squares with water. Fold over each dough square to form a triangle and press down the edges to seal.

Place the triangles on the baking sheet. Make a small hole in the centre of each turnover and brush them with the beaten egg. Place the baking sheet in the oven and bake for 20 minutes or until the pastry is golden brown.

Remove the baking sheet from the oven and allow the turnovers to cool slightly. Serve warm.

Petits Fours

Petits Fours (peh-tee foor) is the French term for little cakes or biscuits [cookies], prettily decorated and usually served with the dessert course or with after-dinner coffee. The name means literally "little ovens" since originally the confection was made in a slow oven which had cooled down after baking larger cakes.

Today, the term petits fours includes little cakes such as fondant-covered Génoise cakes and tiny éclairs; small biscuits [cookies] such as MACAROONS and LANGUES DE CHATS; glacé fruits; fruits covered in fondant icing; marzipan fruit and many other delicacies combining pastry and fruit.

Petits Fours
SMALL ICED CAKES

Light-as-air little sponge cakes coated with icing, Petits Fours (peh-tee foor) are delicious served with tea or coffee. Although we have used red food colouring in this recipe, the fondant icing may be made in a variety of colours — yellow, brown or orange or just left white. Petits Fours may also be filled with flavoured buttercream or jam.

36 CAKES

2 oz. [¼ cup] plus 1 teaspoon unsalted butter, melted
2 oz. [½ cup] plus 2 tablespoons flour
2½ oz. [¼ cup plus 1 tablespoon] castor sugar
2 large eggs, at room temperature
⅛ teaspoon vanilla essence
FONDANT ICING
1 lb. Fondant, softened, diluted with 8 tablespoons of sugar syrup and kept hot
2 drops red food colouring
DECORATION
36 crystallized [candied] rose petals

Preheat the oven to moderate 350°F (Gas Mark 4, 180°C).

Using the teaspoon of butter, grease a 9- x 9-inch square baking tin. Sprinkle in the 2 tablespoons of flour and tip and rotate the tin to distribute the flour evenly.

Petite Marmite is one of the great classic French soups.

Knock out any excess flour and set the tin aside.

Place the sugar, eggs and vanilla essence in a medium-sized heatproof mixing bowl. Place the bowl in a large saucepan half filled with hot water. Set the pan over low heat and cook the mixture, whisking constantly with a wire whisk or rotary beater, until it is pale and frothy and thick enough to hold a ribbon trail on itself when the whisk is lifted.

Remove the pan from the heat and remove the bowl from the pan. Sift the remaining flour and fold it gently into the mixture with a metal spoon. Gradually fold in the remaining melted butter, blending it in thoroughly.

Spoon the batter into the prepared baking tin and smooth it down with a flat-bladed knife or the back of the spoon.

Place the tin in the centre of the oven and bake the sponge for 15 to 20 minutes, or until the centre springs back when lightly pressed with a fingertip.

Remove the cake from the oven and set the sponge aside to cool completely in the tin. Turn the cooled sponge out on to a wire rack and, using a long, sharp knife, cut it into 1½-inch squares. Set aside.

Pour the hot fondant icing into a medium-sized heatproof mixing bowl. Add the red food colouring and beat it in thoroughly. Stand the bowl in a large saucepan half-filled with very hot water — this is to prevent the fondant from cooling and setting while you ice the cakes.

Spear one of the sponge squares on a cocktail stick, being careful not to pierce right through the sponge.

Holding the cocktail stick firmly, quickly dip the sponge in the hot fondant, turning it to evenly coat the top and sides of the sponge.

Carefully remove the cocktail stick from the sponge. Stand the sponge, on its base, on a wire rack. Repeat the spearing and coating process with the remaining sponges and, when they have all been coated, decorate each one with a crystallized [candied] rose petal. Set the petits fours aside for at least 1 hour, or until the fondant icing has cooled and set completely.

Pour any leftover fondant into a screw-top jar and reserve it for future use.

Arrange the petits fours on a serving plate and serve.

Petits Fours Au Chocolat
LITTLE CHOCOLATE BALLS

Delicious melt-in-the-mouth sweetmeats, Petits Fours Au Chocolat (peh-tee foor oh shoh-koh-lah) makes a superb accompaniment to after-dinner coffee. Brandy or rum may be substituted for the coffee, if you like.

ABOUT 40 BALLS

6 oz. dark [semi-sweet] cooking chocolate, broken into pieces
1 tablespoon strong black coffee
4 oz. Fondant, softened, diluted with 2 tablespoons sugar syrup and kept warm
3 oz. [⅜ cup] unsalted butter, cut into small pieces
6 tablespoons cocoa powder

In a double saucepan or in a heatproof mixing bowl placed over a pan of hot water, melt the chocolate with the coffee over low heat, stirring occasionally with a wooden spoon. As soon as the chocolate has melted, remove the pan from the heat. Set the chocolate aside until it has cooled slightly. Add the fondant and, with a wooden spoon, work it into the chocolate mixture. Beat in the butter and continue beating until the mixture becomes smooth and very thick.

Lightly dust your hands with a little of the cocoa powder. Roll teaspoonfuls of the chocolate mixture between the palms of your hands to make little balls.

Roll each ball in the remaining cocoa powder so that each one is generously coated. Store the balls in the refrigerator until you are ready to serve them.

Petits Fours aux Fruits Glacés
GLAZED FRESH FRUIT

These sparkling glazed fruit, Petits Fours aux Fruits Glacés (peh-tee foor oh froo-ee glah-say) must be eaten on the day they are made and great care should be taken in their preparation. The fruit must be perfect and quite dry or the syrup will not coat them. The most suitable fruit are grapes, cherries, tangerine or orange sections and strawberries. Use the stalks of the grapes and cherries to hold them when dipping them in the syrup, and use wooden cocktail sticks to spear and dip the other fruit.

To make these glazed fruit successfully, you must be well organized! Have a bowl of hot water ready to take the pan of hot syrup. The fruit must be ready for dipping on your right and the oiled sheet ready to take the dipped fruit should also be placed close at hand. There may be some wastage of syrup as it will harden by the time the last fruit is being dipped.

ABOUT 20 GLAZED FRUIT

1 teaspoon vegetable oil
1 lb. [2 cups] sugar
10 fl. oz. [1¼ cups] water
⅛ teaspoon cream of tartar
1 lb. grapes, with their stalks

Grease a large baking sheet with the vegetable oil. Set aside.

In a medium-sized, heavy saucepan, dissolve the sugar in the water over low heat, stirring constantly. When the sugar has dissolved, stir in the cream of tartar. Increase the heat to high and bring the syrup to the boil. Continue boiling for 10 to 15 minutes until the temperature of the syrup registers 300°F on a sugar thermometer or until a small amount of the syrup dropped into cold water hardens immediately and can be broken in two. Remove the pan from the heat and place it in a bowl of hot water to prevent the syrup from hardening too quickly.

Working very quickly and holding the grapes by their stalks, dip them into the hot syrup. Place the glazed grapes on the greased baking sheet to cool and harden.

When the grapes are cold, place them in little paper cases and serve.

Petits Fours au Massepain
MARZIPAN BISCUITS [COOKIES]

Serve these delectable Petits Fours au Massepain (peh-tee foor oh mahs-pan) with after-dinner coffee or brandy. The petits fours may be made in different colours. To do this, divide the hot marzipan mixture equally among four small, warmed serving bowls. Add one drop of food colouring to each bowl and beat well. Place each colour in separate forcing bags, or use one bag and rinse it out thoroughly before piping the next colour.

ABOUT 30 BISCUITS [COOKIES]

8 oz. [1⅓ cups] ground almonds
8 oz. [1 cup] castor sugar
1 oz. icing sugar [¼ cup confectioners' sugar], sifted
⅛ teaspoon almond essence
3 egg whites
4 glacé cherries, halved

Preheat the oven to warm 325°F (Gas Mark 3, 170°C).

Line two medium-sized baking sheets with non-stick silicone paper and set them aside.

In a medium-sized, heavy-based saucepan, combine the ground almonds, castor sugar and icing [confectioners'] sugar. With a wooden spoon, beat in the almond essence and two of the egg whites.

Set the pan over low heat and cook the mixture, stirring and scraping the bottom of the pan constantly, for 15 to 20 minutes or until the mixture is smooth and thick, but drops off the end of the spoon easily.

Remove the pan from the heat. Quickly beat in the remaining egg white, blending it in thoroughly. Spoon the hot marzipan mixture into a nylon forcing bag fitted with a medium-sized, star-shaped nozzle. Wrap a tea-towel around the forcing bag if it is too hot to handle.

Working quickly so as not to allow the mixture to cool, pipe the mixture on to the prepared baking sheets in decorative shapes — rounds, rosettes, finger-shapes or star-shapes brought up into peaks. Decorate the shapes with a cherry half. The shapes should be spaced well apart as they spread slightly during baking.

Place the baking sheets in the centre of the oven and bake for 15 to 20 minutes, or until the petits fours are golden and firm to the touch.

Remove the baking sheets from the oven and set them aside to cool for 10 minutes. Using a fish slice or spatula, transfer the petits fours to a wire rack and allow them to cool completely before serving.

Petits Pâtés à la Russe
SALMON AND MUSHROOM PATTIES

These tasty little salmon and mushroom patties are delicious served hot for a light lunch, with a mixed salad or green vegetables. Petits Pâtés à la Russe (peh-tee pah-tay ah lah roos) also make an ideal picnic food, or a snack served cold with pickles and chutneys.

ABOUT 12 PATTIES

1 oz. [2 tablespoons] butter
1 shallot, finely chopped
8 oz. small button mushrooms, wiped clean and sliced
2 tablespoons flour
1 teaspoon salt
½ teaspoon black pepper
⅛ teaspoon cayenne pepper
¼ teaspoon dried dill
4 fl. oz. double cream [½ cup heavy cream]
1 lb. cooked salmon, skinned, boned and flaked
1 teaspoon lemon juice
PASTRY
10 oz. [2½ cups] flour
¼ teaspoon salt
10 oz. [1¼ cups] butter
4 to 5 tablespoons iced water
GLAZE
1 egg yolk, well beaten with 2 tablespoons milk

First, make the filling. In a medium-sized saucepan, melt the butter over moderate heat. When the foam subsides, add the shallot and fry, stirring constantly, for 3 to 4 minutes, or until it is soft and translucent but not brown.

Add the mushrooms to the pan and cook them, stirring frequently, for 3 to 4 minutes, or until they are just tender.

With a slotted spoon, remove the vegetables from the pan and set them aside on a plate. With a wooden spoon, stir the flour, salt, pepper, cayenne and dill into the pan to make a smooth paste. Cook, stirring constantly, for 1 minute.

Remove the pan from the heat and gradually add the cream, stirring constantly and being careful to avoid lumps. Return the pan to the heat and cook the sauce, stirring constantly, for 3 minutes, or until it is very thick.

Remove the pan from the heat and stir in the cooked vegetables, the salmon and lemon juice. Combine the mixture thoroughly and set aside to cool completely.

To make the pastry, sift the flour and salt into a large mixing bowl. Add 2 ounces [¼ cup] of the butter and cut it into small pieces with a table knife. Using your fingertips, rub the butter into the flour until the mixture is crumbly.

Add 4 tablespoons of the water and lightly knead the dough until it is smooth. Add a little more of the water if the dough looks too dry.

Shape the dough into a ball, wrap it in greaseproof or waxed paper and chill it in the refrigerator for 15 minutes.

Place the remaining butter between two sheets of greaseproof or waxed paper and beat it with the back of a wooden spoon or mallet until it forms a flat oblong approximately ¼-inch thick.

Remove the dough from the refrigerator and remove and discard the paper. Place the dough on a lightly floured working surface and roll it out into an oblong approximately ¼-inch thick. Carefully peel off and discard the paper on the butter and place the butter in the centre of the dough. Fold the dough over in half to enclose the butter and chill it in the refrigerator for 10 minutes.

Remove the dough from the refrigerator and place it on the working surface with the open ends facing you. Roll the dough out into an oblong and fold the oblong in three, turning it so that the open ends face you. Roll the dough out again into an oblong and fold it in three. Chill the dough in the refrigerator for 15 minutes, and then repeat the rolling and folding process twice more.

Preheat the oven to hot 425°F (Gas Mark 7, 220°C). Line a large baking sheet with non-stick silicone paper and set it aside.

Roll the dough out into a large circle approximately ⅛-inch thick. Using a 5-inch round pastry cutter, cut the dough into approximately 12 circles. Spoon equal amounts of the salmon and mushroom filling on to one half of each circle to within ½-inch of the edges. Moisten the edges of the circles with a little cold water and fold the circles in half to make semi-circles. Crimp the edges together with your fingers to seal the patties.

Using a fish slice or spatula, carefully transfer the patties to the prepared baking sheet, spacing them apart slightly. With a pastry brush, brush the patties with the egg yolk and milk mixture.

Place the baking sheet in the centre of the oven and bake the patties for 20 to 25 minutes, or until they are puffed up and golden.

Remove the baking sheet from the oven. With a fish slice or spatula, transfer the patties to a warmed serving dish and serve them immediately. Alternatively, cool the patties completely on a wire rack.

Petits Pois
Petits Pois (peh-tee pwah) is the French name for very small, young garden PEAS.

Petits Pois au Beurre
SMALL GARDEN PEAS COOKED WITH BUTTER

Petits Pois au Beurre (peh-tee pwah oh burr) is a simple French way of cooking fresh young peas. Petits Pois au Beurre are particularly good served with roast beef or braised gammon.

4-6 SERVINGS

1½ lb. small fresh garden peas, weighed after shelling or 1½ lb. frozen petits pois
1½ teaspoons salt
2 oz. [¼ cup] butter
1 tablespoon sugar
½ teaspoon black pepper

Place the peas in a large saucepan and sprinkle over 1 teaspoon of the salt. Pour over enough hot water to cover the peas.

Set the pan over high heat and bring the water to the boil. Reduce the heat to moderate and boil for 4 minutes, or until the peas are nearly tender.

Remove the pan from the heat. Drain the peas in a colander and set them aside.

In a medium-sized saucepan, melt the butter with the sugar over moderate heat, stirring constantly. When the sugar has dissolved, stir in the peas, the remaining salt and the pepper. Reduce the heat to low and cook the peas, stirring occasionally, for 4 minutes, or until they are tender.

Remove the pan from the heat. Spoon the peas into a warmed serving dish and serve immediately.

Petits Pois à la Bonne Femme

SMALL GARDEN PEAS WITH BACON AND ONIONS

Petits Pois à la Bonne Femme (peh-tee pwah ah lah bohn fahm) *is a classic French way of preparing garden peas. Serve with grilled [broiled] steaks, roast beef or lamb.*

4-6 SERVINGS

4 streaky bacon slices, diced
1 tablespoon butter
5 small white onions, peeled and finely chopped
2 tablespoons flour
½ teaspoon salt
½ teaspoon black pepper
8 fl. oz. [1 cup] veal or chicken stock
  bouquet garni, consisting of 4 parsley sprigs, 1 thyme spray and 1 bay leaf tied together
1½ lb. small fresh garden peas, weighed after shelling or 1½ lb. frozen petits pois

In a medium-sized saucepan, fry the bacon over moderately high heat, stirring occasionally, for 5 minutes or until it is crisp and has rendered most of its fat.

With a slotted spoon, remove the bacon from the pan and set it aside to drain on kitchen paper towels.

Reduce the heat to moderate and add the butter to the pan. When the foam subsides, add the onions and fry them, stirring occasionally, for 8 to 10 minutes or until they are golden brown.

Remove the pan from the heat. With a slotted spoon, remove the onions from the pan and add them to the bacon. Using a wooden spoon, stir the flour, salt and pepper into the pan to make a smooth paste. Gradually add the stock, stirring constantly and being careful to avoid lumps. Add the bouquet garni and the reserved onions and bacon. Return the pan to the heat.

Bring the liquid to the boil, stirring constantly. Stir in the peas and reduce the heat to low. Cover the pan and simmer for

---

One of the most delicious ways to serve small garden peas, Petits Pois à la Bonne Femme is a tasty mixture of peas, bacon, stock and herbs.

6-8 minutes, stirring occasionally, or until the peas are tender.

Remove the pan from the heat and remove and discard the bouquet garni. Spoon the mixture into a warmed serving dish and serve immediately.

Petits Pois à la Crème

SMALL GARDEN PEAS COOKED WITH CREAM

Small peas cooked in a creamy, paprika-flavoured sauce, Petits Pois à la Crème (peh-tee pwah ah lah krem) *tastes delicious with plain fish dishes such as poached halibut steaks or steamed plaice.*

4-6 SERVINGS

1½ lb. small fresh garden peas, weighed after shelling or 1½ lb. frozen petits pois
2 teaspoons sugar
2 small mint leaves, bruised
1½ teaspoons salt
1 tablespoon butter
1 small shallot, very finely chopped
1½ tablespoons flour
¼ teaspoon black pepper
10 fl. oz. single cream [1¼ cups light cream]
½ teaspoon paprika

Place the peas, sugar, mint leaves and 1 teaspoon of the salt in a large saucepan. Pour over enough hot water to cover the peas.

Set the pan over high heat and bring the water to the boil. Reduce the heat to moderate and boil the peas for 4 minutes, or until they are nearly tender.

Remove the pan from the heat and drain the peas in a colander. Remove and discard the mint leaves and set the peas aside.

In a medium-sized saucepan, melt the butter over moderate heat. When the foam subsides, add the shallot and fry, stirring constantly, for 3 to 4 minutes, or until the shallot is soft and translucent but not brown.

Remove the pan from the heat. With a wooden spoon, stir in the flour, the remaining salt and the pepper to make a smooth paste. Gradually add the cream, stirring constantly and being careful to avoid lumps. When the sauce is smooth, stir in the peas.

Set the pan over low heat and cook the mixture, stirring constantly, for 4 minutes, or until the sauce has thickened and the peas are tender.

Remove the pan from the heat. Spoon the mixture into a warmed serving dish. Sprinkle the paprika over the top and serve immediately.

Petits Pois à la Française

SMALL GARDEN PEAS, FRENCH-STYLE

One of the classic vegetable dishes of French cuisine, Petits Pois à la Française (peh-tee pwah ah la frawn-sehz) is easy both to prepare and to eat! Serve it with omelets, or with grilled [broiled] chops or steaks, or even fish, especially halibut steaks.

4-6 SERVINGS

1½ lb. small fresh garden peas, weighed after shelling or 1½ lb. frozen petits pois
1 teaspoon salt
½ teaspoon black pepper
1 teaspoon sugar
1 medium-sized onion, thinly sliced
4 lettuce leaves, washed, shaken dry and shredded
1 oz. [2 tablespoons] beurre manié

Place the peas, salt, pepper, sugar, onion and lettuce in a large saucepan. Pour over enough hot water to cover the peas and set the pan over moderately high heat. Bring the water to the boil.

Reduce the heat to very low, cover the pan and simmer the pea mixture for 20 to 30 minutes or until the onion is soft and translucent and the peas are very tender. Stir in the beurre manié, a little at a time, stirring constantly. Simmer the mixture for a further 2 minutes or until it has thickened.

Remove the pan from the heat. Spoon the mixture into a warmed serving dish and serve immediately.

Petits Pois aux Oignons

SMALL GARDEN PEAS COOKED WITH ONIONS

A simple vegetable dish, Petits Pois aux Oignons (peh-tee pwah oh-zoh-nyohn) may be served with meat, fish or egg dishes, or as part of a vegetarian meal.

4-6 SERVINGS

1½ lb. small fresh garden peas, weighed after shelling or 1½ lb. frozen petits pois
2 teaspoons sugar
1½ teaspoons salt
2 oz. [¼ cup] butter
4 very small white onions, peeled, blanched and halved
2 shallots, peeled, blanched and thinly sliced
4 small spring onions [scallions], blanched and cut into ¼-inch lengths
½ teaspoon black pepper

Place the peas in a large saucepan and sprinkle over the sugar and 1 teaspoon of the salt. Pour over enough hot water to cover the peas.

Set the pan over high heat and bring the water to the boil. Reduce the heat to moderate and boil the peas for 4 minutes, or until they are nearly tender.

Remove the pan from the heat. Drain the peas in a colander and set them aside.

In a medium-sized saucepan, melt the butter over moderate heat. When the foam subsides, add the onions, shallots and spring onions [scallions]. Sprinkle over the pepper and the remaining salt. Fry, stirring frequently, for 8 to 10 minutes, or until the onions are golden brown. Stir in the peas and reduce the heat to low. Cook the mixture, stirring constantly, for 3 to 4 minutes, or until the peas are tender.

Remove the pan from the heat. Spoon the mixture into a warmed serving dish and serve immediately.

A classic and simple to make vegetable dish from France, Petits Pois aux Oignons may be served with meat, fish or egg dishes.

Petits Pots de Champignons

MUSHROOMS AND BACON COOKED IN
SMALL POTS

*A sophisticated hors d'oeuvre, Petits Pots
de Champignons (peh-tee poh d'sham-
peen-yon) is mushrooms and bacon in a
brandy cream sauce, topped with Gruyère
cheese. It is best followed by a light main
course.*

4 SERVINGS

8 oz. streaky bacon, coarsely
   chopped
1 oz. [2 tablespoons] butter
1 lb. small button mushrooms,
   wiped clean
$\frac{1}{4}$ teaspoon salt
$\frac{1}{8}$ teaspoon black pepper
2 tablespoons brandy
4 tablespoons double [heavy] cream
4 tablespoons grated Gruyère
   cheese
4 parsley sprigs

Preheat the grill [broiler] to high.

In a large frying-pan, fry the bacon
over moderate heat, stirring occasionally,
for 4 to 5 minutes or until it is crisp and
has rendered most of its fat. Add the

butter and, when the foam subsides, add
the mushrooms, salt and pepper. Cook,
stirring frequently, for 3 to 4 minutes or
until the mushrooms are just tender.

Meanwhile, in a ladle, warm the brandy
over a flame or over low heat. Pour the
brandy over the mushroom mixture and
set it alight. When the flames have died
down, stir in the cream.

Remove the pan from the heat. Spoon
the mushroom mixture into 4 flameproof ramekin dishes or cassolettes.
Sprinkle 1 tablespoon of cheese over each
serving.

Place the dishes or cassolettes under
the grill [broiler] and grill [broil] for 3 to
4 minutes or until the cheese has melted
and is lightly browned.

Remove the dishes or cassolettes from
the heat. Garnish each with a parsley
sprig and serve.

Petits Pots de Crème au Chocolat

INDIVIDUAL CHOCOLATE CUSTARDS

*A traditional French dessert, Petits Pots de
Crème au Chocolat (peh-tee poh d'krem*

*Topped with Gruyère cheese and
flavoured with bacon, Petits Pots de
Champignons make a tasty and warming hors d'oeuvre for a dinner party.*

*oh shoh-koh-lah) is also made in other
flavours such as vanilla and coffee. The
custard is usually set in small china or
glazed earthenware pots. Milk may be used
instead of half milk and half cream.*

6 SERVINGS

8 oz. dark [semi-sweet] cooking
   chocolate, broken into small
   pieces
10 fl. oz. single cream [1$\frac{1}{4}$ cups light
   cream]
10 fl. oz. [1$\frac{1}{4}$ cups] milk
1 large egg
4 egg yolks
4 tablespoons castor sugar

Preheat the oven to warm 325°F (Gas
Mark 3, 170°C).

In a medium-sized saucepan, melt the
chocolate with the cream and milk over
very low heat, stirring occasionally with
a wooden spoon. Remove the pan from
the heat. Set the pan aside to cool for 10
minutes.

In a medium-sized mixing bowl, beat the egg, egg yolks and sugar together with a wooden spoon until they are just combined. Stirring constantly with the wooden spoon, gradually pour the chocolate mixture on to the egg mixture, beating until they are well blended. Strain the mixture into a jug or bowl.

Pour the mixture into 6 small ovenproof ramekin dishes or custard cups. Arrange the filled dishes or cups in a baking tin and pour in enough boiling water to come halfway up the sides of the dishes or cups. Cover each dish or cup with aluminium foil.

Place the tin in the lower part of the oven and bake for 30 minutes or until the custards wobble gently.

Remove the tin from the oven and leave to cool, then chill the custards in the refrigerator before serving.

Pets de Nonnes
SWEET FRITTERS

Pets de Nonnes (pet d'nŏhn) are sweet fritters, popular all over France and Belgium. Serve the fritters on their own, or with Crème Chantilly. Pets de Nonnes may also be split in half and filled with various sweet fillings, such as jam or custard.

4-6 SERVINGS

5 fl. oz. [⅝ cup] water
⅛ teaspoon vanilla essence
1½ oz. [3 tablespoons] unsalted butter, cut into small pieces
    finely grated rind of 1 lemon
2 oz. [¼ cup] sugar
5 oz. [1¼ cups] flour
2 eggs
2 egg whites
    sufficient vegetable oil for deep-frying

In a large saucepan, bring the water to the boil over moderate heat. Add the vanilla essence, butter, lemon rind and 2 tablespoons of the sugar to the pan and cook the mixture, stirring constantly, until the butter and sugar have dissolved.

Remove the pan from the heat. Gradually add the flour, beating constantly with a wooden spoon until all the flour has been incorporated and the dough comes away from the sides of the pan.

Quickly beat in the eggs, one at a time, making sure that each egg is thoroughly incorporated before beating in the next. Set aside.

In a small mixing bowl, beat the egg whites with a wire whisk or rotary beater until they form stiff peaks. Using a metal spoon, stir the egg whites into the dough and set aside.

Fill a medium-sized deep-frying pan one-third full with the vegetable oil. Heat the oil over moderate heat until it registers 375°F on a deep-fat thermometer, or until a small cube of stale bread dropped into the oil turns golden in 40 seconds.

Drop four heaped tablespoons of the dough into the hot oil and fry for 3 minutes or until they are puffed up and golden, and have risen to the surface.

With a slotted spoon, remove the fritters from the oil and drain them well on kitchen paper towels. Transfer the fritters to a warmed serving dish and keep them hot while you fry and drain the remaining dough in the same way.

When all the fritters have been cooked, sprinkle over the remaining sugar and serve immediately.

Petticoat Tails

Petticoat Tails are a Scottish biscuit [cookie] dating from the twelfth century. They were mentioned by Sir Walter Scott in his novel

butter lightly grease a medium-sized baking sheet.

Sift the flour into a medium-sized mixing bowl. Add the remaining butter and cut it into small pieces with a table knife. Using your fingers, rub the butter into the flour until the mixture resembles fine breadcrumbs.

Mix in the 2 ounces [¼ cup] of sugar and the milk. Mix and knead the ingredients lightly until they form a soft dough. Add more milk if the dough is too dry. Knead the dough well until it is smooth, then roll it into a ball.

On a lightly floured board, roll out the dough into a circle approximately 10-inches in diameter. Lift the dough on the rolling pin and put it on to the prepared baking sheet. With a 3-inch round pastry cutter, cut a circle out of the centre of the dough. Place the dough circle on one side of the baking sheet. With a sharp knife, cut the remaining dough into 10 equal parts, cutting in a straight line towards the centre so that you have 10 petticoat-shaped pieces. Separate the pieces of dough slightly. With the prongs of a fork, make a decorative edge around the wide end of the pieces.

Dust the top of the dough with the remaining sugar.

Place the baking sheet in the centre of the oven and bake the petticoat tails for 20 to 25 minutes or until they are golden brown.

Remove the baking sheet from the oven and, using a palette knife or spatula, transfer the biscuits [cookies] to a wire rack to cool before serving.

Place the biscuit [cookie] circle on a plate and arrange the petticoat-shaped pieces around it.

Peveragno Lamb Chops

A tasty, colourful family meal, Peveragno (pehr-ver-agnoh) Lamb Chops may be served with jacket potatoes. The vegetables and fruit used grow abundantly in north-western Italy, where this recipe originated.

4 SERVINGS

3 lb. best end of lamb, chined
1 teaspoon salt
½ teaspoon black pepper
3 fl. oz. [⅜ cup] vegetable oil
1 aubergine [eggplant], sliced and dégorged
1 tablespoon butter
1 garlic clove, crushed

4 small courgettes [zucchini], trimmed and sliced
1 green pepper, white pith removed, seeded and cut into strips
3 large tomatoes, blanched, peeled, seeded and chopped
1 large orange, peeled, white pith removed and segmented
1 lemon, peeled, white pith removed and segmented
1 teaspoon grated lemon rind
1 teaspoon chopped fresh basil or ½ teaspoon dried basil
2 teaspoons tomato purée

Remove and discard the chined bones. Using a small sharp knife, cut the meat between the bones into chops.

Rub half of the salt and half of the pepper all over the lamb chops and set aside.

In a large frying-pan, heat 2 fluid ounces [¼ cup] of the oil over moderate heat. When the oil is hot, add the aubergine [eggplant] slices and cook them for 3 minutes on each side or until they are lightly browned. Remove the pan from the heat and, using a slotted spoon, remove the aubergine [eggplant] slices from the pan. Place them on kitchen paper towels to drain.

In a large saucepan, melt the butter over moderate heat. When the foam subsides, add the garlic and cook, stirring constantly, for 1 minute. Add the courgettes [zucchini] to the pan and, stirring frequently, cook them for 2 minutes. Add the aubergine [eggplant] slices, green pepper, tomatoes and the remaining salt and pepper.

Reduce the heat to low and cook the vegetables, stirring frequently, for 5 minutes or until the courgette [zucchini] slices are just tender when pierced with the point of a sharp knife. Remove the pan from the heat and set aside while you cook the chops.

Add the remaining oil to the frying-pan and place it over moderate heat. When the oil is hot, add half of the lamb chops and cook them for 6 minutes on each side. Using a slotted spoon, remove the chops from the pan and drain them on kitchen paper towels. Keep warm while you cook the remaining chops in the same way.

Meanwhile, return the vegetables to low heat, stir in the orange and lemon segments, the lemon rind, basil and tomato purée.

Increase the heat to moderately high and bring the vegetable liquid to the boil. Remove the pan from the heat and pour the vegetable mixture into a large, deep, warmed serving dish. Arrange the chops on top and serve immediately.

The Bride of Lammermoor and are still popular in Scotland today. The biscuits [cookies] are, as the name implies, baked in the shape of a petticoat flounce. Rice flour is often used as part of the flour mixture and caraway seeds may also be added.

10 BISCUITS [COOKIES]

4 oz. [½ cup] plus 1 teaspoon butter
8 oz. [2 cups] flour
2 oz. [¼ cup] plus 1 tablespoon sugar
1 tablespoon milk

Preheat the oven to moderate 350°F (Gas Mark 4, 180°C). With the teaspoon of

Pheasant

One of the finest of the game birds, pheasant is found mainly in Europe and the United States. In Britain, pheasant has its season from October to February, and is at its prime in October. The main breed killed for consumption is the Common Pheasant, but Silver and Golden Pheasants are also still occasionally eaten.

Like most game birds, the older pheasants are, the tougher their meat will be, so they are best eaten when not more than one year old (a wild pheasant will live for up to 15 years, by which time it is virtually inedible!).

Pheasant flesh tends to be very dry and rather flavourless and hanging has been found to increase flavour and improve texture. It is therefore never eaten straight after it has been killed, but is hung for at least one week (or less in warmer weather) before eating — though for those who like their game 'high', pheasant may be hung for two weeks or more, again depending on the weather.

Pheasant should not be plucked until after it has been hung, as the feathers help to retain the flavour and moisture of the flesh. To counteract the natural dryness of the flesh, pheasants are always larded before being cooked — most butchers sell them ready-larded. If you are using pheasant you have shot yourself, tie slices of bacon over the breast.

The oven-ready weight of a young pheasant varies from 1¾ to 2½ pounds — generally speaking, the hen pheasant is smaller. Allow one pheasant for two people.

To roast a young pheasant, have it thoroughly plucked, drawn, larded and trussed. Brush the pheasant all over with melted butter and sprinkle over 1 teaspoon of salt, ½ teaspoon of black pepper and any other seasoning to taste. Place the pheasant, on its back, in a roasting tin and place it in the centre of the oven, which has been preheated to moderate 350°F (Gas Mark 4, 180°C). Roast the pheasant, basting it every 15 minutes with a little melted butter, for 1 hour or until the juices run clear when a thigh is pierced with the point of a sharp knife.

Alternatively, rub the pheasant all over with the salt and pepper and brown it in a little butter in a frying-pan for 6 to 8 minutes, over moderate heat. Then transfer the pheasant to the roasting tin and roast it as in the basic method.

When the pheasant is cooked, remove it from the roasting tin and transfer it to a carving board. Remove and discard the trussing string and larding and carve it like any game or poultry. Traditional accompaniments for roast pheasant include BREAD SAUCE or CRANBERRY SAUCE, GAME CHIPS and braised celery.

Pheasant may also be boned or jointed, stewed, casseroled, grilled [broiled], fried in batter, or used in pies and pâtés.

Pheasants in Almond Batter

Serve Pheasants in Almond Batter with a hot tomato sauce for an unusual and tasty meal. It needs no accompaniment other than a tossed green salad and some smooth claret.

4 SERVINGS

16 fl. oz. [2 cups] Fritter Batter I
2 oz. [⅓ cup] blanched almonds, very finely chopped
sufficient vegetable oil for deep-frying
2 young pheasants, roasted, cut into 8 serving pieces and kept warm
10 fl. oz. [1¼ cups] Coulis de Tomatoes Provençale, hot

Pour the fritter batter into a medium-sized shallow mixing bowl and stir in the chopped almonds. Set aside.

Fill a deep-frying pan one-third full with the vegetable oil. Heat the oil over moderate heat until it reaches 375°F on a deep-fat thermometer, or until a small cube of stale bread dropped into the oil turns golden in 40 seconds.

Dip two or three of the pheasant pieces in the almond batter, coating them thoroughly with the batter and shaking off any excess. Carefully lower the pieces into the hot oil and fry them for 3 to 4 minutes, or until they are crisp and golden brown on the outside.

With a slotted spoon, remove the pieces from the pan and drain them thoroughly on kitchen paper towels. Transfer the fried pheasant pieces to a warmed serving dish and keep them warm while you cook the remaining pieces in the same way.

Pour the hot tomato sauce into a warmed sauceboat and serve immediately, with the fried pheasants.

Pheasant and Chestnut Casserole

Pheasants cooked with orange, thyme, chestnuts and vegetables in a port-flavoured sauce, Pheasant and Chestnut Casserole makes a superb dinner party dish. Serve with creamed potatoes and glazed carrots.

Succulent Roast Pheasant with its traditional accompaniments.

4-6 SERVINGS

2 young pheasants
1 teaspoon salt
½ teaspoon black pepper
2 tablespoons grated orange rind
1 teaspoon dried thyme
4 large streaky bacon slices
1 tablespoon butter
2 tablespoons vegetable oil
1 medium-sized onion, finely chopped
2 small garlic cloves, crushed
6 oz. button mushrooms, wiped clean and sliced
1 lb. chestnuts, blanched, peeled and skinned
8 fl. oz. [1 cup] chicken stock
2 tablespoons orange juice
1 bay leaf
2 tablespoons port
1 tablespoon beurre manié

Rub the pheasants, inside and out, with the salt and pepper and set aside.

In a small saucer, combine the orange rind and thyme. Sprinkle the mixture inside the cavities of the pheasants. Lay two of the bacon slices over the breast of each pheasant. Truss the pheasants with string and set aside.

In a large frying-pan, melt the butter with the oil over moderate heat. When the foam subsides, add the pheasants and fry, turning frequently, for 6 to 8 minutes or until they are golden brown all over.

Remove the pheasants from the pan and place them in a large flameproof casserole. Set aside.

Add the onion and garlic to the frying-pan and fry, stirring occasionally, for 5 to 7 minutes or until the onion is soft and translucent but not brown. Add the mushrooms and chestnuts and fry, stirring frequently, for a further 5 minutes.

Remove the pan from the heat. With a slotted spoon, remove the vegetables and chestnuts from the pan and arrange them around the pheasants in the casserole. Pour the chicken stock and orange juice into the casserole and add the bay leaf.

Set the casserole over moderate heat and bring the liquid to the boil, stirring constantly. Reduce the heat to low, cover the casserole and simmer for 1 hour or until the pheasants are cooked. To test if the pheasants are cooked, pierce one of the thighs with the point of a sharp knife. If the juices run clear, the pheasants are cooked.

Remove the casserole from the heat. Using tongs or two large spoons, lift the pheasants out of the casserole and transfer them to a large, warmed serving dish. Remove and discard the trussing string and bacon. Using a slotted spoon, remove the vegetables and chestnuts from the

Pheasant Pâté, Country-Style is rough textured and makes a delicious appetizer when served with toast.

casserole and arrange them around the pheasants. Set aside and keep warm.

Pour the cooking juices in the casserole through a fine wire strainer held over a medium-sized saucepan. Discard the contents of the strainer. Stir the port into the saucepan and set the pan over moderate heat. Bring the sauce to the boil, stirring constantly. Stir in the beurre manié, a small piece at a time, until the sauce is thick and smooth.

Remove the pan from the heat. Pour the sauce over the pheasants and serve immediately.

Pheasant Pâté, Country-Style

This pâté makes a delicious appetizer for a dinner party or an easy-to-serve snack on toast. Pheasant Pâté takes some time to prepare, but it is well worth making.

6-8 SERVINGS

1 small pheasant
2 oz. [¼ cup] butter
2 tablespoons vegetable oil
4 bacon slices, finely chopped

1 medium-sized onion, finely
   chopped
2 garlic cloves, chopped
2 oz. [1 cup] fresh white
   breadcrumbs
8 oz. pork sausage meat
1 teaspoon grated lemon rind
½ teaspoon grated orange rind
2 tablespoons chopped pistachio
   nuts
2 oz. mushrooms, wiped clean and
   finely chopped
1 teaspoon salt
1 teaspoon black pepper
1 egg, lightly beaten
4 tablespoons brandy

Using a sharp knife, cut the pheasant in
half.

In a large frying-pan or flameproof
casserole, melt the butter with the oil
over moderate heat. When the foam subsides, add the pheasant halves. Reduce
the heat to low and cook the pheasant
halves, turning occasionally, for 35 to 40
minutes or until they are cooked. Test by
piercing the breast with a sharp knife or
skewer. If the juices run clear, the bird is
cooked. With a slotted spoon, remove the
pheasant halves from the pan or casserole
and place them on a chopping board.
Leave them to cool.

Pour off most of the fat in the pan or
casserole so that only a thin film remains.

Add the bacon, onion and garlic and
return the pan or casserole to moderate
heat. Fry, stirring constantly, for 5
minutes. Remove the pan or casserole
from the heat and drain the bacon mixture on kitchen paper towels.

With a sharp knife, remove the pheasant
meat from the bones. Discard the skin,
bones and gristle. Cut half of the meat into
small pieces and set it aside.

Mix the remaining meat with the bacon,
onion and garlic mixture and put it
through a mincer [grinder].

Preheat the oven to fairly hot 375°F
(Gas Mark 5, 190°C).

In a large mixing bowl, combine the
minced [ground] pheasant and bacon mixture, the breadcrumbs, sausage meat,
lemon and orange rinds, pistachio nuts,
mushrooms, salt, pepper and the reserved
pheasant pieces. Using your hands, mix
all of the ingredients together. Add the
egg and brandy and mix well to blend.

Spoon the pâté into a 2-pint [1½-quart]
baking dish. Cover it with a double layer
of aluminium foil.

Place the dish in a roasting tin and pour
in enough boiling water to come about
1-inch up the sides of the dish. Place the
tin in the oven and bake for 5 minutes.
Reduce the oven temperature to moderate
350°F (Gas Mark 4, 180°C) and continue
baking for 1 hour.

Remove the roasting tin from the oven

and remove the dish from the tin. Leave
the pâté to cool to room temperature and
then place it in the refrigerator to chill
for at least 2 hours before serving.

Pheasants with Sauerkraut and Apples

*A tasty and nourishing dish, Pheasants
with Sauerkraut and Apples makes a
warming meal. Serve with boiled potatoes
and cold beer.*

4 SERVINGS

2 young pheasants, trussed
1 teaspoon salt
½ teaspoon black pepper
1 oz. [2 tablespoons] butter
2 medium-sized onions, finely
   chopped
2 tablespoons soft brown sugar
1 lb. canned sauerkraut, drained
2 small cooking apples, peeled,
   cored and chopped
6 fl. oz. [¾ cup] dry white wine
   bouquet garni, consisting of 4
   parsley sprigs, 1 thyme spray
   and 1 bay leaf tied together

*Pheasant with Sauerkraut and Apples
is a simple-to-make casserole which
is excellent accompanied by beer.*

Rub the pheasants all over with the salt and pepper and set aside.

In a large flameproof casserole, melt the butter over moderate heat. When the foam subsides, add the pheasants and fry, turning frequently, for 6 to 8 minutes or until they are golden brown all over.

Using tongs or two large spoons, remove the pheasants from the casserole and set them aside on a plate. Keep warm.

Add the onions to the casserole and fry, stirring occasionally, for 5 to 7 minutes or until they are soft and translucent but not brown. Stir in the sugar and cook for 1 minute. Stir in the sauerkraut and apples and cook, stirring constantly, for a further 5 minutes.

Return the pheasants to the casserole and pour over the wine. Add the bouquet garni and bring the mixture to the boil, stirring constantly. Reduce the heat to low, cover the casserole and simmer for 1 hour or until the pheasants are cooked. To test if the pheasants are cooked, pierce one of the thighs with the point of a sharp knife. If the juices run clear, the pheasants are cooked.

Remove the casserole from the heat and remove and discard the bouquet garni. Using tongs or two large spoons, lift the pheasants out of the casserole and

transfer them to a large, warmed serving dish. Untruss them. Remove the vegetables and apples from the casserole and arrange them around the pheasants in the dish. Serve immediately.

Pheasant Soup

Pheasant Soup is a traditionally British soup and is both tasty and nourishing. It is best made with an old bird which is too tough for cooking by any other method.

4-6 SERVINGS

6 pints [7½ pints] cold water
1 medium-sized onion, quartered
2 large carrots, scraped and coarsely chopped
2 celery stalks, with leaves, halved
1 parsnip, peeled and coarsely chopped
2 leeks, trimmed and coarsely chopped
4 peppercorns
2 teaspoons salt

A classic American soup, Philadelphia Pepper Pot should be served with thin slices of hot toast.

2 teaspoons sugar
1 old pheasant
bouquet garni, consisting of 4 parsley sprigs, 1 thyme spray and 1 bay leaf tied together
4 tablespoons dry sherry
4 tablespoons diced Croûtons

In a large heavy saucepan, bring the water to the boil over high heat. Add the onion, carrots, celery, parsnip, leeks, peppercorns, salt, sugar, pheasant and bouquet garni.

When the water comes to the boil again, cover the pan, reduce the heat to low and simmer the soup for 4 hours.

Remove the pan from the heat. Remove and discard the pheasant. Strain the soup into another large saucepan, discarding the vegetables and seasonings.

Put the pan over moderately high heat, stir in the sherry and bring the soup to the boil. Remove the pan from the heat.

Ladle the soup into a warmed tureen or individual bowls, garnish with the croûtons and serve immediately.

Philadelphia Pepper Pot

A very old, classic American soup, Philadelphia Pepper Pot used to be sold by street hawkers in Philadelphia. Serve Philadelphia Pepper Pot with lots of hot toast. Tripe is available partially pre-cooked or blanched at most butchers and some supermarkets.

6-8 SERVINGS

1 veal knuckle, sawn into 3 pieces
bouquet garni, consisting of 4 parsley sprigs, 1 thyme spray and 1 bay leaf tied together
6 black peppercorns
4 quarts [5 quarts] water
1 lb. blanched tripe, cut into 1-inch pieces
1 medium-sized onion, finely chopped
2 large carrots, scraped and cut into 1-inch pieces
2 celery stalks, trimmed and cut into 1-inch pieces
1 teaspoon salt
1 teaspoon black pepper
½ teaspoon red pepper flakes
2 medium-sized potatoes, peeled and diced
1 oz. [2 tablespoons] beurre manié
2 tablespoons chopped fresh parsley

In a very large saucepan, combine the veal knuckle, bouquet garni, peppercorns and water. Place the pan over moderate heat and bring the liquid to the boil, skimming any scum from the surface with

a slotted spoon. Reduce the heat to low, cover the pan and simmer for 2½ hours.

Remove the pan from the heat and lift out the knuckle. Place the veal pieces on a chopping board and, with a sharp knife, remove the meat from the knuckle. Discard the bones and any fat or gristle. Chop the meat into ½-inch cubes and set aside. Strain the stock through a wire strainer into a large mixing bowl.

Return the strained stock to the pan and add the tripe, onion, carrots, celery, salt, pepper and red pepper flakes. Return the pan to moderate heat and bring the soup to the boil. Reduce the heat to low, cover the pan and simmer for 1 hour. Add the potatoes and the reserved veal cubes and cook for a further 30 minutes or until the potatoes are tender.

Stir in the beurre manié, a small piece at a time, and continue stirring until the mixture thickens slightly. Taste the soup and add more salt and pepper if liked.

Remove the pan from the heat and stir in the chopped parsley. Ladle the soup into a soup tureen or warmed bowls and serve immediately.

Phoenician Honey Cakes

These are little cakes dipped in honey, usually served at Christmas in Greece. They are said to have been introduced into that country by the Phoenicians. Stored in an airtight container, Phoenician Honey Cakes will keep for several days and their flavour improves with keeping.

12 CAKES

1 teaspoon butter
1 lb. [4 cups] flour
2 oz. [¼ cup] sugar
½ teaspoon ground cinnamon
  grated rind and juice of ½ lemon
½ teaspoon ground allspice
8 fl. oz. [1 cup] olive oil
  juice of 1 large orange
2 tablespoons brandy
2 tablespoons sesame seeds
1 teaspoon ground cinnamon
SYRUP
10 fl. oz. [1¼ cups] clear honey
5 fl. oz. [⅝ cup] water
  juice of ½ lemon

Preheat the oven to fairly hot 400°F (Gas Mark 6, 200°C).

Grease a large baking sheet with the butter and set it aside.

Honey syrup soaked little cakes from Greece, Phoenician Honey Cakes are flavoured with allspice, sesame seeds, cinnamon, orange and brandy.

Sift the flour into a large mixing bowl. Add the sugar, cinnamon, lemon rind and allspice. Set aside.

In a medium-sized saucepan, heat the oil over moderate heat until it is just warm. Remove the pan from the heat and stir in the orange juice, lemon juice and brandy.

Make a well in the centre of the flour mixture and pour in the oil mixture, a little at a time. Using a spatula or your hands, mix the liquid into the flour mixture until all the liquid is absorbed and the dough comes away from the sides of the bowl. Knead the dough lightly.

Divide the dough into egg-sized balls and place them on the prepared baking sheet. Place the baking sheet in the oven and cook the cakes for 25 to 30 minutes or until they are golden brown.

Meanwhile, prepare the syrup. In a medium-sized saucepan, bring the honey, water and lemon juice to the boil over moderate heat. Reduce the heat to low and boil the syrup for 5 minutes. Remove the pan from the heat.

Remove the baking sheet from the oven. Using a spoon, remove half of the cakes and drop them into the syrup. Return the pan to the heat. Simmer for 2 minutes. With a slotted spoon, lift out the cakes

and place them on aluminium foil or greaseproof or waxed paper. Repeat this process with the remaining cakes. Remove the pan from the heat.

Sprinkle the cakes with sesame seeds and cinnamon and allow them to cool completely before serving.

Phosphorus

Phosphorus is an important mineral which, when combined with CALCIUM, helps protect and develop bones and teeth.

Phosphorus is found in many foods such as cheese, oatmeal, liver and eggs.

Piatto Freddo di Ortaggi
COLD MIXED VEGETABLES

An Italian salad of cold cooked vegetables with a tart dressing, Piatto Freddo di Ortaggi (pee-yah-toh freh-doh dee ohr-tah-gee) may be served as an hors d'oeuvre or as one of a selection of salads. If you cannot obtain yellow pepper use green pepper instead.

4-6 SERVINGS
3 medium-sized aubergines
[eggplants], cubed and dégorged

1 yellow pepper, white pith removed, seeded and cut into strips
1 red pepper, white pith removed, seeded and cut into strips
1 large onion, chopped
1 teaspoon salt
4 fl. oz. [½ cup] olive oil
6 fl. oz. [¾ cup] water
1 garlic clove, crushed
½ teaspoon dried marjoram
¼ teaspoon dried basil
2 fl. oz. [¼ cup] white wine vinegar
1 teaspoon black pepper
1 teaspoon grated lemon rind

Preheat the oven to fairly hot 375°F (Gas Mark 5, 190°C).

Place the aubergine [eggplant] cubes, yellow and red peppers, onion, salt, olive oil and water in a medium-sized flameproof casserole. Place the casserole over moderate heat and bring the liquid to the boil. Remove the casserole from the heat and stir in the garlic, marjoram and basil.

Cover the casserole and place it in the oven. Bake the mixture for 1 to 1¼ hours or until the vegetables are tender and the cooking liquid has reduced slightly.

Remove the casserole from the oven. Spoon the vegetables into a serving dish. Stir the vinegar into the cooking liquid, then add the pepper and lemon rind. Pour the dressing over the vegetables and set the dish aside to cool.

Place the dish in the refrigerator and chill the mixture for at least 1 hour before serving.

Picardy Rice

Picardy Rice, a tasty mixture of rice, chicken, tomatoes, bacon and vegetables, may be served as a meal in itself. Serve with a light red wine.

4-6 SERVINGS
4 streaky bacon slices, diced
1 oz. [2 tablespoons] butter
2 shallots, finely chopped
2 small green peppers, white pith removed, seeded and cut into julienne strips
2 medium-sized tomatoes, blanched, peeled and coarsely chopped
1 teaspoon salt
½ teaspoon black pepper
½ teaspoon dried thyme
¼ teaspoon dried oregano
12 oz. [2 cups] long-grain rice, washed, soaked in cold water for 30 minutes and drained
1 pint [2½ cups] chicken stock, boiling

1 lb. lean cooked chicken, cut into strips

In a medium-sized flameproof casserole, fry the bacon over moderate heat for 5 minutes or until it is crisp and has rendered most of its fat. Scrape the bottom of the casserole frequently with a wooden spoon to prevent the bacon from sticking.

With a slotted spoon, remove the bacon from the casserole and drain it on kitchen paper towels. Set aside.

Add the butter to the casserole. When the foam subsides, add the shallots and green peppers and fry, stirring frequently, for 3 to 4 minutes or until the shallots are soft and translucent but not brown. Stir in the tomatoes, salt, pepper, thyme and oregano. Add the rice and stir well to thoroughly coat the grains. Pour in the chicken stock and bring the mixture to the boil, stirring occasionally.

Reduce the heat to low and simmer, stirring occasionally, for 15 to 20 minutes. Stir in the chicken and simmer for a further 5 minutes, or until the rice is cooked and tender and has absorbed the cooking liquid.

Remove the casserole from the heat and spoon the rice mixture into a large warmed serving dish. Sprinkle over the fried bacon and serve immediately.

Piccalilli

A traditional English mustard pickle, Piccalilli is made from a variety of vegetables which are first soaked in brine, then pickled in vinegar. The finished pickle is yellow in colour owing to the presence of turmeric and mustard. The pickle may be served immediately it has cooled, but it improves with keeping and may be stored for up to three months. Piccalilli is usually served with cold meats. Use firm red tomatoes if green ones are unavailable.

ABOUT 3 POUNDS
1 medium-sized cauliflower, trimmed and broken into small flowerets
1 cucumber, quartered lengthways and cut into ½-inch pieces
8 oz. pickling [pearl] onions, peeled
1 large Spanish [Bermuda] onion, chopped
4 green tomatoes, blanched, peeled and cut into chunks
6 oz. [1½ cups] coarse salt
1 pint [2½ cups] malt vinegar
SAUCE
1 pint [2½ cups] malt vinegar
3 tablespoons mustard seed, bruised

2-inch piece fresh root ginger, peeled and chopped, or 1 tablespoon ground ginger
4 garlic cloves, halved
1 tablespoon black peppercorns, bruised
1 tablespoon turmeric
1 tablespoon dry mustard
4 oz. [½ cup] sugar
3 tablespoons flour mixed to a paste with 4 tablespoons water

Place the cauliflower, cucumber, pickling [pearl] onions, Spanish [Bermuda] onion and tomatoes in a large bowl. Sprinkle the salt over the vegetables and set them aside for 4 hours.

Drain the vegetables in a colander and discard the liquid.

In a large saucepan, bring the vinegar to the boil over high heat. Add the vegetables and reduce the heat to low. Cover the pan and simmer the vegetables for 15 minutes or until they are almost tender when pierced with the point of a sharp knife.

Remove the pan from the heat and drain the vegetables in the colander. Discard the vinegar. Place the vegetables in a large bowl.

To make the sauce, pour the vinegar into a medium-sized saucepan and stir in the mustard seeds, ginger, garlic, peppercorns, turmeric, mustard and sugar. Place the pan over low heat and stir to dissolve the sugar. When the sugar has dissolved, increase the heat to moderate and bring the vinegar to the boil, stirring frequently. Reduce the heat to low and simmer the mixture for 15 minutes. Remove the pan from the heat and strain the liquid into a medium-sized mixing bowl. Discard the flavourings left in the strainer.

Rinse the pan and return the strained vinegar to it. Stir in the flour mixture and place the pan over moderate heat. Bring the sauce to the boil, stirring constantly, and boil for 2 minutes.

Remove the pan from the heat and pour the sauce over the vegetables in the mixing bowl. Using two spoons, toss the vegetables until they are coated with the sauce.

Spoon the piccalilli into clean, warm, dry jars with screw-top lids. Spoon any sauce remaining in the mixing bowl into the jars, so that they are completely full. Place the lids on the jars and half screw them into position. Set the jars aside until they are completely cold. Screw the lids on firmly and store the jars in a cool, dry place.

A traditional English pickle, Piccalilli is delicious with cold meats.

Pichelsteiner
MEAT AND VEGETABLE CASSEROLE

An unusual stew from Bavaria, Pichel-steiner (pee-shell-styn-air) is made with a mixture of meats and vegetables. The stew was first made during a community picnic with each family contributing something for the pot. The result was so good that the dish is now served in many Bavarian restaurants.

4-6 SERVINGS

4 tablespoons vegetable oil
8 oz. leg of lamb, cut from the
    bone and cut into 1-inch cubes
8 oz. loin of pork, cut from the
    bone and cut into 1-inch cubes
8 oz. stewing steak, cut into ½-inch
    cubes
8 oz. pie veal, cut into ½-inch cubes
2 large carrots, scraped and sliced
½ small cabbage, tough outer leaves
    removed, washed and shredded
4 oz. French beans, trimmed and
    sliced
4 celery stalks, trimmed and sliced
1 medium-sized turnip, peeled and
    chopped
2 medium-sized leeks, white part
    only, sliced
4 oz. fresh peas, weighed after
    shelling
1 large onion, chopped
2 large potatoes, peeled and diced

Pichelsteiner from Bavaria is a mixed meat and vegetable casserole.

4 oz. beef marrow, chopped
2 teaspoons salt
1 teaspoon black pepper
15 fl. oz. [1⅞ cups] beef stock

In a large frying-pan, heat the vegetable oil over moderate heat. When the oil is hot, add the lamb cubes and cook them, turning them frequently, for 3 to 4 minutes, or until they are browned all over. Using a slotted spoon, remove the lamb from the pan and place it on a plate. Fry the remaining meats in the same way.

Meanwhile, combine the carrots, cabbage, French beans, celery, turnip, leeks, peas, onion and potatoes in a large mixing bowl.

Cover the bottom of a large, flameproof casserole with the beef marrow. Over the marrow place layers of the meats and vegetables. Sprinkle each layer with a little of the salt and pepper. Pour over the stock.

Place the casserole over moderate heat and bring the mixture to the boil. Cover the casserole, reduce the heat to low and simmer the stew for 2 hours or until the meat is tender.

Remove the casserole from the heat and serve immediately.

Pichones en Mole
SQUABS WITH CHOCOLATE

An unusual combination of flavours from South America, Pichones en Mole (pitch-on-ays en moh-lay) must be prepared with care so that the birds are succulent and the sauce smooth. If squabs (small pigeons) are not available, partridge may be used instead.

4 SERVINGS

4 squabs, cleaned
2 oz. [¼ cup] butter
1 tablespoon lemon juice
½ teaspoon salt
½ teaspoon black pepper
SAUCE
1 oz. [2 tablespoons] butter
4 shallots, chopped
1 garlic clove, crushed
1 tablespoon flour
5 fl. oz. [⅝ cup] dry white wine
5 fl. oz. [⅝ cup] chicken stock
1 oz. dark [semi-sweet] cooking
    chocolate, grated
½ teaspoon grated lemon rind

Cut the squabs through the back with a sharp, heavy knife and bend the ribs outward until the breastbones crack and the birds lie flat. Remove the backbones completely, using kitchen scissors.

Preheat the grill [broiler] to moderate. In a small saucepan, melt the butter over low heat. Remove the pan from the heat and stir in the lemon juice, salt and pepper.

Place the birds in the grill [broiler] pan, skin sides down, and brush the upper surface generously with the butter mixture. Place the pan under the heat and grill [broil] the birds for 8 minutes or until they are golden brown, brushing frequently with the butter mixture.

Remove the pan from the heat, turn the birds over and brush with the butter mixture. Return the pan to the heat and grill [broil] for 8 minutes or until the birds are golden brown, brushing frequently with the butter mixture again.

Remove the birds from the grill [broiler] pan and transfer them to a heated serving dish. Reserve the cooking juices and remaining butter mixture.

Meanwhile, make the sauce. In a small saucepan, melt the butter over moderate heat. When the foam subsides, add the shallots and garlic and cook, stirring occasionally, for 3 to 4 minutes or until the shallots are soft and translucent but not brown. Stir in the flour and cook the mixture for 1 minute. Remove the pan from the heat and gradually add the wine and stock, stirring constantly with a wooden spoon. Return the pan to the heat and bring the liquids to the boil, stirring constantly. Remove the pan from the heat, stir in the chocolate, lemon rind and the reserved cooking juices and butter mixture. Pour the sauce into a heated sauceboat and serve immediately, with the squabs.

Pickle

A pickle is a vegetable or fruit, or a combination of vegetables and fruit, preserved in spiced vinegar. It is usually served as an accompaniment to cold meat, cheese and meat loaf.

Pickles are easy to make and economical too if you make them when the fruit or vegetables being used are in season. When making pickles, it is important to use only fresh, firm, unblemished fruit and vegetables and good quality vinegar. The saucepan is important too; only stainless steel, aluminium or enamel-coated should be used since the acid in vinegar reacts to metals such as copper and iron.

Pichones en Mole is an unusual dish of squabs with chocolate sauce.

The most suitable containers for pickles are glass preserving jars with vacuum sealed lids. These prevent the pickle from evaporating.

Most pickles will keep for several months.

Pickled Beetroot [Beets]

Pickled Beetroot [Beets] are particularly good served with German sausages, such as knackwurst or frankfurters. They may also be served as part of a mixed salad. Prepared in this way, pickled beetroot [beets] will keep for several weeks if stored in a cool, dark place.

ABOUT 2 POUNDS

2 lb. beetroot [beets], cooked, peeled and sliced
1 medium-sized onion, thinly sliced and pushed out into rings
15 fl. oz. [1⅞ cups] white wine vinegar
6 oz. [¾ cup] sugar
2-inch slice fresh horseradish, peeled
4 black peppercorns

Place the beetroot [beet] slices and onion

rings in earthenware or warmed vacuum-sealed glass preserving jars. Set aside.

In a large saucepan, combine the vinegar, sugar, horseradish and peppercorns. Place the pan over moderate heat and bring the liquid to the boil. Boil for 5 minutes. Remove the pan from the heat and pour the hot liquid over the beetroot [beets]. Seal the jars and store until they are required.

Pickled Chicken

Cold chicken in jelly, Pickled Chicken is a marvellous dish for a cold buffet. It may be accompanied by potato and courgette [zucchini] salads.

4 SERVINGS

3 tablespoons vegetable oil
1 x 4 lb. chicken, cut into serving
   pieces
5 fl. oz. [$\frac{5}{8}$ cup] dry white wine
5 fl. oz. [$\frac{5}{8}$ cup] white wine vinegar
8 fl. oz. [1 cup] strong home-made
   chicken stock

1 celery stalk, halved
2 carrots, scraped and sliced
1 large onion, halved
   bouquet garni, consisting of 4
   parsley sprigs, 1 thyme spray
   and 1 bay leaf tied together
2 teaspoons salt
6 peppercorns
1 garlic clove

In a large frying-pan, heat the oil over moderate heat. When the oil is hot, add the chicken pieces and fry them, turning them frequently, for 8 to 10 minutes or until they are lightly browned.

With tongs, remove the chicken pieces from the pan and transfer them to a large saucepan. Add the wine, vinegar, stock, celery, carrots, onion, bouquet garni, salt, peppercorns and garlic to the pan.

Place the pan over high heat and bring the liquid to the boil. Reduce the heat to low, cover the pan and simmer gently for 25 to 30 minutes or until the chicken is tender.

Remove the pan from the heat. Using the tongs, remove the chicken pieces from the pan and arrange them in a serving dish.

Pour the liquid in the pan through a strainer over the chicken. Discard the vegetables and flavourings. Place the dish in the refrigerator and leave it for at least 8 hours or until the liquid has set to a jelly.

Pickled Cucumbers I

Simple to make, Pickled Cucumbers I have a mild and pleasant taste. Serve with cold meat or cold fish dishes.

3-4 POUNDS

3 large cucumbers, peeled, cut in
   half lengthways with the seeds
   removed
2 tablespoons salt
1$\frac{1}{4}$ pints [3$\frac{1}{8}$ cups] white wine vinegar
1$\frac{1}{4}$ lb. [2$\frac{1}{2}$ cups] sugar
   grated rind of $\frac{1}{2}$ lemon
1 tablespoon dill seed

Cut the cucumbers into chunks. Place the chunks on a tray and scatter over the salt. Leave the cucumber chunks to dégorge for at least 8 hours or overnight.

Drain the cucumber chunks and pat them dry with kitchen paper towels. Pack the cucumber chunks into clean, warm, dry preserving jars.

In a medium-sized saucepan, heat the vinegar, sugar, lemon rind and dill over low heat, stirring constantly until the sugar has dissolved. When the sugar has dissolved, increase the heat to high and boil the vinegar mixture for 4 minutes. Remove the pan from the heat.

Pour the vinegar mixture over the cucumber chunks, filling the jars to the rim. Place the tops on the jars but do not seal them. Set the jars aside until completely cold. Seal the jars and store them in a cool, dry place for at least 6 weeks before using.

Pickled Cucumbers II

These are often known as Dill Pickles or Sour Pickles. They are simple to make and quite delicious, especially served with salt

beef or cold meat. In this recipe, the cucumbers should be stored for three to four weeks before using.

ABOUT 4 POUNDS

2 lb. small pickling cucumbers, well washed
4 fresh dill sprigs
1 pint [2½ cups] white wine vinegar
1 teaspoon dill seed
½ teaspoon allspice berries, bruised
1 mace blade
1 teaspoon mustard seed, bruised
1 teaspoon mixed black and white peppercorns, bruised
½ teaspoon celery seed, bruised
2 garlic cloves
4 dried red chillis
1 bay leaf, crumbled
2 tablespoons rock salt
10 fl. oz. [1¼ cups] water

Prick the cucumbers all over with a fork. Pack them tightly into 4 clean, dry preserving jars. Place 1 dill sprig in each jar.

In a medium-sized saucepan, combine the vinegar, dill seed, allspice berries, mace blade, mustard seed, peppercorns, celery seed, garlic, chillis, bay leaf and salt. Place the pan over moderate heat, bring the liquid to the boil and continue

boiling for 5 minutes. Remove the pan from the heat and set aside at room temperature to cool. Remove and discard the garlic cloves.

Half-fill each preserving jar with the water, adding more water if necessary, then add the cooled spiced vinegar. If necessary, top up the jars with water to cover the cucumbers completely. The liquid should come to within ½-inch of the top of the jars.

Place the lids on the jars but do not seal them. Set the jars aside in a warm place for 4 days. Seal the jars and store them in a cool dark place for at least 3 or 4 weeks or until they are required.

Pickled Eggs

Pickled eggs are marvellous for picnics and they are a welcome addition to a mixed salad too. They should be stored for at least four weeks before using.

12 PICKLED EGGS

12 hard-boiled eggs, shelled
1½ pints [3¾ cups] white wine vinegar
2 green chillis, coarsely chopped
1-inch piece fresh root ginger
2 teaspoons mixed black and white peppercorns, bruised
1 teaspoon allspice berries, bruised
½ teaspoon mustard seed, bruised

Place the eggs in clean, dry preserving jars and set aside.

In a large saucepan, combine the vinegar, chillis, ginger, peppercorns, allspice berries and mustard seed. Place the pan over moderate heat and bring the vinegar to the boil. Boil the mixture for 10 minutes. Remove the pan from the heat and strain the vinegar over the eggs to completely cover them.

Seal the jars and store in a cool, dark place.

Pickled French Beans

An unusual pickle, Pickled French Beans are very good in a salad, well drained and dressed with olive oil. They will keep, unopened, for several months. Use one-pound preserving jars as they are just the right size for French beans. The easiest way to fill the jars is to turn them on their sides and fill them with neat stacks of beans. The cooking time for the beans will vary from 3 minutes for small tender beans to 5 minutes for slightly larger ones.

ABOUT 4 POUNDS

1½ teaspoons salt
1½ pints [3¾ cups] white wine vinegar
4 oz. [½ cup] sugar
4 garlic cloves, peeled
2 bay leaves
2 onions, thinly sliced
6 black peppercorns
2 teaspoons dill seed
2 lb. fresh French beans, trimmed

In a medium-sized saucepan, combine 1 teaspoon of the salt, vinegar, sugar, garlic, bay leaves, onions, peppercorns and dill seed.

Place the pan over moderate heat and bring the liquid to the boil. Reduce the heat to low, cover the pan and simmer for 30 minutes.

Meanwhile, half fill another medium-sized saucepan with water and bring it to the boil over moderate heat. Add the remaining salt and the beans and cook for 3 to 5 minutes or until the beans are cooked. Remove the pan from the heat and drain the beans in a colander.

Place the beans, upright, in clean, dry, preserving jars. Set aside.

Remove the vinegar mixture from the heat. Strain the mixture over the beans up to the tops of the jars. Seal the jars and store in a cool, dark place until they are required.

Pickled Onions

Pickled onions are delicious served with cheese or any cold meat. They should be stored for at least three months before eating.

3-4 POUNDS

8 oz. [2 cups] salt
4 pints [5 pints] water
2 lb. small white onions, peeled
2 oz. [¼ cup] sugar
1 pint [2½ cups] white wine vinegar
1 teaspoon ground allspice
1 teaspoon whole cloves
1 bay leaf

In a large mixing bowl stir half of the salt into half of the water until the salt has dissolved. Add the onions. Cover the bowl and leave the onions to soak for 12 hours.

Drain the onions, discard the brine and wash and dry the bowl. Return the onions to the bowl. Dissolve the remaining salt in the remaining water and pour it over. Cover the bowl and leave for a further 36 hours.

Drain the onions and pack them into clean, dry preserving jars. Set aside.

In a medium-sized saucepan, dissolve the sugar in the vinegar over low heat, stirring constantly. When the sugar has dissolved, add the allspice, cloves and bay leaf and bring the vinegar to the boil. Boil the mixture for 5 minutes.

Remove the pan from the heat. Cover the pan and set it aside to cool.

When the vinegar is cool, pour it over the onions to cover them completely. Seal the jars and store them in a cool, dry place.

Pickled Walnuts

Walnuts used for pickling must be young and green and the insides must not be woody. In Great Britain, they are picked in late June or early July, in warmer climates about a month earlier.

Pickled walnuts are made in the following way: they are pricked all over, then soaked in brine for seven days. They are then drained, re-covered with fresh brine

---

Picnic Patties, stuffed with mushrooms, chicken and ham are ideal for outdoor eating especially when served with a light red Italian wine.

and left for a further seven days. Drained once more, the walnuts are left to dry in an airy, sunny place for two days. By this time they should be quite dry and black.

The nuts are then bottled, covered with spiced vinegar and left to mature for at least six weeks before being served. Pickled walnuts will keep indefinitely.

Pickling Brine

Pickling brine is used to salt meat, generally beef, (silverside or brisket), tongue and pork. Most butchers sell pickled or brined meat, but if they don't it may be possible to order it. Do give the butcher plenty of notice, as it is important that the meat has been in the brine solution long enough for the salt to penetrate and flavour the meat — this usually takes at least three days.

To pickle meat at home, combine 1

gallon [5 quarts] of water, 2 pounds of salt, 8 ounces [1⅓ cups] of brown sugar and 1 ounce [2 tablespoons] saltpetre in a very large pan. Place the pan over low heat and stir constantly until the dry ingredients have dissolved in the water. Increase the heat to high and boil the mixture for 15 minutes, skimming the scum that rises to the surface. Remove the pan from the heat and leave at room temperature to cool. Place the meat in a very large bowl. Strain the brine over it, place a weight on top and leave for at least three days before cooking.

Pickling Spice

Pickling Spice is a commercially prepared combination of spices used, as the name suggests, to flavour various pickles.

The basic recipe varies but most commercial pickling spice contains black and white peppercorns, allspice berries, mustard seed and bay leaves. Celery seed, garlic cloves, dried chillis and dill seed are also often included. Whole spices are usually bruised to release their flavour.

Picnic Patties

As their name suggests, the e tasty little savoury patties are ideal for taking away on picnics. You may, of course, also serve them hot from the oven with green vegetables and a hot tomato sauce for a light meal at home.

12 PATTIES

1½ oz. [3 tablespoons] butter
1 shallot, finely chopped
4 oz. mushrooms, wiped clean and sliced
2 tablespoons flour

1 teaspoon salt
½ teaspoon black pepper
¼ teaspoon grated nutmeg
¼ teaspoon dried oregano
¼ teaspoon Tabasco sauce
4 fl. oz. single cream [½ cup light cream]
8 oz. lean cooked chicken, diced
4 oz. lean ham, in one piece, diced
PASTRY
10 oz. [2½ cups] flour
¼ teaspoon salt
10 oz. [1¼ cups] butter
6 to 7 tablespoons iced water
GLAZE
1 egg yolk, well beaten with 2 tablespoons milk

First, make the filling. In a medium-sized saucepan, melt 1 ounce [2 tablespoons] of the butter over moderate heat. When the foam subsides, add the shallot

and fry, stirring frequently, for 3 to 4 minutes or until it is soft and translucent but not brown.

Add the mushrooms to the pan and cook them, stirring frequently, for 3 to 4 minutes or until they are just tender.

With a slotted spoon, remove the vegetables from the pan and set them aside on a plate. Add the remaining butter to the pan and melt it over moderate heat. When the foam subsides, stir the flour, salt, pepper, nutmeg, oregano and Tabasco sauce into the pan to make a smooth paste. Cook, stirring constantly, for 1 minute.

Remove the pan from the heat and gradually add the cream, stirring constantly and being careful to avoid lumps. Return the pan to the heat and cook the sauce, stirring constantly, for 3 minutes or until it is smooth and very thick.

Remove the pan from the heat and stir in the cooked vegetables, the chicken and ham. Combine the mixture well and set it aside to cool completely.

Meanwhile, make the pastry. Sift the flour and salt into a large mixing bowl.

Add 2 ounces [$\frac{1}{4}$ cup] of the butter and cut it into small pieces with a table knife. Using your fingertips, rub the butter into the flour until the mixture resembles fine breadcrumbs.

Add 6 tablespoons of the water and lightly knead the dough until it is smooth. Add a little more water if the dough looks too dry.

Shape the dough into a ball, wrap it in greaseproof or waxed paper and chill it in the refrigerator for 15 minutes.

Place the remaining butter between two sheets of greaseproof or waxed paper and beat it with the back of a wooden spoon or mallet until it forms a flat oblong approximately $\frac{1}{4}$-inch thick.

Remove the dough from the refrigerator and remove and discard the paper. Place the dough on a lightly floured working surface and roll it out into an oblong approximately $\frac{1}{4}$-inch thick. Carefully peel off and discard the paper on the butter and place the butter in the centre of the dough. Fold the dough over in half to enclose the butter. Chill the dough in the refrigerator for 10 minutes.

Picnic Salad as good to eat now as when it left the kitchen! Serve it with crusty bread for a sustaining and refreshing picnic meal.

Remove the dough from the refrigerator and place it on the working surface with the open ends facing you. Roll the dough out into an oblong and fold the oblong in three, turning it so that the open ends face you. Roll the dough out again into an oblong and fold it in three. Chill the dough in the refrigerator for 15 minutes, and then repeat the rolling and folding process twice more.

Preheat the oven to hot 425°F (Gas Mark 7, 220°C). Line a large baking sheet with non-stick silicone paper and set it aside.

Roll out the dough into a large circle approximately $\frac{1}{8}$-inch thick. Using a 5-inch round pastry cutter, cut the dough into 12 circles. Spoon equal amounts of the chicken and mushroom filling on to one half of each dough circle, to within $\frac{1}{2}$-inch of the edges. Moisten the edges of the circles with a little cold water and fold the circles in half to enclose the filling. Crimp the edges of the dough together to seal the patties.

Using a fish slice or a spatula, carefully transfer the patties to the prepared baking sheet, spacing them apart slightly. With a pastry brush, brush the patties with the egg yolk and milk mixture.

Place the baking sheet in the centre of the oven and bake the patties for 20 to 25 minutes or until they are puffed up and golden.

Remove the baking sheet from the oven. With a fish slice or spatula, transfer the patties to a wire rack to cool completely before serving.

Picnic Salad

This fabulous salad makes a filling picnic meal served with either French bread or rolls and butter. Or serve it at home on its own as a first course to a main meal. To take the salad on your picnic, place it in a plastic bowl and cover with an airtight lid — it is preferable to chill the salad in the refrigerator for at least one hour before the journey.

6 SERVINGS

- 1 lb. lean cooked chicken, diced
- 6 oz. canned sweetcorn, drained
- 4 oz. small button mushrooms, wiped clean and thinly sliced
- 1 large avocado, peeled, stoned and chopped
- 2 medium-sized peaches, blanched, peeled, stoned and coarsely chopped
- 5 oz. [2 cups] cooked long-grain rice, or 6 oz. cooked diced potatoes, cold
- 2 shallots, finely chopped
- 2 tablespoons finely chopped fresh chives
- 1 tablespoon finely chopped fresh parsley

DRESSING
- 6 fl. oz. [¾ cup] mayonnaise
- 2 fl. oz. double cream [¼ cup heavy cream], whipped until thick but not stiff
- 1 tablespoon lemon juice
- 2 teaspoons curry powder
- 1 teaspoon salt
- ½ teaspoon black pepper
- ⅛ teaspoon cayenne pepper

First make the dressing. In a large mixing bowl, beat the mayonnaise, cream and lemon juice together with a wooden spoon. Add the curry powder, salt, pepper and cayenne and stir well to blend.

Add all of the salad ingredients and,

using two large spoons, toss the salad thoroughly. Cover the bowl with aluminium foil and chill the salad in the refrigerator for at least 1 hour before serving, tossing it occasionally.

Pie

A pie is usually made in either a deep or shallow pie dish which is sometimes lined with pastry or other mixtures such as mashed potatoes, crumb crust (made with crushed biscuits [cookies] and butter) or a cake mixture. If pastry is used to line a pie dish, SHORTCRUST is more suitable as it keeps drier and crisper.

Pies may be open-topped, i.e. the dish only is lined, or closed-topped when the filling is covered with pastry or other suitable topping.

Open-topped pies are sometimes called tarts or flans, the latter generally being made in a straight-sided flan ring. Well known open-topped pies are LEMON MERINGUE PIE, custard and syrup tart and fruit flans. Open-topped pies can also have savoury fillings, one of the best-known being the classic French dish, QUICHE LORRAINE. Individual tarts are made in small tartlet tins.

Meat, fish, poultry and game pies may have a double crust, pastry underneath and on top, or just on top. The covering helps to keep the filling moist and succulent. If the pie has pastry only on top then most pastries are suitable — PUFF PASTRY makes a light, crisp and flaky topping which is a particularly pleasant contrast to a more solid filling. Fruit pies can also be made in this way.

Raised pies, such as pork and game, are made with HOT WATER CRUST PASTRY.

Piedmont Salad

A tasty mixed vegetable and salami salad with a distinctly Italian flavour, Piedmont Salad may be served with crusty bread and butter for a light meal.

4-6 SERVINGS

- 6 oz. salami, sliced and cut into large strips
- 3 medium-sized celery stalks, trimmed, and coarsely chopped
- 4 cooked fresh, or canned and drained, artichoke hearts, quartered
- 1 large green pepper, white pith removed, seeded and cut into julienne strips
- 4 oz. small button mushrooms, wiped clean and sliced
- 4 oz. cooked French beans
- 4 medium-sized tomatoes, sliced

- 1 lettuce heart, washed and torn into pieces

DRESSING
- 1 garlic clove, crushed
- ¾ teaspoon salt
- ½ teaspoon sugar
- ½ teaspoon black pepper
- 1 teaspoon prepared French or German mustard
- 4 tablespoons olive oil
- 1½ tablespoons tarragon vinegar

GARNISH
- 8 black olives, halved and stoned
- 3 hard-boiled eggs, thinly sliced
- 2 teaspoons finely chopped fresh tarragon

Place all the salad ingredients in a large serving bowl and toss them together with two large spoons. Set aside.

Place all the dressing ingredients in a small mixing bowl and beat them together with a fork or a small wooden spoon until they are thoroughly blended.

Alternatively, place all the dressing ingredients in a screw-top jar, screw on the lid and shake vigorously for 1 minute, or until the dressing is well blended.

Pour the dressing over the salad ingredients and toss well with the spoons until the salami and vegetables are coated with the dressing.

Place the salad in the refrigerator and chill for 30 minutes.

Remove the salad from the refrigerator and toss it once more with the spoons. Garnish the salad with the olives and hard-boiled eggs and sprinkle over the tarragon. Serve immediately.

Piemontaise, à la

A la Piemontaise (ah lah pee-yeh-mawn-tehz) is the French culinary term for a garnish of little moulds, or timbales, made from risotto and shredded white truffles. The garnish is used with meat or poultry.

Pigeon

Pigeons and doves belong to the *columbidae* family of birds. There are many species, most of them wild and most of them edible. The pigeon which is **domesticated shares a common ancestor,** the rock dove, with those bred for sport and ornament.

Pigeons are best eaten young when the breast is plump and the skin pink. Young pigeons are suitable for roasting and grilling [broiling] and older pigeons for making casseroles and stews. A pigeon **under 5 weeks old is called a** SQUAB. It weighs under a pound, is plump and tender and usually grilled [broiled] or roasted. The pigeon's liver contains no gall, and because of this, it is usually left inside the bird while it is cooking.

When buying pigeons, it is best to buy them oven-ready and prepared for cooking. Allow approximately one pigeon per person.

To roast a pigeon, preheat the oven to moderate 350°F (Gas Mark 4, 180°C). Place the pigeon in a roasting tin. Lay a slice of streaky bacon over the breast. For each pigeon, spoon over 1 ounce [2 tablespoons] of melted butter. Basting occasionally, roast for 50 minutes to 1 hour or until the breast is tender when pierced with the point of a sharp knife. Remove the bacon for the last 20 minutes of the cooking time to allow the breast of the bird to colour. The pigeon may be stuffed or left plain. Serve garnished with watercress.

To grill [broil] a pigeon, preheat the grill [broiler] to high. Cut the pigeon in half and lay the halves on the rack in the grill [broiler] pan. Brush with 1 ounce [2 tablespoons] of melted butter. Place the pan under the grill [broiler] and grill [broil], turning and basting occasionally, for 15 minutes or until the breast is tender when pierced with the point of a sharp knife.

Pigeon Casserole

A tasty dish, Pigeon Casserole may be served with mashed potatoes and steamed French beans.

4 SERVINGS

2 oz. [¼ cup] butter
3 slices lean bacon, chopped
8 spring onions [scallions], trimmed and chopped
8 oz. button mushrooms, wiped clean and halved
4 pigeons, oven-ready
1 pint [2½ cups] water
4 teaspoons tomato purée
grated rind of 1 lemon

Preheat the oven to moderate 350°F (Gas Mark 4, 180°C).

In a large frying-pan, melt the butter over moderate heat. When the foam subsides, add the bacon and spring onions [scallions] and cook, stirring occasionally, for 3 minutes or until the bacon is lightly browned.

Using a slotted spoon, remove the bacon and spring onions [scallions] from the pan and place them in a large oven-proof casserole.

Place the pigeons in the frying-pan and cook them, turning them frequently, for 3 minutes or until they are lightly browned. Using tongs or two large spoons, transfer the pigeons to the casserole.

Add the mushrooms to the pan and cook, stirring constantly with a wooden spoon, for 3 minutes or until they are well coated with the butter.

Tip the contents of the frying-pan over the pigeons. Return the pan to high heat, pour in the water and stir in the tomato purée and lemon rind. When the liquid boils, remove the pan from the heat and pour the contents into the casserole. Cover the casserole and place it in the oven.

Cook the pigeons for 1 hour or until the breasts are tender when pierced with the point of a sharp knife.

Remove the casserole from the oven and serve immediately.

Pigeons aux Cerises

PIGEONS WITH CHERRIES

An unusual combination of flavours, Pigeons aux Cerises (pee-john oh s'reez) should only be made when fresh cherries are available. Serve with creamed potatoes and French beans.

4 SERVINGS

3 oz. [⅜ cup] butter
4 pigeons, oven-ready
6 shallots, chopped
2 tablespoons chopped almonds
1 tablespoon flour
1 pint [2½ cups] chicken stock
bouquet garni, consisting of 4 parsley sprigs, 1 thyme spray and 1 bay leaf tied together
1 lb. cherries, stoned
5 fl. oz. single cream [⅝ cup light cream]
4 triangular Croûtons

In a large saucepan, melt 2 ounces [¼ cup] of the butter over moderate heat. When the foam subsides, add the pigeons and cook them, turning them frequently, for 3 minutes or until they are lightly browned. Using tongs or two large spoons, transfer the pigeons to a plate. Set aside and keep warm.

Add the shallots and almonds to the pan and fry them, stirring occasionally, for 3 to 4 minutes or until the shallots are soft and translucent but not brown.

Sprinkle the flour into the pan and stir with a wooden spoon to make a smooth paste. Cook the paste for 1 minute. Remove the pan from the heat. Gradually pour the stock into the pan, stirring constantly. Return the pan to the heat and bring the sauce to the boil over moderate heat, stirring constantly.

Add the bouquet garni and return the pigeons to the pan. Cover the pan, reduce the heat to low and simmer the pigeons for 1 hour or until the pigeon breasts are tender when pierced with the point of a sharp knife.

Using tongs or two large spoons, transfer the pigeons to a warmed serving dish. Set aside and keep warm while you finish making the sauce. Remove and discard the bouquet garni. Increase the heat to moderately high and boil the sauce until it has reduced by one-quarter of its original quantity.

Meanwhile, in a medium-sized frying-pan, melt the remaining butter over moderate heat. When the foam subsides, add the cherries and cook them for 3 minutes or until they are very hot. Remove the frying-pan from the heat.

Add the cherries, their cooking juices and the cream to the sauce and stir to mix. Cook the sauce for 2 to 3 minutes, stirring constantly, or until it is very hot but not boiling.

Remove the pan from the heat and pour the sauce over the pigeons. Garnish the pigeons with the croûtons and serve immediately.

Pigeons with Chestnuts

A filling, spicy casserole, Pigeons with Chestnuts is an ideal cold weather dish. Serve with Brussels sprouts and mashed potatoes.

4 SERVINGS

1 oz. [2 tablespoons] butter
4 pigeons, oven-ready
16 dried chestnuts, soaked overnight and cooked until almost tender
1 garlic clove, crushed
¼ teaspoon grated nutmeg
¼ teaspoon ground allspice
1 tablespoon flour
1 teaspoon salt
½ teaspoon black pepper
8 fl. oz. [1 cup] dry red wine
8 fl. oz. [1 cup] beef stock

Preheat the oven to moderate 350°F (Gas Mark 4, 180°C).

In a large frying-pan, melt the butter over moderate heat. When the foam subsides, add the pigeons and cook them, turning them frequently, for 3 minutes or until they are lightly browned all over.

Using tongs or two large spoons, remove the pigeons from the pan and

Pigeons coated with a cream and cherry sauce makes Pigeons aux Cerises a delightful dish. Serve the dish with a red Bordeaux wine.

place them in an ovenproof casserole. Add the chestnuts to the casserole and set aside.

Add the garlic, nutmeg and allspice to the pan and cook, stirring frequently, for 2 minutes. Stir in the flour, salt and pepper and cook for 30 seconds. Pour in the wine and stock and bring the liquids to the boil, stirring constantly.

Remove the pan from the heat and pour the wine and stock mixture over the pigeons in the casserole.

Cover the casserole and place it in the oven. Cook the pigeons for 1 hour or until the breasts are tender when pierced with the point of a sharp knife.

Remove the casserole from the oven and serve immediately.

Pigeons with Green Peas

Fresh young peas should be used for this simple but delicious dish.

4 SERVINGS

4 pigeons, oven-ready
4 slices streaky bacon
2 oz. [¼ cup] butter, melted
1½ teaspoons salt
½ teaspoon black pepper
1 lb. fresh peas, weighed after shelling
1 teaspoon sugar
1 round [Boston] lettuce, outer leaves removed, washed and chopped
8 spring onions [scallions], trimmed and chopped
5 fl. oz. [⅝ cup] chicken stock
2 teaspoons cornflour [cornstarch] mixed to a paste with 2 tablespoons water

Preheat the oven to moderate 350°F (Gas Mark 4, 180°C).

Place the pigeons in a roasting tin. Lay the slices of bacon over the pigeon breasts. Pour over 1 ounce [2 tablespoons] of the melted butter. Sprinkle 1 teaspoon of the salt and the pepper over the pigeons. Place the roasting tin in the oven and roast the pigeons, basting occasionally, for 50 minutes to 1 hour or until the breasts are tender when pierced with the point of a sharp knife. Remove the bacon for the last 20 minutes of the cooking time to allow the breasts of the pigeons to colour.

Meanwhile, prepare the peas. Pour the remaining melted butter into a medium-sized, flameproof casserole. Add the peas and sprinkle them with the remaining salt and the sugar. Cover the peas with the lettuce and the spring onions [scallions]. Cover the casserole and place it in the oven with the pigeons. Cook the peas for 30 minutes or until they are tender.

Remove the roasting tin from the oven. Using tongs or two large spoons, transfer the pigeons to a warmed dish. Keep the pigeons warm.

Put the roasting tin over moderately high heat and add the chicken stock. Bring the mixture to the boil, stirring constantly. Remove the roasting tin from the heat and pour the cooking juices through a strainer into a small mixing bowl. Set aside.

Remove the casserole from the oven and, using a slotted spoon, transfer the peas, lettuce and spring onions [scallions] to the serving dish and arrange them around the pigeons.

Add the strained cooking juices to the juices in the casserole. Stir in the cornflour [cornstarch] mixture. Place the casserole over moderate heat and bring the sauce to the boil, stirring constantly. Cook the sauce for 2 minutes. Remove the casserole from the heat and pour the sauce into a warmed sauceboat.

Serve the pigeons immediately, with the sauce.

Pigeons à la Niçoise is ideal for an informal dinner party. The pigeons are served with a wine sauce.

Pigeons à la Niçoise

PIGEONS COOKED WITH GARLIC, ANCHOVIES AND WINE

Pigeons à la Niçoise (pee-john ah la nee-swaz) is ideal for an informal dinner party and may be served with Garlic Bread, steamed broccoli and new potatoes.

4 SERVINGS

3 tablespoons olive oil
4 pigeons, oven-ready
1 tablespoon butter
8 oz. very small white onions, peeled
2 garlic cloves, crushed
6 anchovies, chopped
½ teaspoon dried chervil
10 fl. oz. [1¼ cups] beef stock
10 fl. oz. [1¼ cups] dry white wine
1 tablespoon lemon juice
1 teaspoon salt
½ teaspoon black pepper
1 tablespoon beurre manié
4 tomatoes, blanched, peeled, seeded and chopped
1 tablespoon chopped fresh parsley

In a large saucepan, heat the olive oil over moderate heat. When the oil is hot, add the pigeons and cook them, turning them frequently, for 3 minutes or until they are lightly browned. Reduce the heat to low

Pigeons cooked with apples and cider, Pigeons à la Normande may be served with Duchess Potatoes.

---

and cook the pigeons for 15 minutes.

Meanwhile, in a small frying-pan, melt the butter over moderate heat. When the foam subsides, add the onions and garlic and cook them, stirring occasionally, for 8 to 10 minutes or until the onions are golden brown. Remove the frying-pan from the heat.

Add the onion and garlic mixture to the pigeons, scatter over the anchovies and chervil and pour in the stock, wine and lemon juice. Add the salt and pepper.

Increase the heat to moderate and bring the liquid to the boil.

Cover the pan, reduce the heat to low and cook the pigeons for a further 40 minutes or until the breasts are tender when pierced with the point of a sharp knife.

Using tongs or two large spoons, transfer the pigeons to a heated serving dish.

Add the beurre manié to the sauce, a little at a time, stirring constantly until the sauce is thick and smooth.

Add the tomatoes and cook, stirring constantly, for 5 minutes. Remove the pan from the heat.

Pour the sauce over the pigeons, sprinkle with the parsley and serve immediately.

Pigeons à la Normande

PIGEONS COOKED WITH APPLES AND CIDER

Succulent and flavourful, Pigeons à la Normande (pee-john ah lah nor-mahnd) is a tasty dish from Normandy in France. Serve with Duchess Potatoes and Carottes Vichy.

4 SERVINGS

4 pigeons, oven-ready
4 oz. [½ cup] butter
2 medium-sized onions, chopped
4 medium-sized carrots, scraped and finely diced
4 cooking apples, peeled, cored and sliced
2 slices lean bacon, chopped
2 tablespoons flour
1 pint [2½ cups] beef stock
½ teaspoon salt
½ teaspoon black pepper
16 fl. oz. [2 cups] dry cider
GARNISH
1 tablespoon butter
2 cooking apples, peeled, cored and sliced into rings
4 slices streaky bacon

Pigeons with Orange and Wine Sauce makes an impressive dinner party dish. The pigeons contain a delicate orange-flavoured stuffing.

Preheat the oven to moderate 350°F (Gas Mark 4, 180°C).

Place the pigeons on a board. Using a sharp knife cut them through the breast-bone and backbone. Cut away the backbone with kitchen scissors or a sharp knife and discard it. Set aside.

In a large frying-pan melt 1 ounce [2 tablespoons] of the butter over moderate heat. When the foam subsides, add the onions, carrots, apples and bacon and cook, stirring occasionally, for 5 to 7 minutes or until the onions are soft and translucent but not brown.

Using a slotted spoon, transfer the mixture to an ovenproof casserole.

Place the pigeons in the frying-pan and cook them, turning them frequently, for 3 minutes or until they are lightly browned. Using tongs or two large spoons, transfer the pigeons to the casserole.

Sprinkle the flour into the frying-pan and stir with a wooden spoon to form a smooth paste. Cook, stirring, for 1 minute. Remove the pan from the heat and gradually add the stock, stirring constantly. Stir in the salt, pepper and cider. Return the pan to moderate heat and bring the sauce to the boil, stirring constantly. Remove the pan from the heat and pour the sauce over the pigeons in the casserole.

Cover the casserole and place it in the oven. Cook the pigeons for 1 hour or until the breasts are tender when pierced with the point of a sharp knife.

Preheat the grill [broiler] to high.

Meanwhile prepare the garnish. In a small frying-pan, melt the butter over moderate heat. When the foam subsides, add the apple rings and fry them, turning them once, for 3 minutes or until they are lightly browned. Using a slotted spoon, remove the apple rings and drain them on kitchen paper towels.

Place the bacon on a board and cut each slice in half. Roll up each piece and place the rolls on the grill [broiler] rack. Grill [broil] them, turning them once, for 4 minutes or until they are crisp. Remove the bacon rolls from under the grill [broiler] and set aside.

Remove the casserole from the oven. Arrange the pigeons on a heated serving dish and pour a little of the sauce over them. Pour the remaining sauce into a sauceboat.

Garnish the pigeons with the apple rings and bacon rolls and serve immediately, with the sauce.

Pigeons aux Olives
PIGEONS WITH OLIVES

Young pigeons cooked with a savoury, slightly tart sauce, Pigeons aux Olives (pee-john oh-zaw-leev) makes a fine dinner party dish when served with Savoury Rice or risotto.

4 SERVINGS

4 slices streaky bacon
4 pigeons, oven-ready
2 oz. [¼ cup] butter
1 small onion, sliced
1 teaspoon salt
½ teaspoon black pepper
1 teaspoon grated lemon rind
6 fl. oz. [¾ cup] dry red wine
8 fl. oz. [1 cup] beef stock
1 tablespoon cornflour [cornstarch] dissolved in 4 tablespoons water
2 oz. [¼ cup] green olives, stoned
2 tomatoes, blanched, peeled, seeded and chopped

Place a bacon slice on each pigeon breast. Tie the bacon in place with string. Set aside.

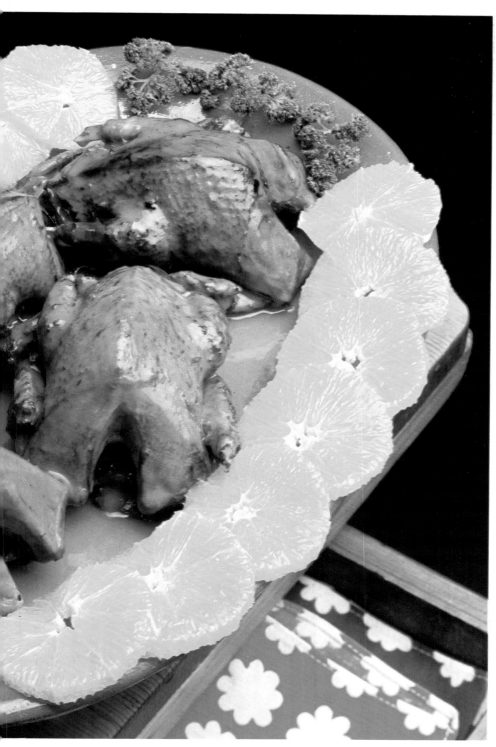

Pigeons with Orange and Wine Sauce

A delicious way to serve this delicate bird, Pigeons with Orange and Wine Sauce is easy to prepare and makes an inexpensive dinner party dish. Serve this dish with pilaff and a crisp green salad.

4 SERVINGS

4 pigeons, oven-ready
6 slices streaky bacon, cut in half
4 oz. [½ cup] butter, melted

STUFFING

1 oz. [2 tablespoons] butter
1 medium-sized onion, finely chopped
2 celery stalks, trimmed and finely chopped
4 oz. white bread, crusts removed and cut into cubes
juice and grated rind of 1 orange
juice and grated rind of 1 medium-sized lemon
1 egg
½ teaspoon salt
¼ teaspoon black pepper
½ teaspoon dried thyme

SAUCE

6 fl. oz. [¾ cup] chicken stock
8 fl. oz. [1 cup] red wine
4 fl. oz. [½ cup] orange juice
¼ teaspoon salt
⅛ teaspoon black pepper
1 tablespoon beurre manié

Preheat the oven to moderate 350°F (Gas Mark 4, 180°C).

First make the stuffing. In a small frying-pan, melt the butter over moderate heat. When the foam subsides, add the onion and celery and fry, stirring occasionally for 5 to 7 minutes, or until the onion is soft and translucent but not brown. Remove the pan from the heat and, with a slotted spoon, transfer the onion and celery to a medium-sized mixing bowl. Set aside.

Put the bread cubes in a small mixing bowl. Pour over the orange and lemon juice. When the bread is soft, add it to the onion and celery mixture. Add the grated orange and lemon rind, egg, salt, pepper and thyme. Using your hands, mix the ingredients well. Spoon the stuffing into the cavity of the birds. Transfer the pigeons to a medium-sized roasting tin. Cover the breasts with the bacon and pour over the melted butter.

Place the roasting tin in the oven and roast the pigeons, basting occasionally, for 50 minutes to 1 hour or until the breast is tender when pierced with the point of a sharp knife. Remove the bacon for the last 20 minutes to allow the breasts of the birds to brown.

In a large saucepan, melt the butter over moderate heat. When the foam subsides, add the onion and cook, stirring occasionally, for 5 to 7 minutes or until it is soft and translucent but not brown.

Add the pigeons, sprinkle with the salt, pepper and lemon rind and cook them, turning them frequently, for 3 minutes or until they are lightly browned. Pour the wine into the pan and cook for 5 minutes. Pour the stock into the pan. Cover the pan, reduce the heat to low and simmer the pigeons for 1 hour or until the breasts are tender when pierced with the point of a sharp knife. Using tongs or two large spoons, transfer the pigeons to a warmed serving dish. Remove and discard the string and bacon. Keep the pigeons warm while you finish making the sauce.

Stir the cornflour [cornstarch] mixture into the cooking juices in the pan. Increase the heat to moderate and bring the sauce to the boil, stirring constantly. Cook the sauce for 2 minutes. Reduce the heat to low, add the olives and tomatoes and cook them for 2 minutes or until they are heated through. Pour the sauce over the pigeons and serve immediately.

Remove the roasting tin from the oven. Transfer the birds to a warmed serving dish and keep hot while you prepare the sauce.

Pour away all but 2 tablespoons of the fat in the roasting tin. Place the roasting tin over high heat, pour in the chicken stock, wine and the orange juice and bring them to the boil, stirring constantly. Boil for 5 to 6 minutes, or until the liquid has reduced by about one-third. Add the salt and pepper. Reduce the heat to low and stir in the beurre manié, a little at a time. Cook for a further 3 minutes, stirring constantly, or until the sauce is smooth and thick. Taste the sauce and add more seasoning if necessary. Strain the sauce, through a strainer, over the pigeons. Serve immediately.

Pigeon Pie I

A delicious pie with a gamey flavour, Pigeon Pie I may be served either hot or cold. Serve it hot with glazed carrots, Brussels sprouts and French beans or cold with a green salad.

4-6 SERVINGS

PASTRY

2 teaspoons butter
12 oz. [3 cups] plus 1 tablespoon flour
1 teaspoon salt
5 fl. oz. [⅝ cup] water
4 oz. [½ cup] vegetable fat
1 egg yolk, lightly beaten
1 egg, lightly beaten

FILLING

8 pigeon breasts, boned and sliced
4 oz. cooked ham, finely chopped
10 oz. pork sausage meat
6 oz. button mushrooms, wiped clean and quartered
1 hard-boiled egg, finely chopped
1 teaspoon salt
½ teaspoon black pepper
1 teaspoon grated lemon rind
⅛ teaspoon cayenne pepper
4 fl. oz. [½ cup] beef stock
2 fl. oz. [¼ cup] dry red wine

Lightly grease the outside of a deep 6-inch pie mould or cake tin with 1 teaspoon of the butter. Lightly dust it with the 1 tablespoon of flour, shaking off any excess. Lightly grease a medium-sized baking sheet with the remaining butter. Set the mould and sheet aside.

Sift the remaining flour and the salt

This imposing Pigeon Pie I tastes as good as it looks. Serve it hot with glazed carrots and Brussels sprouts; or cold with a green salad.

into a large mixing bowl. In a small saucepan, bring the water and vegetable fat to the boil over high heat, stirring frequently until the fat has melted. Remove the pan from the heat.

Make a well in the centre of the flour and pour in the egg yolk and water and fat mixture. With a wooden spoon, gradually draw the flour mixture into the liquid. Continue mixing until all the flour is incorporated and the dough is smooth.

Turn the dough out on to a floured board and knead it well with your hands until it is shiny. Cut off one-third of the dough and set it aside in a warm place. Roll out the remaining dough into a circle approximately 10-inches in diameter. Turn the greased pie mould or cake tin upside-down. Lift the dough on the rolling pin and lay it over the mould. Using your fingers, gently ease the dough down over the sides of the mould.

Place a large piece of greaseproof or waxed paper over the mould and turn it right side up. Gather together the greaseproof or waxed paper and fold it around the mould so that it completely covers the dough. Tie it securely in place with string or strong thread. Place the mould in the refrigerator to chill for 20 to 30 minutes, or until the dough is firm.

Preheat the oven to fairly hot 400°F (Gas Mark 6, 200°C).

In a large mixing bowl, combine the pigeon breasts, ham, sausage meat, mushrooms, egg, salt, pepper, lemon rind and cayenne. Set aside.

Remove the mould from the refrigerator. Gently ease the mould out of the dough case and place the dough case on the baking sheet.

Spoon the filling into the dough case.

Roll out the remaining dough on a lightly floured surface, to a circle slightly larger than the top of the dough case. Lift the dough on the rolling pin and place it over the dough case. Trim the edges of the 'lid' to fit, and dampen the edges of the dough case and the 'lid' with water. With your fingers, firmly press them together to seal the pie.

With a pastry brush, brush the beaten egg over the top of the pie. With a sharp knife, cut a 2-inch slit in the centre of the pie. Place the baking sheet in the centre of the oven and bake the pie for 1 hour.

Reduce the heat to moderate 350°F (Gas Mark 4, 180°C). Remove the baking sheet from the oven. Remove and discard the greaseproof or waxed paper.

In a small saucepan, bring the beef stock and red wine to the boil over high heat. Remove the pan from the heat and carefully pour the stock and wine mixture through the slit in the pie into the filling.

Return the pie to the oven and bake for

a further 1 hour, or until the meat is tender when pierced with the point of a sharp knife.

Remove the pie from the oven and serve at once, if you wish to serve the pie hot.

Pigeon Pie II

Pigeon Pie II makes a tasty dish for a dinner party. Serve with buttered carrots, new potatoes and Brussels sprouts. To give the pie added flavour, a stock may be made from the pigeon carcass and bones.

4-6 SERVINGS

PASTRY

8 oz. [2 cups] flour
1 teaspoon salt
6 oz. [¾ cup] butter, cut into walnut-sized pieces
4 to 5 tablespoons cold water
1 egg, lightly beaten

FILLING

1 oz. [¼ cup] seasoned flour, made with 1 oz. [¼ cup] flour, ¼ teaspoon salt, ⅛ teaspoon black pepper and ¼ teaspoon ground mace
1 lb. rump steak, cut into 1-inch pieces
1 oz. [2 tablespoons] butter
1 tablespoon vegetable oil
1 small onion, finely chopped
8 oz. button mushrooms, wiped clean
8 pigeon breasts, boned and sliced
½ teaspoon salt
¼ teaspoon black pepper
1 tablespoon chopped fresh parsley grated rind and juice of 1 lemon
½ teaspoon dried thyme
12 fl. oz. [1½ cups] chicken stock or stock made from the pigeon carcass and bones

First, make the pastry. Sift the flour and salt into a medium-sized mixing bowl. Add the butter and pour in the water. Mix quickly to a dough, which will be lumpy.

On a floured surface, roll out the dough into an oblong shape. Fold it in three and turn it so that the open edges face you. Roll out again into an oblong shape and turn as before. Repeat this process once more to make three turns in all. Wrap the dough in greaseproof or waxed paper and chill it in the refrigerator for 30 minutes.

Preheat the oven to fairly hot 400°F (Gas Mark 6, 200°C).

Meanwhile, prepare the filling. Place the seasoned flour on a plate and dip each piece of beef in the flour, coating it thoroughly. Shake off any excess flour.

Pig's Trotters with Breadcrumbs may be served with mashed potatoes.

In a large frying-pan, melt the butter with the oil over moderate heat. When the foam subsides, add the beef cubes and fry them, turning them frequently, for 5 minutes or until they are browned all over. Using a slotted spoon, transfer the cubes to a 9-inch pie dish and set aside.

Add the onion to the pan and fry, stirring occasionally, for 5 to 7 minutes or until it is soft and translucent but not brown. Using a slotted spoon, transfer the onion to the pie dish. Add the mushrooms and pigeon slices to the pie dish and season with salt and pepper. Add the parsley, lemon rind and juice and thyme. Pour over the stock.

Remove the dough from the refrigerator. If it looks streaky, roll it out into an oblong shape and fold it in three once again.

On a floured surface, roll out the dough to a circle 1-inch larger than the top of the pie dish. With a knife, cut a ½-inch strip around the dough. Dampen the rim of the dish with water and press the pastry strip on top of the rim. With a pastry brush dipped in water, lightly moisten the strip.

Using the rolling pin, lift the dough on to the dish. With a knife, trim the dough and reserve the trimmings. With your fingers, crimp the edges to seal them to the strip already on the dish. With a sharp knife, cut a fairly large cross in the middle of the dough. Roll out the trimmings and use to make a decoration for the top of the pie. With a pastry brush, coat the surface of the dough with the beaten egg.

Place the dish in the oven and bake the pie for 45 minutes. Cover the top of the pie with a piece of greaseproof or waxed paper. Reduce the oven temperature to moderate 350°F (Gas Mark 4, 180°C) and continue baking for a further 45 minutes to 1 hour. Remove the dish from the oven and remove and discard the paper. Serve at once.

Pig's Head

A little-known meat nowadays, pig's head, including pig's cheek and pig's ear, may be pickled but is mainly used commercially in the manufacture of sausages and meat pies. Pig's tail is generally utilized in the same way.

Pig's Trotters

Pig's trotters, or feet, are nutritious and inexpensive. They are generally sold ready cleaned and prepared for cooking, and are sometimes also blanched or boiled. They generally come in two sizes, medium or large. (There are also very small pig's trotters, called pettittoes, which come only from suckling pigs.)

Although pig's trotters are usually cooked whole, they are sometimes split in half if they are very large. Two medium-sized trotters should be allowed per person.

To boil pig's trotters, first have them cleaned and prepared and, if they have been split, tie them together.

Pour 6 pints [7½ pints] of water into a very large saucepan and add 2 scraped and sliced carrots, 1 large chopped onion, 1 bouquet garni consisting of 4 parsley sprigs, 1 thyme spray and 1 bay leaf tied together, 6 black peppercorns and 2 teaspoons of salt.

Bring the water to the boil over high heat and add the trotters. Reduce the heat to very low, cover the pan and simmer for 3 to 4 hours (depending on the size of the trotters), or until the trotters are very tender. Remove the pan from the heat and drain the trotters in a colander. Either discard the cooking liquid, or strain it and reserve it for future use.

The trotters are now ready to be eaten or they may be cooked further — fried, grilled [broiled], stuffed, jellied, or cut into pieces and used in casseroles and stews.

Pig's Trotters with Breadcrumbs

Pig's Trotters with Breadcrumbs is a simple and economical way of cooking pig's trotters. Serve with mashed potatoes and a green vegetable.

4 SERVINGS

8 medium-sized pig's trotters, cooked, drained and kept hot
4 oz. [½ cup] butter, melted
6 oz. [2 cups] dry white breadcrumbs

Preheat the grill [broiler] to high.

Using a pastry brush, brush the pig's trotters with the melted butter. Place the breadcrumbs on a plate. Roll the pig's trotters, one at a time, in the breadcrumbs to coat them thoroughly, shaking off any excess.

Place the pig's trotters on the grill [broiler] rack. Grill [broil] the trotters, turning them over frequently with tongs, for 4 to 5 minutes or until they are golden brown all over.

Remove the trotters from the heat and transfer them to a warmed serving dish. Serve immediately.

Pikantsas Oxrullader
BEEF ROLLS IN PIQUANT SAUCE

A tasty adaptation of a Scandinavian dish, Pikantsas Oxrullader (pee-kawnt-soss ox-roo-lah-duh) may be served with green beans, creamed potatoes and well chilled lager.

4 SERVINGS

2 oz. [¼ cup] butter
2 tablespoons vegetable oil
2 medium-sized onions, finely chopped
8 oz. sausage meat
6 oz. mushrooms, wiped clean and finely chopped
8 slices of top rump [bottom round], about 6-inches by 4-inches, pounded thin
½ teaspoon salt
½ teaspoon black pepper
½ teaspoon dried dill
SAUCE
1 small onion, finely chopped
1 tablespoon flour
2 tablespoons vinegar
10 fl. oz. [1¼ cups] dry cider
½ teaspoon sugar
½ teaspoon salt
½ teaspoon freshly ground black pepper

Succulent slices of beef, stuffed with onion, sausage meat and mushrooms, Pikantsas Oxrullader is served with a delicious cider sauce.

½ teaspoon dried chervil
2 tablespoons capers
1 tablespoon chopped fresh parsley

In a medium-sized frying-pan, melt 1 tablespoon of the butter with 1 tablespoon of the oil over moderate heat. When the foam subsides, add the onions, and fry, stirring occasionally, for 5 to 7 minutes or until they are soft and translucent but not brown.

Stir in the sausage meat and cook, stirring constantly, for 3 to 4 minutes or until it is evenly browned all over. Add the mushrooms and cook, stirring occasionally, for 3 minutes. Remove the pan from the heat. Set aside.

Lay the beef slices out flat and rub them with the salt, pepper and dill. Spread equal amounts of the onion mixture over each beef slice. Roll up the beef slices and tie the rolls with thread or secure them with small skewers. Set aside.

In a very large frying-pan, melt the remaining butter with the remaining oil over moderate heat. When the foam subsides, add the beef rolls and fry, turning once, for 5 minutes or until they are evenly browned. Using a slotted spoon, remove the beef rolls from the pan and set aside.

To make the sauce, add the onion to the pan and cook, stirring occasionally, for 5 to 7 minutes or until it is soft and translucent but not brown. Stir in the flour and cook, stirring constantly, for 30 seconds. Gradually add the vinegar and cider, stirring constantly, and bring the mixture to the boil. Cook the sauce for 2 minutes. Stir in the sugar, salt, pepper and chervil.

Return the beef rolls to the pan. Baste them well with the sauce. When the sauce comes to the boil again, cover the pan, reduce the heat to low and simmer the beef rolls for 1 to 1½ hours or until the rolls are very tender.

Remove the pan from the heat. Transfer the meat rolls to a warmed serving dish. Remove and discard the thread or skewers.

Stir the capers into the sauce.

Taste the sauce and add more salt and pepper if necessary. Pour the sauce over the beef rolls. Sprinkle over the parsley and serve immediately.

Pike

Pike is a freshwater game fish, belonging to a small family of soft-rayed fish called *esocides*. It is a voracious hunter and is reputed to kill and eat its own kind. It has a long, slightly flattened body and head with a long spatulate snout and large mouth. It can grow to as much as 70 pounds, but for culinary purposes, pike usually weighs from 3 to 6 pounds.

Pike flesh is firm and white but tends to be dry and coarse, with many sharp bones. In Britain, the fish is not popular but in France and North America, it is highly prized.

Pike is cooked in a number of ways but it is most especially used to make QUENELLES (keh-nell) — oval-shaped dumplings made by pounding the flesh of fish with butter, cream and sometimes eggs and flour. All recipes for TURBOT, BRILL, PERCH and CARP are suitable for pike.

To prepare pike for cooking, scrape away the scales, remove the guts and wash the fish thoroughly. Soak the pike in well salted water for 3 hours, then drain. It is now ready to be cooked. All cooking times given here are approximate for a 3-pound pike.

To poach a whole pike, lay it in a large fish kettle. Pour enough warm COURT BOUILLON into the kettle to cover the pike. Place the kettle over high heat and bring the liquid to the boil. Reduce the heat to low, cover the kettle and poach the fish for 25 to 30 minutes or until it is tender. Poached pike may be served with a white or green sauce and garnishes.

To braise filleted pike, preheat the oven to warm 325°F (Gas Mark 3, 170°C). Lay the fillets in a large ovenproof dish. Pour over 8 fluid ounces [1 cup] of concentrated hot COURT BOUILLON. Cook in the oven for 20 minutes until tender.

To bake a pike, preheat the oven to moderate 350°F (Gas Mark 4, 180°C). Wrap the pike in a piece of cheesecloth to preserve its shape. Lay the pike in a greased baking tin. Bake the pike for 45 minutes to 1 hour or until the fish is tender. Alternatively, brush the fish all over with olive oil or melted butter. Wrap it firmly in aluminium foil, folding the edges to seal as well as possible. Place the fish in a baking dish and put it in the oven for 1 hour or until it is tender.

Pike with Anchovy Stuffing

Pike stuffed with veal and anchovies makes a decorative and attractive centrepiece to enhance your dinner table. Serve with petits pois, spinach purée and sautéed potatoes.

4 SERVINGS

2 oz. [¼ cup] plus 1 tablespoon butter, melted
1 x 3 lb. pike, cleaned, prepared, soaked in salted water for 3 hours and drained
1 teaspoon salt
½ teaspoon black pepper
½ teaspoon ground mace
1 lb. forcemeat, made from Forcemeat of Pork recipe, substituting veal for pork
12 anchovy fillets, finely chopped
2 tablespoons chopped fresh parsley

Preheat the oven to moderate 350°F (Gas Mark 4, 180°C). Grease a roasting tin with the tablespoon of butter. Set aside.

Lay the pike on a chopping board. Rub the inside cavity with the salt, pepper and mace.

Place the forcemeat in a medium-sized mixing bowl. Using a fork, mix in the anchovy pieces until they are thoroughly combined with the forcemeat. Spoon the forcemeat mixture into the cavity.

With a pastry brush, brush the pike with the remaining melted butter. Wrap the pike tightly in cheesecloth to preserve its shape and keep the stuffing in place.

Transfer the pike to the roasting tin. Place the tin in the oven and bake the pike for 45 minutes to 1 hour, or until the fish is tender.

Remove the tin from the oven. Carefully lift out the pike, with the help of the cheesecloth, and place it on a large warmed serving dish. Remove the cheesecloth being careful not to break up the fish.

Sprinkle over the parsley and serve at once.

Pilaff

Pilaff, pilau or pulao as it is sometimes called, is a savoury rice dish which originated in the East.

Pilaff is usually cooked with meat, poultry, fish or shellfish, although sometimes dried fruit, nuts and vegetables are substituted or added. The rice may be spiced with ginger, turmeric or saffron.

A pilaff may be served on its own accompanied by salads, chutneys and relishes, or as an accompaniment to roast meat or poultry.

Pilaff with Chicken Liver Ragoût

A plain pilaff served with a tasty ragoût makes an inexpensive and filling dish. Serve it with a green salad and, to drink, a red Spanish Burgundy.

low and simmer the ragoût for 5 minutes.

Remove the pilaff from the heat and remove and discard the bay leaf. Spoon the rice on to a warmed serving platter in a ring and sprinkle over the parsley.

Remove the chicken liver mixture from the heat and spoon it into the middle of the rice ring. Serve immediately.

Pilaff à la Grecque
RICE COOKED WITH MUSHROOMS

Use a good quality long-grain rice, such as Basmati, for this dish to ensure that the grains of rice remain separate when cooked. Pilaff à la Grecque (peel-ahf ah lah grek) may be served with lamb kebabs or with a dish of sautéed aubergines [eggplants].

4-6 SERVINGS

2 oz. [¼ cup] plus 1 tablespoon butter
1 medium-sized onion, finely chopped
2 garlic cloves, crushed
12 oz. [2 cups] long-grain rice, washed, soaked in cold water for 30 minutes and drained
8 oz. button mushrooms, wiped clean
1 teaspoon salt
½ teaspoon black pepper
1½ pints [3¾ cups] home-made chicken stock, hot
1 bay leaf
    thinly pared rind of 1 lemon, in one piece
GARNISH
2 tablespoons slivered almonds
2 tablespoons raisins
8 large black olives, stoned

In a saucepan, melt 2 ounces [¼ cup] of the butter over moderate heat. When the foam subsides, add the onion and garlic and fry for 5 to 7 minutes or until the onion is soft and translucent but not brown.

Add the rice and cook, stirring constantly, for 5 minutes. Add the mushrooms, and cook, stirring constantly, for 3 minutes.

Stir in the salt and pepper and pour in the stock.

Increase the heat to high and add the bay leaf and lemon rind. When the stock is boiling vigorously, cover the pan, reduce the heat to low and simmer the pilaff for 20 to 25 minutes or until the rice is tender and all the liquid has been absorbed.

Meanwhile, in a small frying-pan, melt the remaining butter over moderate heat. When the foam subsides, add the almonds and raisins and fry them, stirring con-

---

4 SERVINGS

PILAFF
1 oz. [2 tablespoons] butter
1 medium-sized onion, thinly sliced
8 oz. [1⅓ cups] long-grain rice, washed, soaked in cold water for 30 minutes and drained
1 teaspoon salt
1 bay leaf
19 fl. oz. [2⅜ cups] chicken stock, boiling
RAGOUT
2 oz. [¼ cup] butter
12 oz. chicken livers, cleaned and halved
1 medium-sized onion, finely chopped
1 garlic clove, crushed
12 oz. button mushrooms, wiped clean
1 tablespoon flour
1 teaspoon salt
¼ teaspoon black pepper
4 fl. oz. [½ cup] red wine
1 tablespoon chopped fresh parsley

First make the pilaff. In a large saucepan, melt the butter over moderate heat. When the foam subsides, add the onion and fry, stirring occasionally, for 5 to 7 minutes or until it is soft and translucent but not brown. Add the rice and cook, stirring constantly, for 5 minutes.

Pike with Anchovy Stuffing — an impressive centrepiece for the table.

Stir in the salt and add the bay leaf. Pour in the stock and bring the mixture to the boil. When the stock is boiling vigorously, cover the pan, reduce the heat to low and simmer the pilaff for 20 to 25 minutes or until the rice is tender and all the liquid has been absorbed.

Meanwhile, make the ragoût. In a large frying-pan, melt 1½ ounces [3 tablespoons] of the butter over moderate heat. When the foam subsides, add the chicken livers and fry them, turning them over frequently, for 4 to 5 minutes or until they are lightly browned.

Using a slotted spoon, transfer the chicken livers to a plate. Set aside.

Add the remaining butter to the pan and melt it over moderate heat. When the foam subsides, add the onion and garlic and fry, stirring occasionally, for 5 to 7 minutes or until the onion is soft and translucent but not brown.

Add the mushrooms and fry them, stirring constantly, for 5 minutes. Stir in the flour, salt and pepper and cook for 30 seconds. Pour in the wine and, stirring constantly, bring the mixture to the boil. Return the chicken livers to the pan. When the mixture comes to the boil again, cover the pan, reduce the heat to

stantly, for 5 minutes or until the almonds are lightly browned and the raisins puffed up.

Remove the pan from the heat and set aside.

Remove the pilaff from the heat. Remove and discard the bay leaf and the lemon rind. Spoon the pilaff on to a warmed serving platter and scatter the almonds, raisins and the olives over the top.

Serve immediately.

Pilaff with Lamb and Almonds

Pilaff with Lamb and Almonds may be served as a complete meal with chutneys, tomato and onion salad or a hot curry sauce.

4 SERVINGS

10 fl. oz. [1¼ cups] sour cream
4 oz. [⅔ cup] ground almonds
1½ teaspoons salt
¼ teaspoon cayenne pepper
2 garlic cloves, crushed
1-inch piece fresh root ginger, peeled and finely chopped
1½ lb. boned leg of lamb, cut into ¾-inch cubes
1½ oz. [3 tablespoons] butter
2 medium-sized onions, finely chopped
2 teaspoons cumin seed
12 oz. [2 cups] long-grain rice, washed, soaked in cold water for 30 minutes and drained
½ teaspoon ground saffron
1 tablespoon melted butter
5 fl. oz. [⅝ cup] boiling water

In a large mixing bowl, combine the sour cream, ground almonds, half of the salt, the cayenne, garlic and ginger. Add the lamb cubes and mix well. Set aside to marinate at room temperature for 30 minutes.

In a large saucepan, melt the butter over moderate heat. When the foam subsides, add the onions and fry, stirring occasionally, for 8 to 10 minutes or until they are golden brown.

Add the cumin seed, and fry for 1 minute. Add the lamb cubes, with the marinade, and cook, stirring and turning frequently, for 8 minutes. Reduce the heat to low, cover the pan and cook the lamb cubes for 30 to 35 minutes or until they are tender when pierced with the point of a sharp knife.

Meanwhile, in a large saucepan, bring 3 pints [7½ cups] of water to the boil. Add the remaining salt and pour in the rice. Boil briskly for 1½ minutes. Remove the

pan from the heat and drain the rice thoroughly.

Preheat the oven to moderate 350°F (Gas Mark 4, 180°C).

Add the rice to the lamb mixture and cook, stirring constantly, for 5 minutes. Stir in the saffron and remove the pan from the heat. Set aside.

Pour the melted butter into a large baking dish. Spoon the lamb and rice mixture into the dish. Pour over the boiling water and stir well to mix. Cover the dish with aluminium foil.

Place the dish in the centre of the oven and bake the pilaff for 20 to 30 minutes, or until the rice is cooked and all the liquid has been absorbed.

Remove the dish from the oven. Serve the pilaff directly from the dish or pile it on to a warmed serving platter.

Serve immediately.

Pilaff with Nuts and Fruit

This is a moist, delicately flavoured pilaff to serve with roast chicken or with a vegetable casserole. Use good quality long-grain rice so that when the pilaff is cooked each grain remains separate.

6-8 SERVINGS

3 oz. [⅜ cup] butter
1 medium-sized onion, chopped
1 green pepper, white pith removed, seeded and chopped
½ teaspoon turmeric
1 teaspoon salt
6 oz. [1 cup] dried apricots, soaked in water for 30 minutes, drained and chopped
3 oz. [½ cup] raisins
12 oz. [2 cups] long-grain rice, washed, soaked in cold water for 30 minutes and drained
1½ pints [3¾ cups] chicken stock, boiling
4 oz. [1 cup] flaked almonds, toasted

In a large saucepan, melt the butter over moderate heat. When the foam subsides, add the onion and green pepper and fry, stirring occasionally, for 5 to 7 minutes or until the onion is soft and translucent but not brown.

Stir in the turmeric and salt. Add the apricots and raisins and cook, stirring constantly, for 2 minutes.

Add the rice and cook, stirring constantly, for 5 minutes. Pour in the chicken stock.

When the mixture comes to the boil, cover the pan, reduce the heat to low and simmer the pilaff for 20 to 25 minutes or until the rice is tender and all the liquid

has been absorbed. Stir in the almonds.

Spoon the pilaff on to a warmed serving platter and serve immediately. Alternatively, cover the pan tightly and put it in a warm oven until you are ready to serve it.

Pilaff with Peppers and Chicken

This fragrant and tasty pilaff may be served with a vegetable or egg curry. Iced lager is the perfect accompaniment. This pilaff may be made an hour or so in advance, placed in an ovenproof serving dish, covered tightly with a lid or aluminium foil and reheated in a moderate oven.

6 SERVINGS

5 fl. oz. [⅝ cup] yogurt
1 teaspoon turmeric
1 tablespoon coriander seeds, crushed
½ teaspoon hot chilli powder
2 tablespoons ground almonds
1½ teaspoons salt
1 oz. [2 tablespoons] butter
2 tablespoons vegetable oil
1 medium-sized onion, finely chopped
2 garlic cloves, crushed
1-inch piece fresh root ginger, peeled and finely chopped
1 green chilli, finely chopped
12 chicken pieces, skin removed
1 lb. green or red peppers, white pith removed, seeded and sliced
1 lb. [2⅔ cups] Basmati or other long-grain rice, washed, soaked in cold water for 30 minutes and drained

In a small mixing bowl, beat the yogurt, turmeric, coriander seeds, chilli powder, ground almonds and salt together. Set aside.

In a large saucepan, melt the butter with the oil over moderate heat. When the foam subsides, add the onion, garlic, ginger and chilli and fry, stirring frequently, for 8 to 10 minutes or until the onion is golden brown.

Add the chicken pieces and fry, turning them frequently, for 6 minutes.

Pour in the yogurt mixture and stir well to mix. Stir in the peppers.

Cover the pan, reduce the heat to low and cook the chicken pieces for 35 to 40 minutes or until they are tender when pierced with a sharp knife. Uncover the pan, increase the heat to moderately high and stir in the rice. Cook the mixture, stirring constantly, for 5 minutes or until the rice has absorbed most of the liquid in the pan.

Pour in enough boiling water to cover the rice and chicken by a ½-inch. When the mixture boils, cover the pan, reduce the heat to very low and cook for 20 to 25 minutes or until the rice is tender and has absorbed all the liquid.

Spoon the pilaff mixture into a warmed serving dish and serve immediately or keep warm until required.

Pilaff with Pineapple and Cashew Nuts

A subtle mixture of taste and texture makes this pilaff an exciting accompaniment to roast lamb. Or serve it on its own, accompanied by a green salad.

4 SERVINGS

3 oz. [⅜ cup] butter
1 small pineapple, peeled, cored and cut into chunks
3 tablespoons raisins
12 spring onions [scallions], chopped
2½ oz. [½ cup] cashew nuts
1 tablespoon coriander seeds, coarsely crushed
¼ teaspoon cayenne pepper
12 oz. [2 cups] long-grain rice, washed, soaked in cold water for 30 minutes and drained
1 teaspoon salt
1 pint [2½ cups] chicken stock
2 hard-boiled eggs, quartered
1 tablespoon chopped coriander leaves

In a medium-sized frying-pan, melt half of the butter over moderate heat. When the foam subsides, add the pineapple chunks and the raisins and fry them, turning them frequently, for 2 to 3 minutes or until the pineapple is lightly coloured. Remove the pan from the heat and set aside.

In a large saucepan, melt the remaining butter over moderate heat. When the foam subsides, add the spring onions [scallions] and fry them, stirring occasionally, for 4 to 5 minutes or until they are golden brown.

Add the cashew nuts, coriander seeds and cayenne and fry, stirring occasionally, for 4 minutes.

Add the rice and the salt and fry, stirring constantly, for 5 minutes. Stir in the pineapple and raisin mixture. Pour in the chicken stock and bring the mixture to the boil.

Cover the pan, reduce the heat to low and cook the pilaff for 20 to 25 minutes or until the rice is tender and all the liquid has been absorbed.

Taste the pilaff and add more salt and pepper if necessary.

Remove the pan from the heat and spoon the pilaff on to a warmed serving platter. Garnish with the hard-boiled eggs and the chopped coriander leaves.

Serve immediately.

Pilaff with Pineapple and Cashew Nuts tastes delicious with roast lamb.

Pilchard

Pilchard is the name for a mature SARDINE, a fish belonging to the herring family. There are many species found all over the world.

Pilchards grow to 10 inches in length and are in season in the northern hemisphere from July to December. Pilchards have a high fat content and because of this do not travel or freeze well. They may be bought fresh on the coasts where they are caught, and cooked by either grilling [broiling] or frying. The bulk of the pilchard catch is canned in oil, tomato sauce or sometimes brine. Canned pilchards are readily available and require no cooking.

Pilchards are valuable sources of vitamins A and D and supply protein and fat.

To grill [broil] fresh pilchards, make three diagonal slits on both sides of the prepared fish. Preheat the grill [broiler] to high. Place the fish in the grill [broiler] pan, sprinkle with a little salt and lemon juice and brush over with a little melted butter. Place the pan under the grill [broiler] and cook the fish for 15 to 20 minutes or until the skin is crisp and the flesh flakes easily when tested with a fork. Turn the fish once during cooking and brush with a little melted butter.

To fry pilchards, bone and fillet the fish, roll them in oatmeal and fry in the same way as HERRING.

Pimento

Also called Jamaica pepper and allspice, pimento is the aromatic berry of a small tropical tree native to the West Indies.

The berries are dried and provide a spice which combines the flavours of nutmeg, cinnamon and clove — hence the name allspice. The spice is sold whole or ground.

Pimiento

A pimiento is a sweet-tasting red pepper or CAPSICUM. Pimientos are sold fresh, canned or bottled in brine and are used in casseroles and meat dishes, as a vegetable or as an ingredient in salads.

Pimiento Chicken

Pimiento Chicken is a simple dish of chicken pieces cooked with pimientos in stock, wine and cream. Serve with boiled rice. A good accompaniment would be a lightly chilled Isabel rosé wine.

4-6 SERVINGS

2 tablespoons seasoned flour made with 2 tablespoons flour, 1 teaspoon salt and $\frac{1}{4}$ teaspoon black pepper
1 x 4 lb. chicken, cut into 8 serving pieces
1 oz. [2 tablespoons] butter

A colourful and flavoursome dish, Pimiento Chicken is cooked in stock, wine and cream. Serve with rosé wine.

2 tablespoons vegetable oil
1 large onion, finely chopped
1 garlic clove, crushed
2 large pimientos or red peppers, white pith removed, seeded and cut into julienne strips
$\frac{1}{2}$ teaspoon dried tarragon
$\frac{1}{2}$ teaspoon salt
$\frac{1}{4}$ teaspoon black pepper
6 fl. oz. [$\frac{3}{4}$ cup] chicken stock
6 fl. oz. [$\frac{3}{4}$ cup] dry white wine
1 tablespoon beurre manié
4 fl. oz. double cream [$\frac{1}{2}$ cup heavy cream]

Place the seasoned flour on a plate. Coat the chicken pieces in it, one by one, shaking off any excess. Set aside.

In a large flameproof casserole, melt the butter with the oil over moderate heat. When the foam subsides, add the chicken pieces and fry for 5 minutes on each side, or until the chicken is browned all over. Using a slotted spoon, remove the chicken from the casserole and set aside on a plate.

Add the onion and garlic to the casserole and fry, stirring occasionally, for 5 to 7 minutes or until the onion is soft and translucent but not brown. Add the pimientos to the pan and cook, stirring occasionally, for a further 5 minutes. Return the chicken to the casserole and add the tarragon, salt and pepper. Pour over the chicken stock and wine. Bring the liquid to the boil over high heat. Reduce the heat to moderately low, cover the casserole and cook for 1 hour or until the chicken is tender.

Remove the casserole from the heat. Using tongs, transfer the chicken pieces to a warmed serving dish.

Pour the cooking liquid through a fine wire strainer set over a medium-sized bowl. Arrange the onion and pimiento strips over and around the chicken pieces. Cover and keep hot while you finish the sauce.

Return the strained liquid to the casserole. Return the casserole to high heat and, stirring constantly, boil the liquid for 3 minutes.

Reduce the heat to low and, with a wooden spoon, stir in the beurre manié, a little at a time, until the sauce is fairly thick and smooth.

Remove the pan from the heat. Stir in the cream. Taste the sauce and add more salt and pepper if necessary. Pour the sauce over the chicken and serve immediately.

Pineapple

A native of tropical America, the pineapple is now also grown in Hawaii (the most intensive producer in the world of the fruit), Malaya, Australia, Africa and many other tropical regions of the world. It is one of the most delicious of tropical fruit.

A yellow or orange spiny skin encloses the pale or clear yellow flesh of the pineapple. A ripe pineapple is slightly soft to the touch and has a pleasantly strong, fragrant smell. Pineapple juice is sold canned and makes a refreshing drink.

Pineapples are exported fresh and canned. Canned pineapples are sold in slices, chunks, tidbits and crushed. The flavour of fresh pineapple is altered by canning, but good quality canned pineapple retains some of the texture of fresh pineapple.

Pineapple may be eaten raw, used in cold desserts, on its own or with other fruit in flans, gâteaux, ice-creams, Bavarian creams and hot and cold soufflés.

Pineapples are also used in savoury dishes, with grilled [broiled] pork, ham and gammon and in sweet and sour sauces, for instance.

To prepare a fresh pineapple, place the pineapple on a chopping board and, using a sharp knife, cut a 1-inch slice from the top and from the bottom.

Stand the pineapple upright and, using a sawing motion, cut thick strips downwards. Turn the pineapple on its side and cut out the prickly pieces or 'eyes' either in a spiral, following the contours of the fruit, or in straight lines. Still holding the pineapple on its side, cut it into thick slices, crosswise. Using a small pastry cutter or knife, remove the core, which is hard and inedible.

To prepare a pineapple so that its outer casing can be used as a container for a dessert or salad, place the pineapple on its side on a board, cut a 1-inch slice from the top of the pineapple and reserve it. Cut a thin slice from the bottom of the pineapple so that it stands firmly. With a serrated knife, cut between the flesh and the peel, following the contours of the pineapple until the flesh can be released from the peel. Chill the case and the flesh for 1 hour in the refrigerator. Cut the flesh into chunks, remove any prickly bits and return it to the pineapple case with other fruit or ingredients. Replace the top of the pineapple and serve immediately.

Pineapple can also be cut in half or quarters lengthways, retaining the leaves. The flesh is then scooped out and the halves or quarters used as containers for any fruit, vegetable or meat and pineapple mixture.

To prepare a fresh pineapple, use a sharp knife and cut a 1-inch slice from the top and bottom.

Stand the pineapple upright on a board and, using a sawing motion, cut thick strips downwards.

Turn the pineapple on its side and cut out the prickly pieces in a spiral, following the shape of the fruit.

Using a small pastry cutter or knife, remove the centre core as this is hard and unpleasant to eat.

To prepare a pineapple as a container, cut between the flesh and the peel, following the fruit's contours.

Carefully ease the flesh from inside the peel. The flesh can now be chopped with other fruit and returned.

Pineapple Bavarian Cream

This is a splendid dessert for a dinner party. Decorate Pineapple Bavarian Cream with poached or candied pineapple or six slices of fresh pineapple soaked in two tablespoons of kirsch.

4-6 SERVINGS

1 teaspoon vegetable oil
1 pint [2½ cups] milk
1 vanilla pod
5 tablespoons sugar
5 egg yolks
½ oz. gelatine dissolved in 3 tablespoons hot water
14 oz. canned, drained pineapple pieces, chopped finely
2 teaspoons kirsch
1 tablespoon chopped angelica
5 fl. oz. double cream [⅝ cup heavy cream]

Using a pastry brush, grease the inside of a 2-pint [1½-quart] mould with the vegetable oil. Place the mould upside-down on kitchen paper towels to drain off the excess oil.

In a medium-sized saucepan, scald the milk with the vanilla pod (bring to just below boiling point) over moderate heat. Remove the pan from the heat, cover it and set aside to infuse for 20 minutes.

Place the sugar in a medium-sized heatproof mixing bowl. Make a well in the centre of the sugar and drop in the egg yolks. With a wooden spoon, slowly incorporate the egg yolks into the sugar until they are well mixed.

Remove the vanilla pod from the milk and reserve it for future use. Pour the milk in a thin stream, stirring constantly, over the egg mixture.

Place the bowl in a saucepan of simmering water over low heat.

Cook the custard, stirring constantly, until it is thick enough to coat the back of the spoon. Remove the pan from the heat and remove the bowl from the pan. Stir the dissolved gelatine into the custard.

Strain the custard through a strainer into a large mixing bowl. Place the bowl over ice cubes placed in a larger bowl. Add the pineapple pieces, kirsch and angelica to the custard and stir constantly until the custard thickens.

In a medium-sized mixing bowl, beat the cream with a wire whisk or rotary beater until it is thick but not stiff. With a metal spoon, lightly fold the cream into the thickening custard and pour the mixture into the prepared mould.

Cover the mould with aluminium foil or greaseproof or waxed paper and place in the refrigerator to chill for 6 hours or until the cream is completely set.

To serve, dip the bottom of the mould quickly into hot water. Run a knife around the edge of the cream and turn it out on to a chilled serving dish.

Serve immediately.

Pineapple Cake

A cake with a fresh taste, Pineapple Cake is easy to make. Serve it with coffee.

ONE 7-INCH CAKE

4 oz. [½ cup] plus 1 teaspoon butter
8 oz. [2 cups] plus 1 tablespoon flour
2 teaspoons baking powder
4 oz. [½ cup] sugar
2 eggs
1 medium-sized fresh pineapple, peeled, cored, chopped and with the juice reserved
FILLING
3 oz. [⅜ cup] butter
12 oz. icing sugar [3 cups confectioners' sugar]
⅛ teaspoon salt
1½ teaspoons vanilla essence
1 oz. dark [semi-sweet] cooking chocolate, grated

Preheat the oven to moderate 350°F (Gas Mark 4, 180°C).

With the teaspoon of butter, grease a 7-inch square cake tin. Sprinkle the tablespoon of flour over the bottom and sides of the tin, tipping and rotating the

Still holding the pineapple on its side, cut it into fairly thick slices, crosswise.

tin to distribute the flour evenly. Knock out any excess flour. Set aside.

Sift the remaining flour and the baking powder into a medium-sized mixing bowl.

In another medium-sized mixing bowl, beat the remaining butter with a wooden spoon until it is soft and creamy. Add the sugar and cream it with the butter until the mixture is light and fluffy. Beat in the eggs, one at a time, with a tablespoon of the flour mixture.

Using a metal spoon, fold in the remaining flour mixture. Stir half of the pineapple pieces into the cake batter.

Spoon the batter into the prepared cake tin and smooth the top with a table knife or the back of a spoon.

Place the tin in the oven and bake the cake for 1 to 1¼ hours or until a skewer inserted into the centre of the cake comes out clean.

Remove the cake from the oven. Run a knife around the edge of the cake and turn it out on to a wire rack to cool completely.

Meanwhile, make the filling. In a medium-sized mixing bowl, beat the butter with a wooden spoon until it is soft and creamy. Stir in the icing [confectioners'] sugar and beat the mixture well until it is light and fluffy. Beat in the salt, vanilla essence, grated chocolate and the remaining pineapple and the juice.

Using a long sharp knife, cut the cake into three layers. Place the base of the

Pineapple Bavarian Cream makes a splendid dessert for a dinner party. It can be decorated with more pineapple or with cream piped around the edge.

cake on a serving dish and spread it with half of the buttercream. Place the next layer on top and spread it with the remaining buttercream. Cover with the remaining layer of cake.

Serve immediately or store the cake in an airtight tin.

Pineapple Cheesecake

Ricotta cheese, shortbread biscuits [cookies], allspice and pineapple combine to make Pineapple Cheesecake a delectable dessert or coffee-time treat.

ONE 9-INCH CAKE

4 oz. [½ cup] plus 1 teaspoon butter
8 oz. [2 cups] crushed shortbread biscuits [cookies]
2 tablespoons castor sugar
½ teaspoon ground allspice
FILLING
2½ lb. ricotta cheese
2 oz. [¼ cup] castor sugar
2 tablespoons flour
½ teaspoon vanilla essence
very finely grated rind of 2 small lemons
⅛ teaspoon ground allspice
3 egg yolks
1 large fresh pineapple, peeled, cored and very finely chopped
6 walnut halves

Preheat the oven to moderate 350°F (Gas Mark 4, 180°C).

Using the teaspoon of butter, lightly grease a 9-inch loose-bottomed cake tin. Set it aside.

In a medium-sized saucepan, melt the remaining butter over moderate heat.

Remove the pan from the heat and add the crushed biscuits [cookies], sugar and allspice. Beat the mixture with a wooden spoon until the biscuit [cookie] crumbs are thoroughly coated with the melted butter.

Spoon the mixture into the prepared cake tin. Using the back of the spoon or your fingers, press the mixture down so that it evenly lines the bottom of the tin. Set aside.

To make the filling, place the ricotta cheese in a large fine wire strainer held over a medium-sized mixing bowl. Using the back of a wooden spoon, rub the cheese through the strainer. Add the sugar, flour, vanilla essence, lemon rind and allspice. Beat the mixture with the wooden spoon until it is well blended. Beat in the egg yolks, one at a time, beating until the mixture is smooth.

Spoon half of the filling over the biscuit [cookie] base. Using a flat-bladed knife or the back of the spoon, spread the

filling evenly over the base. Spoon over the chopped pineapple and spread it over the filling. Spoon over the remaining ricotta filling and smooth it over the pineapple to cover it completely.

Place the tin in the centre of the oven and bake the cheesecake for 20 minutes.

Remove the cheesecake from the oven and arrange the walnuts decoratively over the top.

Return the cheesecake to the oven and bake for a further 10 to 15 minutes or until the filling is firm.

Remove the cheesecake from the oven and set it aside to cool completely. Then lift off the sides of the tin. Very carefully slide the cheesecake off the base of the tin on to a chilled serving plate.

Place the cheesecake in the refrigerator and chill it for at least 1 hour before serving.

Pineapple and Cheese Salad

This is a delightful salad which combines soft and crunchy textures. Serve it as a light luncheon dish, preceded by hot soup.

4 SERVINGS

½ fresh pineapple, peeled, cored and chopped
6 oz. Caerphilly or Cheshire cheese, cut into ¼-inch dice
1 ripe pear, peeled, cored and chopped
12 small radishes, trimmed
2 celery stalks, trimmed and cut into ¼-inch pieces
1 head of chicory [French or Belgian endive], cut into ½-inch slices
8 watercress sprigs
DRESSING
4 tablespoons olive oil
1 teaspoon salt
½ teaspoon sugar
½ teaspoon black pepper
2 tablespoons single [light] cream
1½ tablespoons lemon juice
½ teaspoon chopped fresh tarragon or ½ teaspoon dried tarragon

In a large mixing bowl, combine the pineapple, cheese, pear, radishes, celery and chicory [French or Belgian endive]. Set aside.

To make the dressing, in a small mixing bowl, combine the olive oil, salt, sugar and pepper together. Using a fork, gradually beat in the cream, lemon juice

Fresh pineapple, sandwiched between a creamy cheese mixture, Pineapple Cheesecake is a delightful dessert.

Pineapple Fruit Salad, made with fresh fruit and served in a shell, and Pineapple and Honey Sorbet — a mouth-watering dessert.

and tarragon. Pour the dressing over the fruit and vegetables and, using two forks, toss them until they are well coated.

Spoon the salad into individual serving dishes and garnish with the watercress sprigs. Serve immediately.

Pineapple Cream

Pineapple Cream makes a delectable dessert for a special dinner party.

6 SERVINGS

1 pint [2½ cups] milk
4 egg yolks, at room temperature
3 tablespoons castor sugar
6 tablespoons flour
2 teaspoons vanilla essence
1 tablespoon butter
8 oz. canned crushed pineapple, in thick syrup
4 egg whites
1 tablespoon sugar

In a small saucepan, scald the milk over moderate heat (bring to just under boiling point). Remove the pan from the heat and set aside to cool.

In a medium-sized mixing bowl, beat the egg yolks and castor sugar together with a wire whisk or rotary beater until the mixture is pale and thick. Whisk in the flour, then the milk, a little at a time.

Pour the mixture into a medium-sized, heavy-based saucepan and place the pan over moderate heat. Cook, stirring constantly, for 2 minutes or until the custard is thick.

Remove the pan from the heat and beat in the vanilla essence and the butter, stirring until the butter has melted. Pour the custard into a large mixing bowl and set aside.

Drain 3 fluid ounces [⅜ cup] of the pineapple syrup into a small saucepan and cook over moderate heat for 5 minutes. Add the crushed pineapple to the pan and cook for 5 minutes, stirring occasionally. Drain the pineapple, reserving the liquid. Set both the pineapple and the reserved liquid aside.

In a medium-sized mixing bowl, beat the egg whites with a wire whisk or rotary beater until they form soft peaks. Sprinkle on the sugar and beat until they form stiff peaks. Set aside.

Spoon 2 tablespoons of the reserved cooked syrup into the custard mixture and mix well. With a rubber spatula, fold

in the egg whites, then the pineapple, reserving about 2 tablespoons of the pineapple for decoration.

Spoon the custard mixture into a deep serving dish. Cover the dish with aluminium foil and place in the refrigerator to chill for 3 hours.

Just before serving, sprinkle the remaining pineapple over the top.

Pineapple Delight

A refreshing dessert, Pineapple Delight is best made with fresh fruit. If strawberries are not available, other fruit, such as grapes or raspberries may be used instead.

4 SERVINGS

15 fl. oz. [1⅞ cups] sour cream
12 macaroons, crumbled
3 tablespoons sugar
1 medium-sized fresh pineapple, peeled, cored and cut into chunks
2 oranges, peeled, pith removed and sliced
8 oz. strawberries, washed, hulled and halved
2 tablespoons brandy
2 tablespoons slivered almonds, toasted

In a small mixing bowl, combine the sour cream, macaroons and sugar together. Put the bowl in the refrigerator for 2 hours.

Layer the pineapple, oranges and strawberries with the sour cream mixture in a glass serving bowl. Sprinkle over the brandy and scatter the almonds over the top.

Serve immediately.

Pineapple Flan

A light sponge flan case filled with fresh pineapple, brandy, almonds and cream, Pineapple Flan is ideal for a dinner party dessert. The flan case may be made in advance and the dessert assembled at the last minute.

4-6 SERVINGS

1 x 9-inch Flan Case made with sponge, baked blind and cooled
1 fresh pineapple, peeled, cored and finely chopped
4 tablespoons brandy
4 tablespoons ground almonds
10 fl. oz. double cream [1¼ cups heavy cream], beaten until stiff
1 tablespoon icing [confectioners'] sugar
1 oz. [¼ cup] slivered almonds, toasted

Preheat the grill [broiler] to high.

Place the flan case on a heatproof serving dish. Arrange the pineapple in the flan case. Set aside.

In a small mixing bowl, combine the brandy and the ground almonds together. Spoon the mixture over the pineapple.

Pile the cream on top, sprinkle over the sugar and scatter the slivered almonds on top.

Place the dish under the grill [broiler] for 1 minute or until the sugar has caramelized and the cream has melted.

Remove the dish from under the grill [broiler] and set it aside for 10 minutes or until it is quite cold.

Serve immediately.

Pineapple Fruit Salad

This colourful dessert should ideally be made with fresh fruit, but if this is not possible, use a mixture of fresh and canned fruit. Serve Pineapple Fruit Salad with whipped cream or Crème Chantilly.

4-6 SERVINGS

2 bananas, sliced
1 tablespoon lemon juice
1 large fresh pineapple
8 oz. strawberries, hulled and sliced
2 large oranges, peeled, white pith removed and segmented
2 tablespoons kirsch
4 tablespoons icing [confectioners'] sugar
1 pint [2½ cups] vanilla ice-cream

In a medium-sized mixing bowl, combine the banana slices and the lemon juice together. Set aside.

Place the pineapple on a chopping board. Cut a 1-inch slice from the top of the pineapple and reserve it. Cut a thin slice from the bottom of the pineapple so that it stands firmly. With a sharp knife or spoon, scoop out the flesh, being careful not to cut the shell or pierce the bottom. Remove and discard the core and cut the flesh into chunks. Reserve the shell.

Add the pineapple chunks to the bananas in the bowl, then add the strawberries and oranges. Pour the kirsch over the fruit and sprinkle them with the icing [confectioners'] sugar. Stir the fruit, cover the bowl and place it in the refrigerator.

Wrap the pineapple shell and the reserved top in aluminium foil and put them in the refrigerator. Chill both the fruit mixture and reserved pineapple shell and top for at least 6 hours or overnight.

Remove the pineapple shell and top

and the fruit mixture from the refrigerator. Remove and discard the aluminium foil from the shell and top. Place the pineapple shell on a chilled serving dish. Spoon 2 tablespoons of the fruit mixture into the shell, cover with 2 tablespoons of ice-cream and continue making layers in this way until all the ingredients are used up. Place the top on the pineapple shell and serve immediately.

Any leftover ice-cream and fruit mixture may be used to refill the shell for second helpings.

Pineapple and Honey Sorbet

This delicately-flavoured sorbet makes a superb summer dessert — for a more luxurious sorbet, dissolve the gelatine in 2 tablespoons of hot rum instead of water.

4 SERVINGS

10 fl. oz. [1¼ cups] fresh or canned pineapple juice
3 fl. oz. [⅜ cup] water
2 fl. oz. [¼ cup] clear orange-blossom honey
2 tablespoons castor sugar
finely grated rind and juice of 1 large lemon
½ oz. gelatine dissolved in 2 tablespoons hot water
1 egg white

Set the thermostat of the refrigerator to its coldest setting.

In a medium-sized saucepan, combine the pineapple juice, water, honey, sugar and lemon rind. Set the pan over moderately high heat and bring the mixture to the boil, stirring constantly. Boil the mixture, without stirring, for 4 minutes.

Remove the pan from the heat and stir in the lemon juice and the dissolved gelatine mixture. Pour the mixture through a fine wire strainer into a freezer tray. Set the mixture aside to cool completely, and then place it in the frozen food storage compartment of the refrigerator to freeze for 30 minutes.

In a medium-sized mixing bowl, beat the egg white with a wire whisk or rotary beater until it forms stiff peaks.

Remove the pineapple juice mixture from the refrigerator and whisk it into the egg white until the mixture is smooth. Spoon the mixture back into the freezer tray and return the tray to the frozen food storage compartment. Freeze the mixture for 1 hour.

Remove the freezer tray from the refrigerator and turn the pineapple mixture into a medium-sized chilled mixing bowl. Whisk it with a wire whisk or rotary beater for 1 minute or until it is smooth.

Spoon the mixture back into the freezer tray and return it to the storage compartment. Continue whisking the mixture every hour for 4 hours and then leave it to freeze in the frozen food storage compartment overnight.

The next day, chill 4 individual serving glasses or dishes in the refrigerator for 30 minutes.

Remove the glasses or dishes from the refrigerator. Remove the sorbet from the storage compartment and, using a tablespoon which has been dipped in hot water, spoon the sorbet into the glasses or dishes.

Serve the sorbet immediately.

Pineapple Jam

Pineapple Jam is easy to make and tastes absolutely delicious spread on fresh white bread or home-made scones [biscuits]. Remember that the weight of the pineapple is calculated after peeling and coring. Three medium-sized pineapples give about 3 pounds of prepared fruit.

ABOUT 6 POUNDS

3 lemons
3 lb. fresh pineapples, peeled, cored and chopped into small pieces
1 pint [2½ cups] water
3 lb. [6 cups] sugar

Squeeze the juice from the lemons and set it aside. Tie the squeezed out lemons and the pips in a cheesecloth bag.

Place the chopped pineapples, the reserved lemon juice, the cheesecloth bag and the water in a preserving pan or large saucepan. Set the pan over moderately high heat and bring the liquid to the boil. Reduce the heat to low, cover the pan and simmer for 2 hours or until the pineapple pieces are tender. Remove the cheesecloth bag, squeezing it against the side of the pan with the back of a wooden spoon to extract as much juice as possible.

Add the sugar to the pan and cook the jam, stirring constantly, until the sugar has dissolved.

Increase the heat to moderately high and boil the jam, without stirring, for 15 to 20 minutes or until setting point is reached. If you are using a sugar thermometer, setting point is reached when the jam registers 220°F to 222°F on the thermometer.

Alternatively, remove the pan from the heat and drop a teaspoon of the jam on to a cold saucer. Allow the jam to cool. If the surface of the jam wrinkles when gently pushed with your index finger, setting point has been reached.

If the jam has not set, return the pan to the heat and continue boiling the jam, testing it every 5 minutes.

Remove the pan from the heat and let it stand for 5 minutes.

Ladle the jam into clean, warm, dry jam jars. Place a circle of greaseproof or waxed paper over the surface of the jam in each jar. Cover the jars with jam covers and secure with rubber bands. Label the jars and store them in a cool, dark, dry place.

Pineapple and Lettuce Salad

A simple salad made with fresh ingredients, Pineapple and Lettuce Salad may be served as a refreshing first course.

6 SERVINGS

1 fresh pineapple, peeled and cored
2 small round [Boston] lettuce hearts, cut into ½-inch slices

1 tablespoon capers
3 fl. oz. [$\frac{3}{8}$ cup] sour cream
2 tablespoons mayonnaise
1 tablespoon lemon juice
2 teaspoons light rum
$\frac{1}{4}$ teaspoon salt
$\frac{1}{4}$ teaspoon black pepper
$\frac{1}{4}$ teaspoon sugar
1 tablespoon chopped fresh chives
6 watercress sprigs

Place the pineapple on a chopping board and, using a sharp knife, cut it into thin slices. Halve three of the slices and set them aside. Chop the remainder into small pieces.

Place the lettuce, chopped pineapple and capers in a large mixing bowl. Set aside.

In a small mixing bowl, combine the sour cream, mayonnaise, lemon juice, rum, salt, pepper, sugar and chives, beating well with a fork until the ingredients are well mixed.

An easy-to-make Pineapple Jam and a smooth, delicate Pineapple Liqueur- just two of the unusual recipes to try using fresh pineapples.

Pour the dressing over the lettuce and pineapple mixture and toss well with two forks.

Arrange the salad on individual glass dishes. Garnish each dish with the reserved pineapple and the watercress sprigs.

Serve immediately:

Pineapple Liqueur
A liqueur with a fine and delicate flavour, Pineapple Liqueur becomes smoother the longer you keep it. The weight of the pineapple is calculated after peeling and coring.
ABOUT 3 PINTS [7$\frac{1}{2}$ CUPS]
1 lb. fresh pineapple, peeled and
    cored

2 pints [5 cups] gin
4 oz. [$\frac{1}{2}$ cup] sugar
2 tablespoons kirsch

On a wooden board, chop the pineapple into chunks. Put the pineapple chunks into an electric blender, a few at a time. Blend at high speed until the pineapple is completely crushed. Put the crushed pineapple into a large mixing bowl. Pour over the gin, add the sugar and kirsch and stir to blend.

Pour the mixture into a large jug or crock and cork it tightly.

Set the jug or crock aside in a warm place and allow the mixture to infuse for 60 days.

Thoroughly clean and dry two bottles. Uncork the jug or crock and filter the liqueur, through a layer of fine cheese-cloth, into the bottles.

Seal the bottles and set them aside for at least 1 week before serving. The longer you leave the liqueur to mature, the better.

Pineapple and Pork Casserole

This delicately-flavoured dish of pork fillets cooked with herbs, pineapple, orange, wine and green peppers makes a superb Sunday lunch. Serve with creamed potatoes and buttered green beans.

4 SERVINGS

2 lb. pork fillets, beaten until thin
1 garlic clove, halved
1 teaspoon salt
½ teaspoon black pepper
1 tablespoon finely grated orange rind
½ teaspoon dried marjoram
½ teaspoon dried sage
1 oz. [2 tablespoons] butter
2 medium-sized green peppers, white pith removed, seeded and cut into julienne strips
10 fl. oz. [1¼ cups] dry white wine
16 oz. canned pineapple rings, drained and coarsely chopped
1 tablespoon cornflour [cornstarch] dissolved in 2 tablespoons orange juice

Rub the pork fillets all over with the garlic clove halves and half of the salt and pepper. Discard the garlic clove halves and lay the pork fillets flat on a working surface. Sprinkle over the orange rind, marjoram and sage. Roll up the fillets and secure the rolls with trussing thread or string. Set aside.

In a medium-sized flameproof casserole, melt the butter over moderate heat. When the foam subsides, add the green peppers and fry them, stirring frequently, for 4 minutes. With a slotted spoon, remove the peppers from the casserole and set them aside.

Add the pork fillets to the casserole and fry for 6 to 8 minutes, turning the rolls occasionally with tongs, or until they are lightly browned.

Pour the wine into the casserole and stir in the remaining salt and pepper, the pineapple pieces and fried green peppers. Bring the liquid to the boil, stirring constantly. Reduce the heat to low, cover the casserole and simmer for 30 to 40 minutes, or until the pork fillets are cooked and tender when pierced with the point of a sharp knife.

Remove the casserole from the heat. Using a slotted spoon, remove the pork rolls from the casserole and transfer them to a warmed serving dish. Remove and discard the trussing thread or string. Remove the pineapple pieces and green peppers from the casserole and arrange them around the meat. Keep the dish warm.

With a metal spoon, skim off and discard any fat from the surface of the cooking liquid in the casserole. Pour the liquid through a fine wire strainer into a medium-sized saucepan and stir in the cornflour [cornstarch] mixture. Set the pan over moderate heat and cook the sauce, stirring constantly with a wooden spoon, for 5 minutes or until it is thick and smooth.

Remove the pan from the heat. Pour the sauce over the pork rolls and serve immediately.

Pineapple Sauce

Pineapple Sauce may be served with steamed puddings or ice-cream. It will keep for up to two days in the refrigerator in a screw-top jar.

16 FLUID OUNCES [2 CUPS]

½ fresh pineapple, peeled, cored, very finely chopped and the juice reserved
juice of 1 lemon
juice of 1 orange
1 teaspoon grated lemon rind
1 tablespoon sugar
10 fl. oz. [1¼ cups] water
2 tablespoons arrowroot dissolved in 3 tablespoons water
1 tablespoon orange-flavoured liqueur

In a medium-sized saucepan, combine the pineapple, pineapple juice, lemon and orange juices, lemon rind, sugar, water and arrowroot mixture. Place the pan over moderate heat and bring the sauce to the boil, stirring constantly. Cook the sauce for 2 minutes, stirring frequently. Remove the pan from the heat and stir in the liqueur. Pour the sauce into a warmed sauceboat and serve immediately.

Pineapple Shrub

Like all liqueurs, this shrub improves with keeping. The finished drink is very evocative of warm Hawaiian evenings, so serve it well chilled with ice.

ABOUT 5 PINTS [6¼ PINTS]

3 medium-sized pineapples, peeled, cored and chopped
4 pints [5 pints] rum
9 oz. [1⅛ cups] sugar

Put the chopped pineapples into an electric blender, a little at a time. Blend at high speed until the pineapples are completely crushed.

In a large mixing bowl, combine the blended pineapples, rum and sugar together, stirring until the sugar dissolves.

Strain the shrub through a layer of fine cheesecloth into clean, dry bottles. Seal the bottles and set them aside for at least 2 months before serving.

Pineapple Soufflé

This feather-light, sweet soufflé should be served hot, on its own or with a bowl of whipped cream. The weight of the fresh pineapple is calculated after peeling and coring.

4 SERVINGS

2 oz. [¼ cup] plus 1 tablespoon butter
1 lb. fresh pineapple, peeled and cored or 1 lb. canned and drained pineapple
2 oz. [½ cup] flour
¾ teaspoon ground allspice
8 fl. oz. single cream [1 cup light cream]
2 fl. oz. [¼ cup] kirsch
2 oz. [¼ cup] castor sugar
4 egg yolks
5 egg whites

Preheat the oven to fairly hot 375°F (Gas Mark 5, 190°C).

Using the tablespoon of butter, grease a 3-pint [2-quart] soufflé dish. Tie a strip of greaseproof or waxed paper around the rim of the dish so that it projects 2-inches above the top. Set aside.

Place the pineapple on a chopping board and, using a sharp knife, chop it finely. Set aside.

In a medium-sized, heavy-based saucepan, melt the remaining butter over moderate heat. When the foam subsides, stir in the flour and allspice with a wooden spoon to make a smooth paste. Cook the mixture, stirring constantly, for 1 minute.

Remove the pan from the heat. Gradually add the cream, stirring constantly and being careful to avoid lumps. Stir in the kirsch, sugar and pineapple. Set the pan over moderately low heat and cook the mixture, stirring constantly, for 6 minutes or until it is very thick.

Remove the pan from the heat and set the mixture aside to cool to lukewarm. Beat in the egg yolks, one at a time, with a wooden spoon. Set aside.

In a large mixing bowl, beat the egg whites with a wire whisk or rotary beater until they form stiff peaks.

Using a metal spoon, fold the egg whites into the pineapple mixture.

Pineapple and Pork Casserole — a delicately flavoured dish for lunch.

A popular American cake, Pineapple Upside-down Cake is made by pouring batter over pineapple arranged on the bottom of the cake tin.

Spoon the mixture into the prepared soufflé dish. Place the dish in the centre of the oven and bake for 35 to 40 minutes, or until the soufflé has risen and is golden on top.

Remove the dish from the oven and quickly remove and discard the grease-proof or waxed paper strip. Serve the soufflé immediately, straight from the dish.

Pineapple and Turkey Salad

An attractive and refreshing dish, Pine-apple and Turkey Salad is the perfect way to use up leftover roast turkey. Serve it with a lightly chilled Mateus rosé wine.

4 SERVINGS

2 medium-sized fresh pineapples, cut in half lengthways, leaving green tops on, with the flesh scooped out and reserved
1½ lb. cooked turkey meat, diced
4 celery stalks, trimmed and diced
1 large banana, cut into ¼-inch slices
2 oz. [⅓ cup] salted peanuts
6 fl. oz. [¾ cup] mayonnaise
2 fl. oz. double cream [¼ cup heavy cream]
1 tablespoon apricot jam
1 teaspoon curry powder
1 teaspoon salt
½ teaspoon black pepper
GARNISH
2 tablespoons coarsely desiccated [shredded] coconut
1 orange, peeled, pith removed and cut into thin slices

Dry the pineapple shells thoroughly with kitchen paper towels. Wrap them in aluminium foil and put them in the refrigerator to chill for 1 hour.

Cut half of the pineapple flesh into cubes. Reserve the remaining half for other uses. In a large mixing bowl, combine the cubed pineapple, turkey meat, celery, banana and peanuts together. Set aside.

In a small mixing-bowl, combine the mayonnaise, cream, apricot jam, curry, salt and pepper. Taste the dressing and add more seasoning if necessary.

Pour the mayonnaise mixture over the fruit and turkey and, using two large spoons, lightly toss the ingredients together.

Remove the pineapple shells from the refrigerator. Remove and discard the aluminium foil. Spoon the pineapple and turkey salad into the pineapple shells.

Garnish with the desiccated [shredded] coconut and orange slices. Serve immediately.

Pineapple Upside-down Cake

This is a well-known American cake in which the fruit is arranged decoratively on the bottom of the cake tin and the batter is poured over the top. When the cake is baked it is turned out, upside-down, to display the fruit. Serve it with whipped cream.

6 SERVINGS

5 oz. [⅝ cup] plus 1 teaspoon butter
2 tablespoons soft brown sugar
1 medium-sized fresh pineapple, peeled, cored and cut into 9 rings or 14 oz. canned pineapple rings, drained
9 glacé cherries
4 oz. [½ cup] sugar
2 eggs
6 oz. [1½ cups] self-raising flour, sifted
3 tablespoons milk
1-inch piece angelica cut into 18 leaves (optional)

Preheat the oven to moderate 350°F (Gas Mark 4, 180°C).

With the teaspoon of the butter, grease the sides of a 8- x 8-inch cake tin. Cut 1 ounce [2 tablespoons] of the remaining butter into small pieces and dot them over the base of the tin. Sprinkle the brown sugar over the top. Arrange the pineapple slices decoratively on top of the sugar, and place a cherry in the centre of each ring. Set aside.

In a medium-sized mixing bowl, beat the remaining butter with a wooden spoon until it is soft and creamy. Add the sugar and cream it with the butter until the mixture is light and fluffy. Add the eggs, one at a time, beating well until they are thoroughly blended. Using a large metal spoon, fold in the flour. Stir in enough of the milk to give the batter a dropping consistency.

Spoon the batter into the cake tin, being careful not to dislodge the cherries. Smooth down the top of the batter with a table knife. Place the cake tin in the oven and bake the cake for 50 minutes to 1 hour or until the cake is golden brown and a skewer inserted into the centre of the cake comes out clean.

Remove the tin from the oven and allow the cake to cool for 5 minutes. Run a knife around the sides of the cake. Invert a serving dish over the cake tin and reverse the two. The cake should slide out easily. Decorate each cherry with two angelica leaves, if desired.

Serve the cake immediately or set it aside to cool before serving.

Pineapple and Walnut Ice-Cream

This decorative, pale yellow Pineapple and Walnut Ice-Cream is flavoured with rum and is frozen in a rounded mould. It tastes delicious cut into thick slices and served with crisp wafers or Krumkaker.

4 SERVINGS

1 pint [2½ cups] milk
1 vanilla pod, split in half
1 egg yolk
1 tablespoon custard powder
3 tablespoons sugar
1½ teaspoons gelatine dissolved in 2 tablespoons hot water
1 egg white
2 drops yellow food colouring
½ medium-sized fresh pineapple, peeled, cored and very finely chopped
1 tablespoon rum
1 oz. [¼ cup] finely chopped walnuts

Set the thermostat of the refrigerator to its coldest setting. Place a 2-pint [1½-quart] mould with rounded sides in the refrigerator.

In a medium-sized saucepan, scald the milk with the vanilla pod (bring to just under boiling point) over moderate heat. Remove the pan from the heat, cover it and set the milk aside to infuse for 20 minutes.

In a medium-sized mixing bowl beat the egg yolk, custard powder, sugar and 2 tablespoons of the scalded milk together with a wooden spoon. Strain the remaining milk on to the mixture, stirring constantly.

Pour the mixture back into the sauce-pan and return it to moderately low heat. Cook, stirring constantly, for 5 minutes or until the custard starts to simmer and becomes thick enough to coat the back of the spoon.

Remove the pan from the heat and carefully stir in the dissolved gelatine. Pour the custard into a bowl and set it aside to cool completely, stirring occasionally. When the custard is cool cover the bowl and place it in the refrigerator to chill for 1 hour.

Pour the chilled custard into a cold freezing tray and put it in the frozen food storage compartment of the refrigerator to freeze for 30 minutes.

Remove the tray from the compartment and spoon the custard mixture into a medium-sized chilled mixing bowl. Beat well with a wire whisk or rotary beater.

In a small mixing bowl, beat the egg white with a wire whisk or rotary beater until it forms stiff peaks. With a metal spoon, fold the egg white into the custard and blend the mixture thoroughly. Spoon the mixture back into the freezing tray and return it to the storage compartment to freeze for 1 hour, or until the mixture is firm.

Remove the ice-cream from the compartment. Place it in the mixing bowl and beat it well. With a wooden spoon, stir in the food colouring, then fold in the chopped pineapple, rum and walnuts. Beat the mixture until it is evenly coloured.

Remove the chilled mould from the refrigerator and spoon in the ice-cream. Smooth the ice-cream down with the back of the spoon.

Place the mould in the frozen food storage compartment of the refrigerator and freeze for 1 hour, or until the ice-cream is completely firm.

Remove the ice-cream from the refrigerator. Run a sharp-edged knife around the edge of the mould to loosen the sides. Quickly dip the bottom of the mould in boiling water. Hold a chilled serving plate, inverted, over the top of the mould and reverse the two, giving a sharp shake. The ice-cream should slide out easily.

Serve the ice-cream immediately.

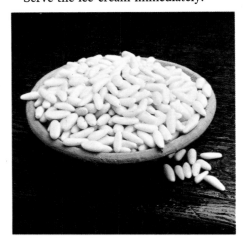

Pine Nuts

Pine Nuts, also known as pine seeds or pine kernels, are the edible seeds of a variety of pine tree. Encased in a hard brown shell, the nut is small, white and capsule-shaped.

Pine nuts are softer than most other nuts and have a delicate pine flavour. They may be eaten raw, or roasted and salted and are often used in confectionery and baking.

Pintades aux Cerises — guinea fowls served with a rich, cherry sauce.

Pine nuts are usually sold shelled and ready for use.

Pink Lady

A gin-based cocktail, Pink Lady, as with most cocktails, has many variations. In this recipe we suggest adding lime juice but this may be omitted if preferred.

1 SERVING

2 fl. oz. [¼ cup] gin
2 tablespoons brandy
1 teaspoon grenadine
1 egg white, lightly beaten
    juice of ½ lime (optional)
1 mint sprig (optional)

Place the gin, brandy and grenadine in a cocktail shaker or large screw-topped jar. Add the beaten egg white and lime juice, if you are using it. Screw the cocktail shaker together or screw the top on the jar, and shake well.

Pour the mixture into a cocktail glass, garnish with the mint sprig if you are using it, and serve at once.

Pintades aux Cerises

GUINEA FOWLS WITH CHERRY SAUCE

Pintades aux Cerises (pahn-tahd oh sey-reez) *is a superbly rich dish, combining Morello cherries with the delicate flavour of guinea fowl. Serve Pintades aux Cerises with croquette potatoes and Broccoli with Almonds.*

4 SERVINGS

2 x 1½ lb. guinea fowls, cleaned
1 teaspoon salt
½ teaspoon black pepper
4 oz. salt pork, diced
1 medium-sized onion, finely
    chopped
½ teaspoon dried sage
2 teaspoons grated orange rind
2½ oz. [1 cup] cooked rice
8 fl. oz. [1 cup] chicken stock
1 lb. canned stoned Morello
    cherries, drained
4 tablespoons double [heavy] cream
1 tablespoon brandy

Rub the birds all over with half of the salt and pepper. Set aside.

In a large flameproof casserole, fry the pork dice over moderate heat, stirring frequently, for 8 to 10 minutes, or until they are golden brown and have rendered most of their fat. With a slotted spoon, transfer the salt pork to a medium-sized

mixing bowl. Set aside.

Add the onion to the pork fat and fry, stirring occasionally, for 5 to 7 minutes, or until it is soft and translucent but not brown. Remove the casserole from the heat. With a slotted spoon, remove the onion from the casserole and add it to the pork.

Add the remaining salt and pepper, the sage, orange rind and rice to the salt pork

mixture and mix well to blend. Spoon half of the mixture into the cavity of each bird. Close the cavities with a trussing needle and string, or with skewers.

Return the casserole to moderate heat and reheat the pork fat. When the fat is hot, add the guinea fowls and fry them, turning frequently with two large spoons, for 8 to 10 minutes, or until they are evenly browned.

Pour in the stock and bring the liquid to the boil over high heat. Cover the casserole, reduce the heat to low and cook for 50 minutes to 1 hour or until the guinea fowls are tender, and the juice that runs out when the thighs are pierced with a skewer is only faintly rosy. Remove the guinea fowls to a warmed serving dish and keep hot while you prepare the sauce.

Increase the heat to high and bring the cooking juices in the casserole to the boil. Boil for 5 minutes, or until the liquid has reduced by about half. Reduce the heat to moderate. Stir in the cherries, cream and brandy and cook for a further 2 to 3 minutes or until the cherries are heated through and the sauce is hot.

Remove the casserole from the heat. Pour the sauce over the guinea gowls and serve immediately.

Pintades Farcies
STUFFED GUINEA FOWLS

  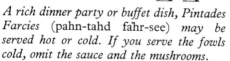

A rich dinner party or buffet dish, Pintades Farcies (pahn-tahd fahr-see) may be served hot or cold. If you serve the fowls cold, omit the sauce and the mushrooms.

6 SERVINGS

8 oz. minced [ground] veal
6 oz. chicken livers, coarsely chopped
1 oz. [¼ cup] shelled pistachios
1 tablespoon chopped fresh parsley
1 tablespoon chopped fresh tarragon
1 teaspoon salt
½ teaspoon black pepper
1 tablespoon brandy
2 x 1½ lb. guinea fowls, cleaned and boned
6 streaky bacon slices
4 oz. [½ cup] butter
1 medium-sized onion, sliced
½ teaspoon dried thyme
1 bay leaf

8 fl. oz. [1 cup] chicken stock
1 lb. mushrooms, wiped clean and with the stalks removed
1 egg yolk mixed with 2 tablespoons double [heavy] cream

In a medium-sized mixing bowl, combine the veal, chicken livers, pistachios, parsley, tarragon, salt, pepper and brandy together and mix well.

Lay the guinea fowls out on a flat surface and spoon half of the veal and liver stuffing into the centre of each one. Wrap the guinea fowls around the stuffing and sew them up with a trussing needle and string. Place three bacon slices over the breast of each fowl and tie them on with string.

In a large flameproof casserole, melt half of the butter over moderate heat. When the foam subsides, place the guinea fowls in the casserole and cook, turning them frequently with two large spoons, for 8 to 10 minutes or until they are evenly browned.

Add the onion, thyme, bay leaf and

Pintades Farcies is an unusual rich dish which is delicious served hot or cold for a special dinner party.

stock to the casserole and bring the liquid to the boil. Cover the casserole, reduce the heat to low and cook for 50 minutes to 1 hour or until the guinea fowls are tender and the juice that runs out when the centre of the stuffing is pierced with a skewer is only faintly rosy.

Five minutes before the guinea fowls are ready, in a large saucepan, melt the remaining butter over moderate heat. When the foam subsides, add the mushrooms and cook, shaking the pan frequently, for 3 minutes or until the mushrooms are just tender.

Remove the pan from the heat. Set aside and keep warm.

Remove the casserole from the heat. Carefully transfer the guinea fowls to a warmed serving dish. Remove and discard the bacon. Arrange the mushrooms around the guinea fowls. Set aside and

A classic French omelet, Pipérade is made with a mixture of green and red peppers and tomatoes.

---

keep warm.

Strain the cooking liquid into a small saucepan. With a metal spoon, skim any scum and the excess fat from the surface. Place the pan over low heat and stir in the egg yolk mixture. Cook gently, stirring constantly, for 2 to 3 minutes or until the sauce thickens slightly. Do not let the sauce come to the boil or it will curdle.

Remove the pan from the heat. Pour the sauce into a warmed sauceboat and serve immediately, with the guinea fowls.

Pintail

The pintail, also known as sea pheasant, gray duck and sea widgeon among others, is a popular species of wild duck. It is considered to be one of the most delicate of all wild ducks.

Pipérade

PEPPER AND TOMATO OMELET

One of the great classic French regional dishes, Pipérade (pee-pehr-add) originated in the Basque country near Béarn, although it is now popular all over France. Serve Pipérade with some crusty French bread, a tossed lettuce salad and some vin ordinaire.

2-3 SERVINGS

2 fl. oz. [¼ cup] olive oil
1 small onion, finely chopped
2 garlic cloves, crushed
1 medium-sized green pepper, white pith removed, seeded and chopped
1 medium-sized red pepper, white pith removed, seeded and chopped
3 tomatoes, blanched, peeled, seeded and chopped
6 eggs
¼ teaspoon salt
¼ teaspoon black pepper
2 tablespoons water

In a large omelet pan or frying-pan, heat the oil over moderate heat. When the oil is hot, add the onion, garlic and peppers and cook, stirring occasionally, for 5 to 7 minutes or until the onion is soft and translucent but not brown. Stir in the tomatoes and cook, stirring occasionally, for 5 minutes.

Meanwhile, in a large mixing bowl, beat the eggs, salt, pepper and water together until they are well mixed.

Pour the egg mixture into the pan. Stir the eggs, then leave them for a few seconds until the bottom sets. Reduce the heat to low. Using a palette knife or spatula, lift the edges of the omelet and, at the same time, tilt the pan away from you so that the liquid egg escapes from the top and runs on to the pan. Put the pan down flat over the heat and leave until the omelet begins to set again.

Remove the pan from the heat and, with the help of the palette knife, slide the pipérade quickly on to a warmed serving dish. Cut into two or three and serve at once.

Piping

Piping is a method of decorating by forcing a soft mixture, such as cream, icing, meringue, or creamed potatoes through a greaseproof paper or fabric bag fitted with a nozzle, into decorative shapes.

Whether you are using a sweet or savoury mixture, it is very important that it is the right consistency. It must be free of lumps and thin enough to be forced through the pipe, yet thick enough to hold its shape once it is piped.

There are many different sizes and types of piping nozzles. For example, when piping eclairs, a plain $\frac{5}{8}$-inch nozzle is most often used. Meringues require a plain $\frac{1}{2}$-inch nozzle and duchess potatoes, savoury cream cheese or sweet cream for decorating desserts, can be piped with star nozzles of different sizes.

For cake decoration the variety is endless, from writing nozzles, to shell nozzles and flat sided nozzles for making petals and flowers. Depending on the type of cake and how intricate the decoration, either royal or butter cream icing is generally used.

An example of how a selection of icing nozzles make different designs and patterns. Top to bottom the numbers are: 3, 33, 16, 22, 34, 32, 2, 4, 35, 20 and 21.

This shell border makes an attractive edging around a cake. Put a No: 34 nozzle into a paper icing bag.

Fill the bag with royal icing, hold the bag firmly and start by piping the icing to about ½-inch.

Gently lift the pipe and press it down again to make another ½-inch. Continue until the border is complete.

Butter Cream icing may also be piped. Cover the cake with the icing and coat the side with chopped nuts.

Place a large plain nozzle in a nylon icing bag and pipe lines across the top of the cake.

With an up-and-down movement pipe a border of the butter cream icing around the top and bottom of the cake.

To make roses, secure a piece of paper, on to a piping nail. Using a No. 18 nozzle, pipe a circle of royal icing.

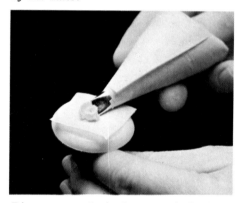

Pipe a second circle around the first, making sure the circles are upright (the icing should be stiff).

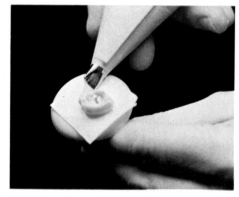

Continue to make circles, 4 or 5, until the rose is complete. Leave the rose on the paper until it is dry.

Other flowers may be made with the same nozzle. For a flat flower, pipe the petals on to the paper.

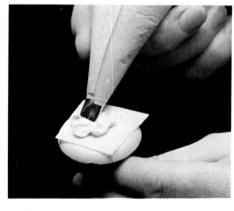

Being careful not to separate the petals, continue to make the petal shapes into a circle.

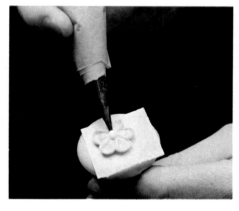

To complete the flower, pipe a centre using a No: 2 nozzle. Set the paper aside until the flower is dry.

Pip

A simple yet effective design for a birthday cake with an easy-to-do trellis pattern and decorated with roses.

With a No: 2 nozzle, pipe lines around the top and bottom edges of the cake. Continue by crossing the first lines.

Allow the first trellis to dry then colour a little royal icing a pale pink. Wash and dry the icing nozzle.

Repeat the pattern with the pink icing building up the criss-cross trellis on the top and bottom of the cake.

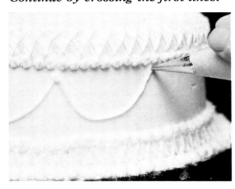

Using a No: 20 nozzle pipe rosettes around the cake. Make loops with the No: 2 nozzle around the cake.

To finish the cake, secure icing roses on the side, with a little icing, and pipe Happy Birthday on the top.

Piquant Beef

A quick and delicious way to cook entrecôte, Piquant Beef is a good dinner party dish for a busy hostess to make. After the preliminary browning of the meat, the cooking time will vary according to how well-done you like your beef — 15 minutes will leave the beef rare and 30 minutes, medium to well-done. Ask the butcher to trim off most of the fat leaving only a thin layer on one side. Serve Piquant Beef with fluffy creamed potatoes and French beans. A good red wine such as St. Emilion makes the perfect accompaniment.

6 SERVINGS

1 tablespoon butter
1 tablespoon vegetable oil
1 x 3 lb. entrecôte steak
½ teaspoon freshly ground black pepper
1 teaspoon prepared mustard
1 teaspoon sugar
1 teaspoon salt
1 tablespoon wine vinegar
6 fl. oz. [¾ cup] dry red wine
1 tablespoon beurre manié
2 tablespoons capers

In a large frying-pan, melt the butter with the oil over moderate heat. When the foam subsides, add the entrecôte, sprinkle the pepper on top, and cook it for 7 minutes on each side, or until it is evenly browned.

Leave the beef fat side down, cover the pan, reduce the heat to low and cook the meat for 15 minutes, if you wish the meat to be rare.

Piquant Beef, as well as looking and tasting delicious, is surprisingly quick and easy to prepare.

Meanwhile, in a cup or measuring jug combine the mustard, sugar, salt, vinegar and wine. Set aside.

When the beef is cooked, transfer it to a warmed plate, cover with aluminium foil and keep it hot while you finish the sauce.

Increase the heat to high and pour the wine mixture into the frying-pan.

Stirring frequently, bring the sauce to the boil. Reduce the heat to low and add the beurre manié, a little at a time, stirring constantly until the sauce is smooth.

Stir in the capers and cook the sauce for 2 minutes. Pour the sauce into a warmed sauceboat. Transfer the beef to a carving board. Carve the beef into thick slices and serve, with the sauce.

Piquant Dip

Tangy Piquant Dip is delicious as an appetizer. Serve with raw vegetables such as cauliflower, broccoli, mushrooms and carrots.

12 FLUID OUNCES [1½ CUPS]

4 oz. cream cheese
8 fl. oz. [1 cup] sour cream
1 hard-boiled egg, finely chopped
4 tablespoons tomato ketchup
1 teaspoon horseradish sauce
1 teaspoon Worcestershire sauce
1 garlic clove, crushed
1 teaspoon prepared mustard
½ teaspoon salt
1 teaspoon lemon juice
¼ teaspoon Tabasco sauce

In a medium-sized mixing bowl, beat the cream cheese and sour cream together with a wooden spoon until they are smooth and creamy. Stir in the egg, tomato ketchup, horseradish sauce, Worcestershire sauce, garlic clove, mustard, salt, lemon juice and Tabasco. Mix all the ingredients together until they are thoroughly combined.

Place the bowl in the refrigerator and chill the dip for 2 hours before serving.

Piquant Meat Loaf

Piquant Meat Loaf is quick and easy to prepare and tastes absolutely delicious. Serve with creamed potatoes and a rich tomato sauce.

6-8 SERVINGS

1 teaspoon vegetable oil
3 oz. [1½ cups] fresh breadcrumbs
8 fl. oz. [1 cup] milk
1 lb. lean pork, minced [ground]
1 lb. lean beef, minced [ground]
1 large onion, finely chopped
4 oz. canned pimiento, drained and chopped
3 tablespoons prepared French mustard
1 teaspoon dried basil

An ideal dish to make for a family supper, Piquant Meat Loaf may be served with creamed potatoes.

⅛ teaspoon cayenne pepper
1 tablespoon paprika pepper
1 teaspoon salt
½ teaspoon black pepper
2 eggs, lightly beaten

Preheat the oven to moderate 350°F (Gas Mark 4, 180°C). Grease a 2-pound loaf tin with the teaspoon of oil. Set aside.

Place the breadcrumbs in a medium-sized mixing bowl. Pour over the milk and set aside for 15 minutes, or until the bread has soaked up most of the milk.

Place the breadcrumb mixture in a large mixing bowl. Add all the remaining ingredients. With your hands, mix and knead the ingredients until they are thoroughly combined. Spoon the meat mixture into the prepared tin.

Half-fill a baking tin with boiling water. Place the meat loaf in the baking tin. Place the tin in the centre of the oven and bake the meat loaf for 1¼ to 1½ hours or until it is cooked through.

Remove the tin from the oven and unmould the meat loaf by running a knife around the edges of the tin and turning it out on to a plate. Serve at once, or allow the meat loaf to cool in the tin, cover it, put it in the refrigerator and serve cold.